The 70-297 Cram Sheet

This cram sheet provides you with the distilled facts about Exam 70-297, "Designing a Windows Server 2003 Active Directory and Network Infrastructure." Review these important points as the last thing you do before entering the test center. Pay close attention to those facts you feel you need to review. A good exam strategy is to transfer all the information you can recall from this cram sheet to a piece of paper after you enter the testing room. You can also refer to the glossary at the end of the book for more information regarding key terms.

CREATING THE CONCEPTUAL DESIGN BY GATHERING AND ANALYZING BUSINESS AND TECHNICAL REQUIREMENTS

1. A forest is a single domain, but can contain multiple domains depending on the requirements of the business. The first domain installed becomes the forest root domain.

2. A domain added to the forest may inherit a portion of its namespace from its parent domain. A new domain tree will start its own namespace inside the forest.

3. Two-way transitive trust relationships are automatically established between all parent and child domains within the same forest.

4. An explicit trust must be defined between two forests.

5. Domains within the same tree share a contiguous namespace (that is, a child domain inherits a portion of its namespace from its parent domain).

6. Domains requiring a unique namespace can be established as a new tree within a forest.

7. Two-way transitive trusts are automatically established between any new trees established within the forest and the forest root domain; this creates a trust path throughout the forest, making resources available forest-wide.

8. Windows Server 2003 can interoperate with vendors' versions of DNS. DNS versions BIND 4.9.7 and later support SRV records. BIND 8.2.2 and later support dynamic update.

9. Windows Server 2003 supports a forest trust. This allows two separate forests to be linked together with a one-way or two-way transitive trust. Doing so can form a transitive trust between every domain in each forest.

CREATING THE LOGICAL DESIGN FOR AN ACTIVE DIRECTORY INFRASTRUCTURE

10. The administrative model deployed by a company will affect the Active Directory design. There are two main administrative models, centralized administration and decentralized administration.

11. The model for administration that is chosen determines the organization of the Active Directory structure. There are four models: functional, geographical, organizational, and hybrid.

12. Multiple forests might be required if a company requires separate schemas. To update the schema, you must be a member of the Schema Admins group

13. Security policies are applied at the domain level. If multiple security policies are required, multiple domains must be created. Only one security policy can exist within a domain.

14. Multiple trees can be created if a business needs to maintain more than one namespace.

15. Organizational units are created within a domain to logically group objects for administrative purposes—more specifically, for applying Group Policy Objects (GPOs) and delegating authority.

16. *Delegation* is the process of decentralizing network administration by assigning some of the administrative duties to other individuals or groups within the business. This is another reason for creating organizational units.

17. GPOs can be applied locally or at the site, domain, and OU level. GPOs are applied in the following order: local, site, domain, OU.

43. Incremental Zone Transfer (IXFR) allows for more frequent zone transfer and thereby increases accuracy of zone information.

44. Caching-only DNS servers should be used with a small remote office that has a relatively slow link back to the main office. These servers are not authoritative for a zone and therefore do not perform zone transfer. This conserves available bandwidth on the slow link.

45. Conditional forwarding is new to Windows Server 2003. This service allows all queries for a particular namespace to be forwarded directly to the server that hosts that namespace. Doing so increases the efficiency of name resolution on a network

46. The Global Catalog (GC) contains all the objects in the Active Directory forest. It is used by computers, users, and applications to search the Active Directory. Domain controllers can be set to also be a GC server. You should have at least one GC server per site.

47. The schema is a list of all the object classes and attributes in the Active Directory and the rules associated with combining them to create objects. There is only one schema per Active Directory. You should only modify the schema when no other alternative exists.

48. Flexible Single Master Operation (FSMO) roles include the schema master and domain naming master (one per forest) and the PDC emulator, RID master, and infrastructure master (one per domain).

49. To make changes to the schema, a person with an account in the Schema Admins group must be able to make contact with server holding the schema master role.

50. To add or delete a domain from a forest, a person with an account in the Enterprise Admins group must be able to make contact with the server holding the role of domain naming master.

51. The PDC emulator emulates the NT 4.0 BDC for mixed mode domains, keeps the time, and is the final authority of password changes for each domain. There is only one PDC emulator per domain.

52. The RID master ensures that all domain security IDs remain unique for each domain.

53. The infrastructure master keeps track of group-to-name references in each domain.

54. Seizing an FSMO role from a computer is a risky operation and should be performed only as a last resort. The most likely role to be seized is the PDC emulator role because it is the role that will be missed the soonest.

55. There are four editions of Windows Server 2003: Standard, Web, Enterprise, and Datacenter. Web Edition cannot be used as a domain controller.

56. The L2TP and PPTP tunneling protocols are used for VPNs. PPTP is the oldest of the two. Windows 2000 Professional and later clients support L2TP natively. Windows 98 and Windows NT have an L2TP client that can be downloaded from Microsoft.

57. Physically placing a server between the Internet and the other servers on a private network can provide additional authentication and security for a network while letting the other servers keep more services available for those who are authorized.

58. Public IP addresses should be registered through the Internet Corporation of Assigned Names and Numbers (ICANN) or one of its registries located throughout the world.

18. *Filtering* is a feature that allows an administrator to exclude certain groups from being affected by a group policy by limiting the scope of the policy. By removing the Apply Group Policy permission for a user or group, that entity can be made exempt from the policy settings.

19. Using a feature called *block policy inheritance*, the inheritance of a GPO can be modified so that it is not passed on from parent container to child container. Any policy applied at the site, domain, or OU level can be blocked.

20. The No Override option means exactly that. If the option is set, any group policies linked to a parent container will be applied to the child containers, regardless of whether the Block Policy Inheritance option is set.

21. Windows Server 2003 supports four different types of security groups: local, domain local, global, and universal groups.

22. Windows Server 2003 supports Kerberos, public key infrastructure, and smart cards for authentication.

23. Migration paths to Windows Server 2003 include an in-place upgrade, domain restructuring, and a new Active Directory environment.

24. An Active Directory *site* is basically a collection of well-connected IP subnets. The links between the subnets within a site are generally fast, reliable, and capable of supporting replication.

25. The properties of a site link are transport, schedule, cost, and interval.

26. RPC over IP or SMTP can be used to replicate information between sites. The schedule determines the time and day that a site link can be used for replication.

27. SMTP is recommended for slow, unreliable WAN connections. SMTP ignores all schedules configured for a site link.

CREATING THE LOGICAL DESIGN FOR A NETWORK SERVICES INFRASTRUCTURE

28. Administrators have three choices for the name of an Active Directory network: the same name as the public name, a delegated subdomain, and a completely different name. The choice will be based on the inherent advantages and disadvantages of each. It will affect administration, security, and ease of use of the network.

29. Windows Server 2003 requires TCP/IP and DNS to operate at all. This is partially because it uses SRV (Service) records in DNS to locate domain controllers and Global Catalog servers.

30. A *zone* is a discrete, contiguous portion of a DNS namespace. Zone information is contained in a zone database file. Adding the words *database file* to the word *zone* sometimes helps tremendously when answering a question relating to zones.

31. A standard primary zone database file is the original database file of a zone. It can be written to and read from as well.

32. A standard secondary zone database file is a copy of the original database for a zone. It can be read but not written to, except through zone transfer. Standard secondary zones are used for load balancing between DNS servers.

33. Servers that host a standard primary zone can be master servers for other servers that host the standard secondary database for that zone.

34. DHCP can interoperate with DNS and thereby register hostnames of clients in the DNS database. Clients that can register their own A (host) records include Windows 2000 Professional and Windows XP Professional.

35. Active Directory–integrated zones are preferred when available. Active Directory–integrated zones do not use zone transfer, but instead piggy-back their zone change information on Active Directory replication. Active Directory zones are all primary, but they can be set for only secure updates.

36. Stub zones are special zones that contain only the SRV record, name server record, and glue A host record (IP address) for the zone. These zones are used in networks with noncontiguous namespaces to make DNS name resolution more efficient.

37. Windows Internet Name Service (WINS) is still used in Windows Server 2003. It provides NetBIOS name resolution for legacy clients and applications. WINS will be needed until all legacy clients and applications are removed from the network.

38. Push replication occurs between two WINS servers after a specified number of changes on a database. Pull replication occurs on a specific interval, regardless of the number of changes.

39. Remote access policies define when, where, and how a user can gain access to a network from a remote location. They contain the elements of conditions, permissions, and profile.

40. Internet authentication services centralize authentication and logging for multiple RAS servers. In regard to IAS services, the RAS servers are the client of an IAS server.

41. Servers, network printers, and router interfaces should always have static IP addresses. Clients should have addresses that are assigned by a DHCP server whenever possible.

CREATING THE PHYSICAL DESIGN FOR AN ACTIVE DIRECTORY AND NETWORK INFRASTRUCTURE

42. To host an Active Directory–integrated zone, a DNS server must also be a domain controller.

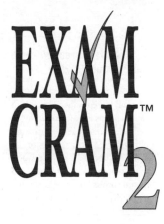

Designing a Windows® Server™ 2003 Active Directory™ and Network Infrastructure

Diana Huggins

Bill Ferguson

CERTIFICATION

Designing a Windows® Server™ 2003 Active Directory™ and Network Infrastructure Exam Cram 2 (Exam 70-297)

International Standard Book Number: 0-7897-3015-4

Library of Congress Catalog Card Number: 2003103929

Printed in the United States of America

First Printing: December 2003

07 06 05   7 6 5 4 3 2

Trademarks

All terms mentioned in this book that are known to be trademarks or service marks have been appropriately capitalized. Que Publishing cannot attest to the accuracy of this information. Use of a term in this book should not be regarded as affecting the validity of any trademark or service mark.

Windows is a registered trademark of Microsoft Corporation. Active Directory is a trademark of Microsoft Corporation.

Warning and Disclaimer

Every effort has been made to make this book as complete and as accurate as possible, but no warranty or fitness is implied. The information provided is on an "as is" basis. The authors and the publisher shall have neither liability nor responsibility to any person or entity with respect to any loss or damages arising from the information contained in this book or from the use of the CD or programs accompanying it.

Bulk Sales

Que Publishing offers excellent discounts on this book when ordered in quantity for bulk purchases or special sales. For more information, please contact

> U.S. Corporate and Government Sales
> 1-800-382-3419
> corpsales@pearsontechgroup.com

For sales outside the U.S., please contact

> International Sales
> international@pearsoned.com

Publisher
Paul Boger

Executive Editor
Jeff Riley

Development Editor
Susan Brown Zahn

Managing Editor
Charlotte Clapp

Project Editor
Tonya Simpson

Copy Editor
Mike Henry

Indexer
John Sleeva

Proofreader
Tracy Donhardt

Technical Editors
Brian McCann
David Neilan

Publishing Coordinator
Pamalee Nelson

Multimedia Developer
Dan Scherf

Page Layout
Stacey Richwine-DeRome

CERTIFICATION

Que Certification • 800 East 96th Street • Indianapolis, Indiana 46240

A Note from Series Editor Ed Tittel

You know better than to trust your certification preparation to just anybody. That's why you, and more than two million others, have purchased an Exam Cram book. As Series Editor for the new and improved Exam Cram 2 series, I have worked with the staff at Que Certification to ensure you won't be disappointed. That's why we've taken the world's best-selling certification product—a finalist for "Best Study Guide" in a CertCities reader poll in 2002—and made it even better.

As a "Favorite Study Guide Author" finalist in a 2002 poll of CertCities readers, I know the value of good books. You'll be impressed with Que Certification's stringent review process, which ensures the books are high-quality, relevant, and technically accurate. Rest assured that at least a dozen industry experts have reviewed this material, helping us deliver an excellent solution to your exam preparation needs.

Best Study Guides

We've also added a preview edition of PrepLogic's powerful, full-featured test engine, which is trusted by certification students throughout the world.

As a 20-year-plus veteran of the computing industry and the original creator and editor of the Exam Cram series, I've brought my IT experience to bear on these books. During my tenure at Novell from 1989 to 1994, I worked with and around its excellent education and certification department. This experience helped push my writing and teaching activities heavily in the certification direction. Since then, I've worked on more than 70 certification-related books, and I write about certification topics for numerous Web sites and for *Certification* magazine.

In 1996, while studying for various MCP exams, I became frustrated with the huge, unwieldy study guides that were the only preparation tools available. As an experienced IT professional and former instructor, I wanted "nothing but the facts" necessary to prepare for the exams. From this impetus, Exam Cram emerged in 1997. It quickly became the best-selling computer book series since "...*For Dummies*," and the best-selling certification book series ever. By maintaining an intense focus on subject matter, tracking errata and updates quickly, and following the certification market closely, Exam Cram was able to establish the dominant position in cert prep books.

You will not be disappointed in your decision to purchase this book. If you are, please contact me at etittel@jump.net. All suggestions, ideas, input, or constructive criticism are welcome!

Ed Tittel

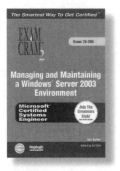

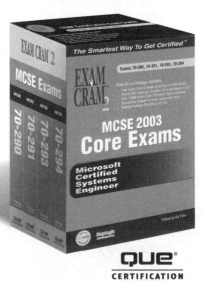

This book is dedicated with all my love to my son, Brandon.
—Diana Huggins

ॐ

This book is dedicated to my wife, Wilma, who put up with the long hours and encouraged me throughout its production.
—Bill Ferguson

ॐ

About the Authors

Diana Huggins is currently an independent contractor providing both technical writing and consulting services. Prior to this, she worked as a senior systems consultant. Some of the projects she worked on included a security review of Microsoft's official curriculum and content development for private companies, as well as network infrastructure design and implementation projects.

Diana's main focus over the past few years has been writing certification study guides. To complement her efforts, she also spends a portion of her time consulting for small- to medium-sized companies in a variety of areas and continues to work as an independent technical trainer.

Diana currently has her Microsoft Certified Systems Engineer (MCSE) and Microsoft Certified Trainer (MCT), along with several other certifications from different vendors. Although her focus is on the information technology industry, she also holds a bachelor's degree in education. Diana runs her own company, DKB Consulting Services. The main focus of the company is developing certification training courseware and online practice exams, as well as content delivery.

Bill Ferguson, MCT, MCSE, MCP+I, CCNA, A+, Network+, Server+, has been in the computer industry for more than 15 years. Originally in technical sales and sales management with Sprint, Bill made his transition to Certified Technical Trainer in 1997 with ExecuTrain. Bill now runs his own company as an independent contractor in Birmingham, Alabama, teaching classes for most of the national training companies and some regional training companies and corporations. In addition, Bill writes and produces technical training videos for Virtual Training Company, Inc. and Specialized Solutions, Inc. His current titles include A+, Network+, Windows 2000 Management, Windows XP Management, Windows 2000 Security, Server+, and Interconnecting Cisco Network Devices. Bill keeps his skills sharp by being a technical reviewer for books and sample tests. Bill says, "My job is to understand the material so well that I can make it easier for my students to learn than it was for me to learn."

About the Technical Editors

Brian McCann, MCSE, MCT, is a trainer and consultant specializing in Active Directory and network security. He is the owner of Diesel Technologies, a training and consulting company dedicated to helping small- to medium-sized businesses with their IT needs.

Brian has worked in the IT field for 10 years and started his career in the U.S. Army. His teaching experience comes from local training centers and community colleges and also from just under 3 years of doing live synchronous training over the Web. Brian has spent the last 5 years teaching students from all over the world on technologies such as Active Directory, PKI, DNS, IIS and many others.

Brian has been recognized by Microsoft as one of its "Go to Trainers."

David Neilan is an experienced MCSE (+Security) who has been working in the computer/network industry for more than 12 years—the last 6 years dealing primarily with network/Internet connectivity and security. He is currently running a business, Security Technologies, in the network/security realm, working with local companies to enable and secure their networks. He has been designing network infrastructures to support secure LAN/WAN connectivity for various companies utilizing Microsoft 2000 and Cisco products, and the Internet to create secure virtual private networks. David is currently involved in many infrastructure upgrades, including domain and email systems.

David has also been beta testing Microsoft operating systems since Windows for Workgroups (WFW3.11), and has worked as a technical editor on numerous Microsoft/networking/security books.

David and his wife Susan (also in the computer industry) live in Winnipeg, Canada. They and their two dogs love spending time at the cabin in the great outdoors.

Acknowledgments

I'd like to first of all thank my son, Brandon, for always being so understanding and patient when I have deadlines to meet.

Thanks to Jeff Riley and Que Publishing for giving me the opportunity to work on this title and for seeing the value in the *Exam Cram 2* series. Thanks to Susan Brown-Zahn for keeping the project on track. Also, a huge thanks to Bill Ferguson for taking on the project at the last minute.

To all those people in my life who support me and encourage me when I'm struggling to get things done and that one person who always manages to drag me away from work when I do need to get things done. Finally, I would like to thank my dear friend, David, for motivating me indirectly through your own drive and determination. Thanks to you all!

—*Diana Huggins*

I'd like to first of all thank my wife, Wilma, who encouraged me and gave me the inspiration to take on this project. Thanks for putting up with the long "late night" hours that it took to complete it.

Thanks to Jeff Riley for bringing me in on the project and keeping me on target at each step. Thanks to Susan Brown-Zahn for keeping the project on track and providing me with direction.

Thanks to Diana Huggins for coordinating with me to produce a product of which we can both be proud.

Finally, thanks to all who have encouraged me in my technical classes and Sunday School classes and given me the determination to step out and tackle something new. I sincerely appreciate all of your thoughts and prayers.

—*Bill Ferguson*

We Want to Hear from You!

As the reader of this book, *you* are our most important critic and commentator. We value your opinion and want to know what we're doing right, what we could do better, what areas you'd like to see us publish in, and any other words of wisdom you're willing to pass our way.

As an executive editor for Que Publishing, I welcome your comments. You can email or write me directly to let me know what you did or didn't like about this book—as well as what we can do to make our books better.

Please note that I cannot help you with technical problems related to the topic of this book. We do have a User Services group, however, where I will forward specific technical questions related to the book.

When you write, please be sure to include this book's title and author as well as your name, email address, and phone number. I will carefully review your comments and share them with the author and editors who worked on the book.

Email: feedback@quepublishing.com

Mail: Jeff Riley
          Executive Editor
          Que Publishing
          800 East 96th Street
          Indianapolis, IN 46240 USA

For more information about this book or another Que Publishing title, visit our Web site at www.examcram2.com. Type the ISBN (excluding hyphens) or the title of a book in the Search field to find the page you're looking for.

Contents at a Glance

Table of Contents

Introduction

Welcome to *MCSE Exam Cram 2 (Exam 70-297)*! Whether this is your first or your fifteenth *Exam Cram 2* series book, you'll find information here that will help ensure your success as you pursue knowledge, experience, and certification. This introduction explains Microsoft's certification programs in general and talks about how the *Exam Cram 2* series can help you prepare for Microsoft's Certified Systems Engineer and Microsoft's Certified Systems Administrator exams.

Chapter 1 discusses the basics of Microsoft certification exams, including a description of the testing environment and a discussion of test-taking strategies. Chapters 2 through 6 are designed to remind you of everything you'll need to know to take and pass the 70-297 Microsoft MCSE certification exam. The two practice exams at the end of the book should give you a reasonably accurate assessment of your knowledge and, yes, we've provided the answers and their explanations. Read the book and understand the material, and you stand a very good chance of passing the test.

Exam Cram 2 books help you understand and appreciate the subjects and materials you need to pass Microsoft certification exams. *Exam Cram 2* books are aimed strictly at test preparation and review. They do not teach you everything you need to know about a topic. Instead, they present and dissect the questions and problems that you're likely to encounter on a test. We've worked to bring together as much information as possible about Microsoft certification exams.

Nevertheless, to completely prepare yourself for any Microsoft test, we recommend that you begin by taking the self-assessment that immediately follows this introduction. The self-assessment tool will help you evaluate your knowledge base against the requirements for a Microsoft Certified Systems Engineer (MCSE) under both ideal and real-world circumstances.

Based on what you learn from the self-assessment, you might decide to begin your studies with some classroom training, some practice with Windows Server 2003, or some background reading. On the other hand, you might decide to pick up and read one of the many study guides available from Microsoft or third-party vendors on certain topics. We also recommend that you supplement your study program with visits to www.examcram2.com to receive additional practice questions, get advice, and track the MCSE program.

We also strongly recommend that you install, configure, and play around with the software that you'll be tested on, because when it comes to understanding the questions you're likely to encounter on a certification test, nothing beats hands-on experience and familiarity. Book learning is essential, but without a doubt, hands-on experience is the best teacher of all!

Many of the chapters include step-by-step instructions on how to perform various tasks in Windows Server 2003 to assist you in becoming familiar with the product. The CD-ROM that accompanies the book contains a searchable PDF version of the book and the PrepLogic Practice Exams, Preview Edition exam simulation software. The preview edition exhibits the full functionality of the Premium Edition, but offers only one exam's worth of questions. To get the complete set of practice questions, visit www.preplogic.com.

Taking a Certification Exam

After you've prepared for your exam, you need to register with a testing center. Each computer-based MCP exam costs $125. If you don't pass, you can retest for an additional $125 for each subsequent try. In the United States and Canada, tests are administered by Prometric and by Pearson VUE. Here's how you can contact them:

➤ *Pearson VUE*—You can sign up for a test or get the phone numbers for local testing centers through the Web at www.vue.com/ms.

➤ *Prometric*—You can sign up for a test through the company's Web site, at www.2test.com. Within the United States and Canada, you can register by phone by calling 800-755-3926. If you live outside this region, you should check the Prometric Web site for the appropriate phone number.

To sign up for a test, you must possess a valid credit card or contact either Pearson VUE or Prometric for mailing instructions to send a check (in the United States). Only when payment has been verified or your check has cleared can you actually register for the test.

To schedule an exam, you need to call the number or visit either of the Web pages at least one day in advance. To cancel or reschedule an exam, you must call before 7 p.m. Pacific standard time the day before the scheduled test time (or you might be charged, even if you don't show up to take the test). When you want to schedule a test, you should have the following information ready:

➤ Your name, organization, and mailing address.

➤ Your Microsoft test ID. Inside the United States, this usually means your Social Security number; citizens of other nations should call ahead to find out what type of identification number is required to register for a test.

➤ The name and number of the exam you want to take.

➤ A method of payment. As mentioned previously, a credit card is the most convenient method, but alternative means can be arranged in advance, if necessary.

After you've signed up for a test, you'll be told when and where the test is scheduled. You should try to arrive at least 15 minutes early. You must supply two forms of identification—one of which must be a photo ID—and sign a nondisclosure agreement to be admitted into the testing room.

All Microsoft exams are completely closed book. In fact, you are not permitted to take anything with you into the testing area, but you are given a blank sheet of paper and a pen (or in some cases an erasable plastic sheet and an erasable pen). We suggest that you immediately write down on that sheet of paper all the information that you've memorized for the test. In *Exam Cram 2* books, this information appears on a tear-out sheet, the cram sheet, that's inside the front cover of each book. You're given some time to compose yourself, record this information, and take a sample orientation exam before you begin the real thing. We suggest that you take the orientation test before taking your first exam, but because all the certification exams are more or less identical in layout, behavior, and controls, you probably don't need to do this more than once.

When you complete a Microsoft certification exam, the software tells you immediately whether you've passed or failed. If you need to retake an exam, you have to schedule a new test with Pearson VUE or Prometric and pay another $125.

NOTE   In the unlikely event that you fail the test on the first attempt, you can retake the test as soon as the next day. However, if you fail a second time, you must wait 14 days before retaking that test. The 14-day waiting period remains in effect for all retakes after the second failure.

Tracking MCP Status

As soon as you pass any Microsoft exam, you attain MCP status. Microsoft generates transcripts that indicate which exams you've passed. You can view a copy of your transcript at any time by going to the MCP secured site and selecting Transcript Tool. This tool enables you to print a copy of your current transcript and confirm your certification status.

After you pass the necessary set of exams, you are certified. Official certification is normally granted after three to six weeks, so you shouldn't expect to get your credentials overnight. The package for official certification includes a Welcome Kit that contains a number of elements (see Microsoft's Web site for other benefits of specific certifications):

➤ A certificate that is suitable for framing, along with a wallet card and lapel pin.

➤ A license to use the applicable logo, which means you can use the logo in advertisements, promotions, and documents, as well as on letterhead, business cards, and so on. Along with the license comes a logo sheet, which includes camera-ready artwork. Note that before you use any of the artwork, you must sign and return a licensing agreement that indicates you'll abide by its terms and conditions.

➤ A subscription to *Microsoft Certified Professional Magazine*, which provides ongoing data about testing and certification activities, requirements, and changes to the program.

Many people believe that the benefits of MCP certification go well beyond the perks that Microsoft provides to newly anointed members of this elite group. We're starting to see more job listings that request or require applicants to have MCP, MCSA, and other certifications, and many individuals who complete Microsoft certification programs can qualify for increases in pay and/or responsibility. As an official recognition of hard work and broad knowledge, one of the MCP credentials is a badge of honor in many IT organizations.

How to Prepare for an Exam

Preparing for any MCSE-related test (including Exam 70-297) requires that you obtain and study materials designed to provide comprehensive information about the product and its capabilities that will appear on the specific exam for which you are preparing. The following list of materials can help you study and prepare:

➤ The Windows Server 2003 product CD. Some of the best resources you can use when preparing for an exam are the help files included with the operating system. They usually cover different aspects of all the technologies included with the operating system.

➤ The exam preparation materials, practice tests, and self-assessment exams on the Microsoft Training & Services page at www.microsoft.com/traincert. The Exam Resources link offers examples of the new question types found on the MCSE exams. You should find the materials, download them, and use them!

➤ The exam preparation advice, practice tests, questions of the day, and discussion groups on the www.examcram2.com e-learning and certification destination Web site.

In addition, you might find any or all the following materials useful in your quest for Windows Server 2003 expertise:

➤ *Microsoft training kits*—Microsoft Press offers a training kit that specifically targets Exam 70-297. For more information, visit http://www.microsoft.com/ mspress/certification/mcse.asp. This training kit contains information that you will find useful in preparing for the test.

➤ *Microsoft TechNet*—This monthly publication provides information on the latest technologies and topics some of which pertain to the exam topics covered in 70-297.

➤ *Study guides*—Several publishers, including Que Publishing, offer certification titles. Que Publishing offers the following:

  ➤ *The* Exam Cram 2 *series*—These books give you information about the material you need to know to pass the tests.

  ➤ *The* MCSE Training Guide *series*—These books provide a greater level of detail than the *Exam Cram 2* books and are designed to teach you everything you need to know about the subject covered by an exam. Each book comes with a CD-ROM that contains interactive practice exams in a variety of testing formats.

  Together, these two series make a perfect pair.

➤ *Classroom training*—Microsoft Certified Technical Education Centers (CTECs), online partners, and third-party training companies all offer classroom training on Windows Server 2003. These companies aim to help you prepare to pass Exam 70-297 (and other exams). Although such training costs more than $350 per day in class, most of the individuals lucky enough to partake find this training to be quite worthwhile.

➤ *Other publications*—There's no shortage of materials available about Windows Server 2003. The "Need to Know More?" resource section at the end of each chapter in this book will give you an idea of where we think you should look for further discussion.

This set of required and recommended materials represents an unparalleled collection of sources and resources for Windows Server 2003 and related topics. We hope you'll find that this book belongs in this company.

What This Book Will Not Do

This book will *not* teach you everything you need to know about computers, or even about a given topic. Nor is this book an introduction to computer technology. If you're new to network administration or networking in general and looking for an initial preparation guide, check out www.quepublishing.com, where you will find a whole section dedicated to the MCSE certifications. This book will review what you need to know before you take the test, with the fundamental purpose dedicated to reviewing the information needed on the Microsoft 70-297 certification exam.

This book uses a variety of teaching and memorization techniques to analyze the exam-related topics and to provide you with ways to input, index, and retrieve everything you'll need to know to pass the test. Again, this book is *not* an introduction to networking and network administration, nor does it cover introductory topics as they pertain to Windows Server 2003.

What This Book Is Designed to Do

This book is designed to be read as a pointer to the areas of knowledge you will be tested on. In other words, you might want to read the book one time, just to get an insight into how comprehensive your knowledge of computers is. The book is also designed to be read shortly before you go for the actual test and to give you a distillation of the entire field of designing a Windows Server 2003 Active Directory and network infrastructure in as few pages as possible. We think you can use this book to get a sense of the underlying context of any topic in the chapters or to skim-read for exam alerts, bulleted points, summaries, and topic headings.

The material covered in this book is based on Microsoft's own listing of exam objectives. These are the topics that Microsoft intends to test you on during the exam. The book also covers a number of other topics you're likely to encounter both on the exam and on the job.

The 70-297 exam makes the assumption that you already have a strong background of experience with Windows Server 2003 and its related technologies. On the other hand, because the platform is so new, no one can be a complete expert. We've tried to demystify the jargon, acronyms, terms, and concepts. Also, wherever we think you're likely to blur past an important concept, we've defined the assumptions and premises behind that concept.

About This Book

The topics in this book have been structured around the objectives outlined by Microsoft for Exam 70-297. This ensures that you will be familiar with the topics that you'll encounter on the exam.

Some of the topics covered later in the book might require an understanding of topics covered in earlier chapters. Therefore, we recommend that you read the book from start to finish for your initial reading. After you've read the book, you can brush up on certain areas by using the index or the table of contents to go straight to the topics and questions that you want to reexamine. We've tried to use the headings and subheadings to provide outline information about each given topic.

After you've been certified, we think you'll find this book useful as a tightly focused reference and an essential foundation of Windows Server 2003 reference material.

Chapter Formats

Each *Exam Cram 2* chapter follows a regular structure, along with graphical cues about especially important or useful material. The structure of a typical chapter is as follows:

➤ *Opening hotlists*—Each chapter begins with lists of the terms you'll need to understand and the concepts you'll need to master before you can be fully conversant with the chapter's subject matter. We follow the hotlists with a few introductory paragraphs that set the stage for the rest of the chapter.

➤ *Topical coverage*—After the opening hotlists, each chapter covers the topics related to the chapter's subject.

➤ *Exam alerts*—Throughout the topical coverage section, we highlight the material most likely to appear on the exam by using a special exam alert layout that looks like this:

 This is what an exam alert looks like. An exam alert stresses concepts, terms, software, or activities that will most likely appear in one or more certification exam questions. For that reason, we think any information offset in exam alert format is worthy of extra attentiveness on your part.

Even if material isn't flagged as an exam alert, *all* the content in this book is associated in some way with test-related material. What appears in the chapter content is critical knowledge.

➤ *Notes*—This book is an overall examination of computers. As such, we dip into many aspects of Windows Server 2003. Where a body of knowledge is deeper than the scope of the book, we use notes to indicate areas of concern or specialty training.

Cramming for an exam will get you through a test, but it won't make you a competent IT professional. Although you can memorize just the facts you need to become certified, your daily work in the field will rapidly put you in water over your head if you don't know the underlying principles of application development.

➤ *Tips*—We provide tips that help you build a better foundation of knowledge or focus your attention on an important concept that will reappear later in the book. Tips provide a helpful way to remind you of the context surrounding a particular area of a topic under discussion.

You should also read Chapter 1, "Microsoft Certification Exams," for helpful strategies used in taking a test. The introduction to Practice Exam 1 in Chapter 7 contains additional tips on how to figure out the correct response to a question and what to do if you draw a complete blank.

➤ *Practice questions*—This section presents a short list of test questions related to the specific chapter topic. Each question has a following explanation of both correct and incorrect answers. The practice questions highlight the areas we found to be most important on the exam.

➤ *Need to Know More?*—Each chapter ends with a list of additional resources that offer more details about the chapter topics.

The bulk of the book follows this chapter structure, but there are a few other elements that we would like to point out:

➤ *Practice exams*—The practice exams, which appear in Chapters 7 and 9 (with answer keys in Chapters 8 and 10), are very close approximations of the types of questions you're likely to see on the current 70-297 exam.

➤ *Answer keys*—These provide the answers to the sample tests, complete with explanations of both the correct responses and the incorrect responses.

➤ *Glossary*—This is an extensive glossary of important terms used in this book.

➤ *The cram sheet*—This appears as a tear-away sheet inside the front cover of this *Exam Cram 2* book. It is a valuable tool that represents a collection of the most difficult-to-remember facts and numbers that we think you should memorize before you take the test. Remember, you can dump this information out of your head onto a piece of paper as soon as you enter the testing room. These are usually facts that we've found require brute-force memorization. You need to remember this information only long enough to write it down when you walk into the test room. Be advised that you will be asked to surrender all personal belongings before you enter the exam room itself.

You might want to look at the cram sheet in your car or in the lobby of the testing center just before you walk into the testing center. The cram sheet is divided under headings so that you can review the appropriate parts just before each test.

➤ *The CD-ROM*—The CD-ROM includes a searchable PDF copy of the book. The CD-ROM also contains the PrepLogic Practice Exams, Preview Edition exam simulation software. The Preview Edition exhibits all of the full functionality of the Premium Edition, but offers only enough questions for one practice exam. To get the complete set of practice questions and exam functionality, visit `www.preplogic.com`.

Contacting the Authors

We've tried to create a real-world tool that you can use to prepare for and pass the 70-297 MCSE certification exam. We're interested in any feedback that you care to share about the book, especially if you have ideas about how we can improve it for future test-takers. We'll carefully consider everything you say and will respond to all reasonable suggestions and comments. You can reach us via email at `dhuggins@skyweb.ca` or `billferguson@charter.net`.

Let us know if you found this book to be helpful in your preparation efforts. We'd also like to know how you felt about your chances of passing the exam *before* you read the book and then *after* you read the book. Of course, we'd love to hear that you passed the exam and even if you just want to share your triumph, we'd be happy to hear from you.

Thanks for choosing us as your personal trainers, and enjoy the book. We would wish you luck on the exam, but we know that if you read through all the chapters and work with the product, you won't need luck—you'll pass the test on the strength of real knowledge!

Self-Assessment

We included a self-assessment in this *Exam Cram 2* book to help you evaluate your readiness to tackle Microsoft certifications. This should also help you understand what you need to know to master the topic of this book: Exam 70-297 "Designing a Microsoft Windows Server 2003 Active Directory and Network Infrastructure." But before you tackle this self-assessment, let's address concerns you might face when pursuing an MCSE (Microsoft Certified Systems Engineer) or MCSA (Microsoft Certified Systems Administrator) certification for the Windows Server 2003 and what an ideal MCSE candidate might look like.

MCSEs in the Real World

In this section, we describe an ideal MCSE candidate, knowing full well that only a few candidates will meet this ideal. In fact, our description of that ideal candidate might seem downright scary. But take heart: Although the requirements to obtain an MCSE might seem formidable, they are by no means impossible to meet. However, be keenly aware that it does take time, involves some expense, and requires real effort to get through the process.

More than 200,000 MCSEs are already certified, so it's obviously an attainable goal. You can get all the real-world motivation you need from knowing that many others have gone before; you will be able to follow in their footsteps. If you're willing to tackle the process seriously and do what it takes to obtain the necessary experience and knowledge, you can take—and pass—all the certification tests involved in obtaining an MCSE. In fact, we've designed *Exam Cram 2* to make it as easy on you as possible to prepare for these exams. But prepare you must!

The same, of course, is true for other Microsoft certifications, including these:

➤ *MCSA (Microsoft Certified Systems Administrator)*—This is the brand-new certification that Microsoft has provided for Microsoft professionals who will administer networks rather than design them. This certification includes three core exams and a single elective.

➤ *MCSD (Microsoft Certified Solutions Developer)*—This is aimed at software developers and requires one specific exam, two more exams on client and distributed topics, plus a fourth elective exam drawn from a different but limited pool of options.

➤ *MCAD (Microsoft Certified Application Developer)*—This is aimed at software developers functioning at a departmental level with one to two years of experience in application development. The MCAD certification requires two specific exams, plus a third elective exam drawn from a limited pool of options. The 70-306 exam is a core exam for the MCAD credential.

➤ *MCDBA (Microsoft Certified Database Administrator)*—This is aimed at database administrators and developers who work with Microsoft SQL Server. The MCDBA certification requires three core exams and one elective exam.

The Ideal MCSE Candidate

Just to give you some idea of what an ideal MCSE candidate is like, here are some relevant statistics about the background and experience that such an individual might have. Don't worry if you don't meet these qualifications or don't come that close. This is a far-from-ideal world, and where you fall short is simply where you'll have more work to do.

➤ Academic or professional training in network theory, concepts, and operations. This includes everything from networking media and transmission techniques through network operating systems, services, and applications.

➤ More than three years of professional networking experience, including experience with Ethernet, token ring, modems, and other networking media. This must include installation, configuration, upgrade, and troubleshooting experience.

➤ More than two years in a networked environment that includes hands-on experience with Windows Server 2003, Windows XP, Windows 2000 Server, Windows 2000 Professional, Windows NT Server, Windows NT Workstation, Windows 95, or Windows 98. A solid understanding of each system's architecture, installation, configuration, maintenance, and troubleshooting is also essential.

➤ Knowledge of the various methods for installing Windows Server 2003, including manual and unattended installations.

➤ A thorough understanding of key networking protocols, addressing, and name resolution, including TCP/IP, IPX/SPX, and NetBEUI.

➤ A thorough understanding of DNS naming conventions fully qualified domain names, and the Domain Name Service (DNS).

➤ Familiarity with key Windows Server 2003 TCP/IP–based services, including HTTP (Web servers), DHCP, WINS, and DNS, plus familiarity with one or more of the following: Internet Information Server (IIS), Index Server, and ISA Server.

➤ An understanding of how to implement different connectivity models, such as remote access, IP routing, Internet Connection Sharing (ICS), Network Address Translation (NAT), and virtual private networks (VPNs).

➤ An understanding of how to implement security for key network data in a Windows Server 2003 environment.

➤ Working knowledge of NetWare 3.*x* and 4.*x*, including IPX/SPX frame formats; NetWare file, print, and directory services; and both Novell and Microsoft client software. Working knowledge of Microsoft's Client Service for NetWare (CSNW), Gateway Service for NetWare (GSNW), Services for NetWare (SFN) and the NetWare Client for Windows (Windows NT, Windows 95, and Windows 98) is essential.

Fundamentally, this boils down to a bachelor's degree in computer science, plus three years of experience working in a position involving network design, installation, configuration, and maintenance. We believe that well under half of all certification candidates meet these requirements and that, in fact, most meet less than half of these requirements—at least when they begin the certification process. But because all 200,000 people who already have been certified have survived this ordeal, you can survive it, especially if you heed what our self-assessment can tell you about what you already know and what you need to learn.

Put Yourself to the Test

The following series of questions and observations is designed to help you figure out how much work you must do to pursue Microsoft certification and what kinds of resources you should consult on your quest. Be absolutely honest in your answers; otherwise, you'll end up wasting money on exams you're not yet ready to take. There are no right or wrong answers, only steps along the path to certification. Only you can decide where you really belong in the broad spectrum of aspiring candidates. Two things should be clear from the outset, however:

➤ Even a modest background in computer science and programming will be helpful.

➤ Hands-on experience with Microsoft products and technologies is an essential ingredient to Microsoft certification success.

Educational Background

Following are questions related to your education:

1. Have you ever taken any computer-related classes? [Yes or No]

   If your answer is Yes, proceed to question 2; if your answer is No, proceed to question 4.

2. Have you taken any classes about computer operating systems? [Yes or No]

   If your answer is Yes, you will probably be able to handle Microsoft's architecture and system component discussions. If you're rusty, brush up on basic operating system concepts and general computer security topics.

   If your answer is No, consider some basic reading in this area. We strongly recommend a good general operating systems book, such as *Operating System Concepts, 6th Edition*, by Abraham Silberschatz, Peter Baer Galvin, and Greg Gagne (John Wiley & Sons, 2001). If this title doesn't appeal to you, check out reviews for similar titles at your favorite online bookstore.

3. Have you taken any networking concepts or technology classes? [Yes or No]

   If your answer is Yes, you will probably be able to handle Microsoft's networking terminology, concepts, and technologies (brace yourself for frequent departures from normal usage). If you're rusty, brush up on basic networking concepts and terminology, especially networking media, transmission types, the OSI Reference Model, and networking technologies such as Ethernet, token ring, FDDI, and WAN links. Skip to the next section, "Hands-On Experience."

   If your answer is No, you might want to read one or two books in this topic area. The two best books that we know of are *Computer Networks, 4th Edition*, by Andrew S. Tanenbaum (Prentice-Hall, 2002) and *Computer Networks and Internets, 3rd Edition*, by Douglas E. Comer (Prentice-Hall, 2001).

4. Have you read operating system or network publications? [Yes or No]

If your answer is No, consult the recommended reading for both topics. A strong background will help you prepare for the Microsoft exams better than just about anything else.

Hands-On Experience

The most important key to success on all the Microsoft tests is hands-on experience, especially with Windows Server 2003, plus the many add-on services and BackOffice components around which so many of the Microsoft certification exams revolve. If we leave you with only one realization after taking this self-assessment, it should be that there's no substitute for time spent installing, configuring, and using the various Microsoft products upon which you'll be tested repeatedly and in depth.

5. Have you installed, configured, and worked with Windows Server 2003 Server? [Yes or No]

If your answer is Yes, make sure you're familiar with not only installing and configuring the operating system, but also with using the different services included. When studying for Exam 70-297, you should pay close attention to DNS, DHCP, WINS, RRAS, and Certificate Services. The exam requires in-depth knowledge of and a fair amount of experience with each one.

 You can download objectives, practice exams, and other data about Microsoft exams from the Training and Certification page at **www.microsoft.com/train_cert/**. Use the Find an Exam link to obtain specific exam information.

If you haven't worked with Windows Server 2003, TCP/IP, and IIS (or whatever product you choose for your final elective), you must obtain one or two machines and a copy of Windows Server 2003. Then learn the operating system. Do the same for TCP/IP and whatever other software components you'll be tested on.

In fact, we recommend that you obtain two computers, each with a network interface, and set up a two-node network on which to practice. With decent Windows Server 2003–capable computers selling for about $500 to $600 apiece these days, this shouldn't be too much of a financial hardship. You might have to scrounge to come up with the necessary software, but if you scour the Microsoft Web site, you can usually find low-cost options to obtain evaluation copies of most of the software that you'll need.

For any and all of these Microsoft exams, the Resource Kits for the topics involved are a good study resource. You can purchase soft-cover Resource Kits from Microsoft Press (search for them at **www.microsoft.com/mspress/**), but they also appear on the TechNet CDs (**www.microsoft.com/technet**). We believe that Resource Kits, along with *Exam Cram 2* series of books, are among the best preparation tools available.

6. For any specific Microsoft product that is not itself an operating system (for example, FrontPage 2000, SQL Server, and so on), have you installed, configured, used, and upgraded this software? [Yes or No]

If your answer is Yes, skip to the "Testing Your Exam-Readiness" section. If your answer is No, you must get some experience. Read on for suggestions on how to do this.

Experience is a must with any Microsoft product exam, whether something as simple as FrontPage or as challenging as Exchange Server or SQL Server. For trial copies of other software, search Microsoft's Web site using the name of the product as your search term. Also search for bundles such as BackOffice or Small Business Server.

If you have the funds or your employer will pay your way, consider taking a class at a Microsoft Certified Training and Education Center (CTEC) or at an IT academy. In addition to classroom exposure to the topic of your choice, you get a copy of the software that is the focus of your course, along with a trial version of whatever operating system it needs, with the training materials for that class.

Before you even think about taking any Microsoft exam, make sure you've spent enough time with the related software to understand how it can be installed and configured (depending on the exam, this could be an operating system or specific services and applications), how to maintain such an installation, and how to troubleshoot that software when things go wrong. This will help you in the exam and in real life!

Testing Your Exam-Readiness

Whether you attend a formal class on a specific topic to get ready for an exam or use written materials to study on your own, some preparation for the Microsoft certification exams is essential. At $125 a try, pass or fail, you want to do everything you can to pass on your first try. That's where studying comes in.

We've included two practice exams in this book (Chapters 7 and 9) so that if you don't score that well on the first, you can study more and then tackle the second.

For any given subject, consider taking a class if you've tackled self-study materials, taken the test, and failed anyway. The opportunity to interact with an instructor and fellow students could make all the difference in the world, if you can afford that privilege. For information about Microsoft classes, visit the Training and Certification page at for Microsoft Certified Training and Education Centers.

If you can't afford to take a class, visit the Training page at www.microsoft.com/traincert/training/find/default.asp anyway—it also includes pointers to free practice exams and to Microsoft Certified Professional Approved Study Guides and other self-study tools. Even if you can't afford to spend much at all, you should still invest in some low-cost practice exams from commercial vendors.

7. Have you taken a practice exam on your chosen test subject? [Yes or No]

If your answer is Yes and you scored 70% or better, you're probably ready to tackle the real thing. If your score isn't above that threshold, keep at it until you break that barrier.

If your answer is No, obtain all the free and low-price practice tests you can find and get to work. Keep at it until you can break the passing threshold comfortably.

 When it comes to assessing your test-readiness, there is no better way than to take a good-quality practice exam and pass with a score of 70% or better. When we're preparing for exams, we shoot for 80% or more, just to leave room for the fact that we might encounter a question or two on the exam that makes little sense due to its wording.

Assessing Readiness for Exam 70-297

In addition to following the general exam-readiness information in the previous section, you can do several things to prepare for Exam 70-297. We suggest that you join an active Microsoft mailing list, obtain a Microsoft TechNet subscription, and regularly visit the Windows Server 2003 Web site for new information (see www.microsoft.com/windowsserver2003/default.mspx).

Microsoft exam mavens also recommend checking the Microsoft Knowledge Base (integrated into the TechNet CD-ROM, or on the Microsoft Web site at support.microsoft.com/support/) for "meaningful technical support issues" that relate to your exam's topics. Although we're not sure exactly what the quoted phrase means, we've noticed some overlap between technical support questions on particular products and troubleshooting questions on the exams for those products.

What's Next?

After you've assessed your readiness, undertaken the right background studies, obtained the hands-on experience that will help you understand the products and technologies at work, and reviewed the many sources of information to help you prepare for a test, you're ready to take a round of practice tests. When your scores come back positive enough to get you through the exam, you're ready to go after the real thing. If you follow our assessment regime, you'll know not only what you need to study, but you'll also know when you're ready to make a test date at Pearson VUE (www.vue.com) or Prometric (www.2test.com). Good luck!

Microsoft Certification Exams

Terms you'll need to understand:

✓ Case study
✓ Multiple-choice question format
✓ Build-list-and-reorder question format
✓ Create-a-tree question format
✓ Drag-and-connect question format
✓ Select-and-place question format
✓ Hot area question format
✓ Active screen question format
✓ Fixed-length test
✓ Simulation
✓ Adaptive test
✓ Short-form test

Techniques you'll need to master:

✓ Assessing your exam-readiness
✓ Answering Microsoft's various question types
✓ Altering your test strategy depending on the exam format
✓ Practicing to make perfect
✓ Making the best use of the testing software
✓ Budgeting your time
✓ Guessing as a last resort

Exam taking is not something that most people look forward to, no matter how well prepared they are. In most cases, familiarity helps offset test anxiety. In plain English, that means you probably won't be as nervous when you take your fourth or fifth Microsoft certification exam as you'll be when you take your first one.

Whether it's your first exam or your tenth, understanding the details of taking the new exams (how much time to spend on questions, the environment you'll be in, and so on) and the new exam software will help you concentrate on the material rather than on the setting. Likewise, mastering a few basic exam-taking skills should help you recognize and perhaps even outfox some of the tricks and snares you're bound to find in some exam questions.

This chapter, in addition to explaining the exam environment and software, describes some proven exam-taking strategies that you should be able to use to your advantage. Taking the time to read through the information and recommendations presented in this chapter will bring you one step closer to achieving success on a Microsoft exam.

Assessing Exam-Readiness

We strongly recommend that you read through and take the self-assessment included with this book (it appears just before this chapter). Doing so will help you compare your knowledge base to the requirements for obtaining MCSE certification, and it will also help you identify parts of your background or experience that are in need of improvement, enhancement, or further learning. If you get the right set of basics under your belt, obtaining Microsoft certification will be that much easier.

After you've gone through the self-assessment, you can remedy those topical areas where your background or experience might not measure up to those of an ideal certification candidate. But you can also tackle subject matter for individual tests at the same time, so you can continue making progress while you're catching up in some areas.

After you've worked through an *Exam Cram 2* series book, have read the supplementary materials, and have taken the practice test, you'll have a pretty clear idea of when you should be ready to take the real exam. Although we strongly recommend that you keep practicing until your scores top the 75% mark, 80% is a good goal, to give yourself some margin for error in a real exam situation (where stress will play more of a role than when you practice). After you hit that point, you should be ready to challenge the exam. But if you get through the practice exam in this book without attaining that score, you should keep taking practice tests and studying the materials until you get there. You'll find more pointers on how to study and prepare in the self-assessment. At this point, let's talk about the exam itself.

What to Expect at the Testing Center

When you arrive at the testing center where you scheduled your exam, you need to sign in with an exam coordinator. The coordinator asks you to show two forms of identification, one of which must be a photo ID. After you sign in and your time slot arrives, you're asked to deposit any books, bags, and other items that you brought with you. Then you are escorted into a closed room.

All exams are completely closed book. In fact, you aren't permitted to take anything with you into the testing area. But you are furnished with a blank sheet of paper and a pen or, in some cases, an erasable plastic sheet and an erasable pen. Before the exam, be sure to carefully review this book's cram sheet, located in the very front of the book. You should memorize as much of the important material as you can so that you can write that information on the blank sheet as soon as you're seated in front of the computer. You can refer to that piece of paper anytime you like during the test, but you have to surrender the sheet when you leave the room.

You're given some time to compose yourself, to record important information, and to take a sample exam before you begin the real thing. We suggest that you take the sample test before taking your first exam, but because all exams are more or less identical in layout, behavior, and controls   you prob ably won't need to do this more than once.

The testing room is typically furnished with anywhere from one to six computers, and each workstation is separated from the others by dividers designed to keep you from seeing what's happening on someone else's computer. Most testing rooms feature a wall with a large picture window. The window permits the exam coordinator to monitor the room, to prevent exam-takers from talking to one another, and to observe anything out of the ordinary that might go on. The exam coordinator will have preloaded the appropriate Microsoft certification exam—for this book, that's Exam 70-297 "Designing a Microsoft Windows Server 2003 Active Directory and Network Infrastructure"—and you're permitted to start as soon as you're seated in front of the computer.

All Microsoft certification exams allow a certain maximum amount of testing time (this time is indicated on the exam by an onscreen timer clock, so you can check the time remaining whenever you like). All Microsoft certification exams are computer generated. In addition to multiple choice, most exams contain select-and-place (drag-and-drop), create-a-tree (categorization and prioritization), drag-and-connect, and build-list-and-reorder (list prioritization) types of questions. Although this might sound quite simple, the questions are constructed not only to check your mastery of basic facts and figures about a Windows Server 2003 Active Directory and network infrastructure, but to also require you to evaluate one or more sets of circumstances or requirements. You are often asked to give more than one answer to a question. Likewise, you might be asked to select the best or most effective solution to a problem from a range of choices, all of which are technically correct. Taking the exam is quite an adventure, and it involves real thinking. This book shows you what to expect and how to deal with the potential problems, puzzles, and predicaments.

Exam Layout and Design

The format of Microsoft's Windows Server 2003 and Windows 2000 MCSA and MCSE series of exams is different from that of its previous exams covering Windows NT 4.0. For the design exams, each exam consists entirely of a series of case studies, and the questions can be of six types. The MCSE design exams include the following:

➤ *70-219*—Designing a Microsoft Windows 2000 Directory Services Infrastructure

➤ *70-220*—Designing Security for a Microsoft Windows 2000 Network

➤ *70-221*—Designing a Microsoft Windows 2000 Network Infrastructure

➤ *70-226*—Designing Highly Available Web Solutions with Microsoft Windows 2000 Server Technologies

➤ *70-229*—Designing and Implementing Databases with Microsoft SQL Server 2000 Enterprise Edition

➤ *70-297*—Designing a Microsoft Windows Server 2003 Active Directory and Network Infrastructure

➤ *70-298*—Designing Security for a Microsoft Windows Server 2003 Network

For design exams, each case study or testlet presents a detailed problem that you must read and analyze. Figure 1.1 shows an example of what a case study looks like. You must select the different tabs in the case study to view the entire case.

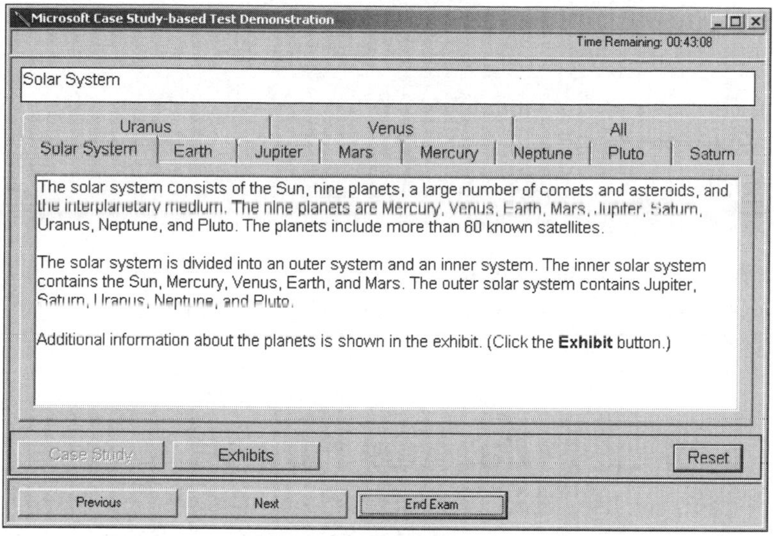

Figure 1.1   The format for case study questions.

Following each case study is a set of questions related to the case study; these questions can be one of six types (which are discussed in the following sections). Careful attention to details provided in the case study is the key to success. You should be prepared to toggle frequently between the case study and the questions as you work. Some of the case studies include diagrams (called *exhibits*), which you'll need to examine closely to understand how to answer the questions.

After you complete a case study, you can review all the questions and your answers. However, after you move on to the next case study, you might not be able to return to the previous case study to make any changes.

For the MCSA and MCSE core exams and the upgrade exams, the same six types of questions might appear, but you aren't likely to encounter complex, multi-question case studies. The MCSA/MCSE core exams and upgrade exams for the Windows Server 2003 track include the following:

➤ *70-210*—Installing, Configuring, and Administering Microsoft Windows 2000 Professional

➤ *70-270*—Installing, Configuring, and Administering Microsoft Windows XP Professional

➤ *70-290*—Managing and Maintaining a Microsoft Windows Server 2003 Environment

➤ *70-291*—Implementing, Managing, and Maintaining a Microsoft Windows Server 2003 Network Infrastructure

➤ *70-292*—Managing and Maintaining a Microsoft Windows Server 2003 Environment for an MCSA Certified on Windows 2000

➤ *70-293*—Planning and Maintaining a Microsoft Windows Server 2003 Network Infrastructure

➤ *70-294*—Planning, Implementing, and Maintaining a Microsoft Windows Server 2003 Active Directory Infrastructure

➤ *70-296*—Planning, Implementing, and Maintaining a Microsoft Windows Server 2003 Environment for an MCSE Certified on Windows 2000

Traditional Exam Question Formats

Six question formats have historically appeared on Microsoft certification exams. For the 70-297 exam, be prepared to be presented with various case studies followed by questions in all six formats. You can download a demo from the Microsoft Web site to further familiarize yourself with the new types of exam questions. These types of questions continue to appear on current Microsoft tests and are discussed in the following sections:

➤ Multiple-choice, single answer

➤ Multiple-choice, multiple answers

➤ Build-list-and-reorder (list prioritization)

➤ Create-a-tree

➤ Drag-and-connect

➤ Select-and-place (drag-and-drop)

The Single-Answer and Multiple-Answer Multiple-Choice Question Formats

Some exam questions require you to select a single answer, whereas others ask you to select multiple correct answers. The following multiple-choice question requires you to select a single correct answer. Following the question is a brief summary of each potential answer and why it is either right or wrong.

Question 1

> You have three domains connected to an empty root domain under one con-
> tiguous domain name: **tutu.com**. This organization is formed into a forest
> arrangement, with a secondary domain called **frog.com**. How many schema
> masters exist for this arrangement?
>
> O A. 1
> O B. 2
> O C. 3
> O D. 4

Answer A is correct because only one schema master is necessary for a forest
arrangement. The other answers (answers B, C, and D) are misleading because
they try to make you believe that schema masters might be in each domain, or
perhaps that you should have one for each contiguous namespace domain.

This sample question format corresponds closely to the Microsoft certification exam format. The only difference is that on the exam, the questions are
not followed by answers and their explanations. To select an answer, you
position the cursor over the radio button next to the answer you want to
select, and then click the mouse button to select the answer.

Let's examine a question where one or more answers are possible. This type
of question provides check boxes rather than option buttons for marking all
appropriate selections.

Question 2

> What can you use to seize FSMO roles? (Select all the correct answers.)
> ❑ A. The **ntdsutil.exe** utility
> ❑ B. The Replication Monitor
> ❑ C. The **secedit.exe** utility
> ❑ D. Active Directory domains and trusts

Answers A and D are correct. In the case of a server failure, you can seize
roles with the ntdsutil.exe utility. Active Directory domains and trusts can be
used to change the location of the Domain Naming Master (which is one of
the five FSMO roles). The secedit.exe utility is used to force group policies
into play; therefore, answer C is incorrect. Replication Monitor can be used
to view which servers are holding the FSMO roles.

For this particular question, two answers are required. Microsoft sometimes
gives partial credit for partially correct answers. For question 2, you have to

mark the checkboxes next to answers A and B to obtain credit for a correct answer. Notice that choosing the right answers also means knowing why the other answers are wrong!

The Build-List-and-Reorder Question Format

Questions in the build-list-and-reorder format present two lists of items, one on the left and one on the right. To answer the question, you must move items from the list on the right to the list on the left. The final list must then be reordered into a specific order.

These questions generally sound like this: "From the following list of choices, pick the choices that answer the question. Arrange the list in a certain order." To give you practice with this type of question, some questions of this type are included in this book. Question 3 shows an example of how they appear in this book; for an example of how they appear on the test, see Figure 1.2.

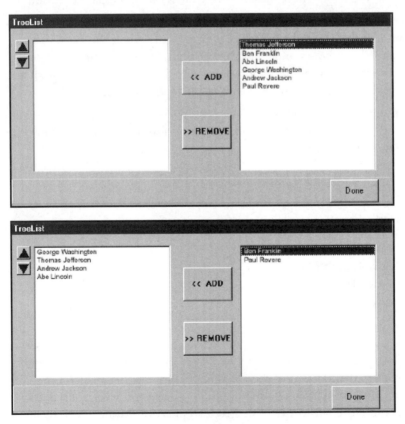

Figure 1.2   The format for build-list-and-reorder questions.

Question 3

From the following list of famous people, choose those that have been elected president of the United States. Arrange the list in the order in which the presidents served.

Thomas Jefferson

Ben Franklin

Abe Lincoln

George Washington

Andrew Jackson

Paul Revere

The correct answer is

George Washington

Thomas Jefferson

Andrew Jackson

Abe Lincoln

On an actual exam, the entire list of famous people would initially appear in the list on the right. You would move the four correct answers to the list on the left and then reorder the list on the left. Notice that the answer to question 3 does not include all items from the initial list. However, that might not always be the case.

To move an item from the right list to the left list on the exam, you first select the item by clicking it, and then you click the Add button (left arrow). After you move an item from one list to the other, you can move the item back by first selecting the item and then clicking the appropriate button (either the Add button or the Remove button). After items have been moved to the left list, you can move an item by selecting the item and clicking the up or down button.

The Create-a-Tree Question Format

Questions in the create-a-tree format also present two lists, one on the left side of the screen and one on the right side. The list on the right consists of individual items, and the list on the left consists of nodes in a tree. To answer the question, you must move items from the list on the right to the appropriate node in the tree.

These questions can best be characterized as simply a matching exercise. Items from the list on the right are placed under the appropriate category in the list on the left. Question 4 shows an example of how they appear in this book; for a sample of how they appear on the test, see Figure 1.3.

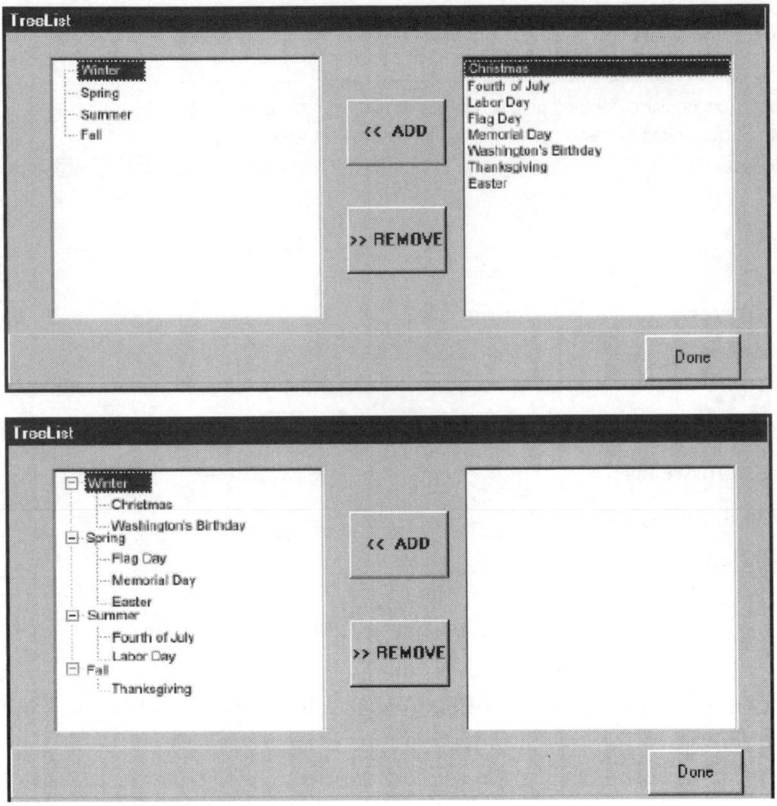

Figure 1.3   The create-a-tree question format.

Question 4

The calendar year is divided into four seasons:

Winter   Summer

Spring   Fall

Identify the season during which each of the following holidays occurs:

Christmas   Memorial Day

Fourth of July   Washington's Birthday

Labor Day   Thanksgiving

Flag Day   Easter

The correct answer is

➤ Winter

  Christmas

  Washington's Birthday

➤ Spring

  Flag Day

  Memorial Day

  Easter

➤ Summer

  Fourth of July

  Labor Day

➤ Fall

  Thanksgiving

In this case, all the items in the list are used. However, that might not always happen.

To move an item from the right list to its appropriate location in the tree, you must first select the appropriate tree node by clicking it. Then you select the item to be moved and click the Add button. If one or more items have been added to a tree node, the node is displayed with a + icon to the left of the node name. You can click this icon to expand the node and view the items that have been added. If any item has been added to the wrong tree node, you can remove it by selecting it and clicking the Remove button.

The Drag-and-Connect Question Format

Questions in the drag-and-connect format present a group of objects and a list of connections. To answer the question, you must move the appropriate connections between the objects.

This type of question is best described using graphics. Question 5 shows an example.

Question 5

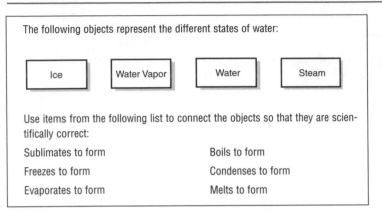

The following objects represent the different states of water:

The correct answer is

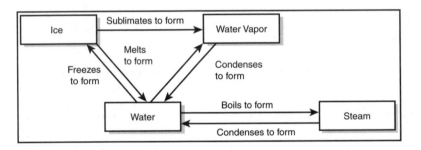

For this type of question, it's not necessary to use every object, and each connection can be used multiple times.

The Select-and-Place Question Format

Questions in the select-and-place (drag-and-drop) format present a diagram with blank boxes and a list of labels that need to be dragged to correctly fill in the blank boxes. To answer such a question, you must move the labels to their appropriate positions on the diagram.

This type of question is best described using graphics. Question 6 shows an example.

Question 6

Place the items in their proper order, by number, on the following flowchart. Some items might be used more than once, and some items might not be used at all:

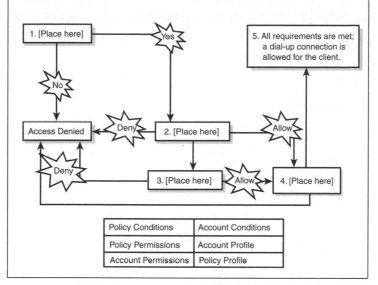

Policy Conditions	Account Conditions
Policy Permissions	Account Profile
Account Permissions	Policy Profile

The correct answer is

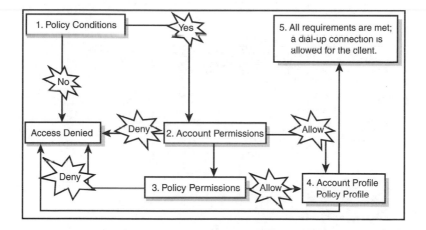

New Exam Question Formats

Microsoft is introducing several new question types in addition to the more traditional types of questions that are still widely used on all Microsoft exams. These new, innovative question types have been highly researched and tested by Microsoft before they were chosen to be included in many of the newer exams for the MCSA/MCSE on Windows 2000 track and the MCSA/MCSE on Windows Server 2003 track. These new question types are as follows:

➤ Hot area questions

➤ Active screen questions

➤ New drag-and-drop type questions

➤ Simulation questions

Hot Area Question Types

Hot area questions ask you to indicate the correct answer by selecting one or more elements within a graphic. For example, you might be asked to select multiple objects within a list, as shown in Figure 1.4.

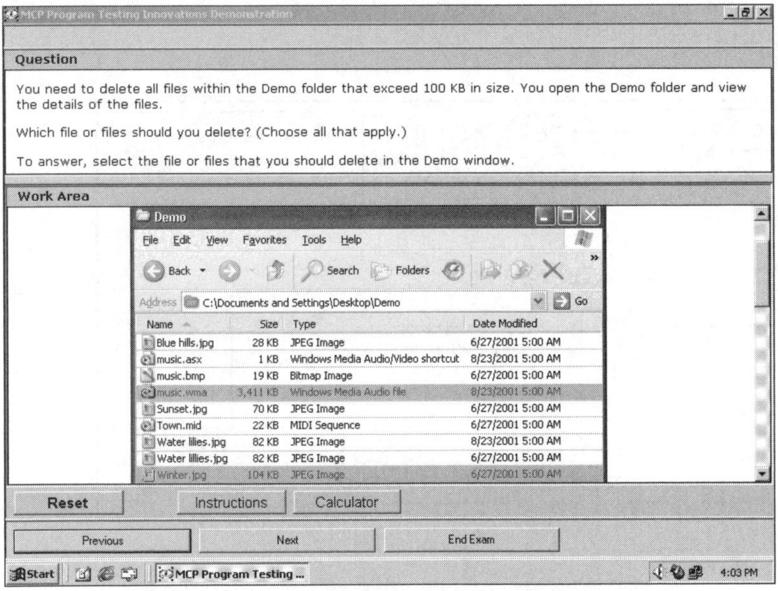

Figure 1.4 Selecting objects within a list box to answer a hot area question.

Active Screen Question Types

Active screen questions ask you to configure a dialog box by modifying one or more elements. These types of questions offer a realistic interface in which you must properly configure various settings, just as you would within the actual software product. For example, you might be asked to select the proper option within a drop-down list box, as shown in Figure 1.5.

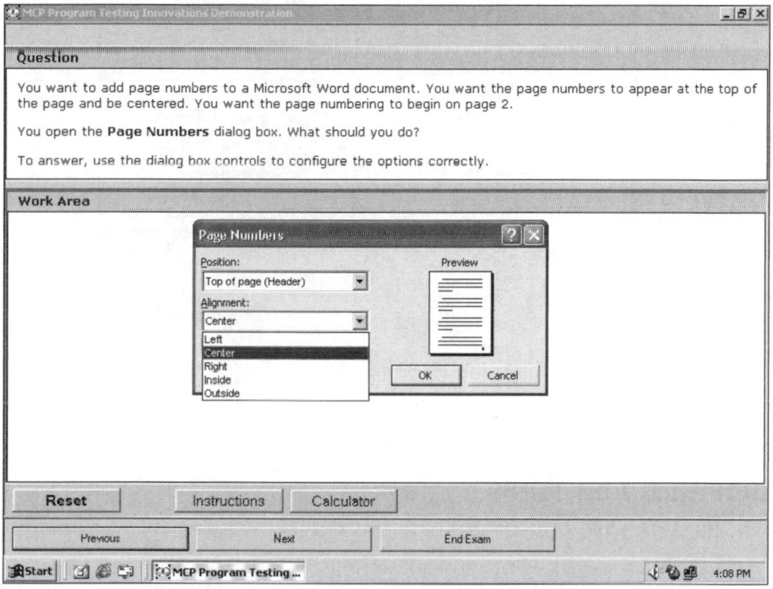

Figure 1.5   Configuring an option from a dialog box's drop-down list box to answer an active screen question.

New Drag-and-Drop Question Types

New drag-and-drop questions ask you to drag source elements to their appropriate corresponding targets within a work area. These types of questions test your knowledge of specific concepts and their definitions or descriptions. For example, you might be asked to match a description of a computer program to the actual software application, as shown in Figure 1.6.

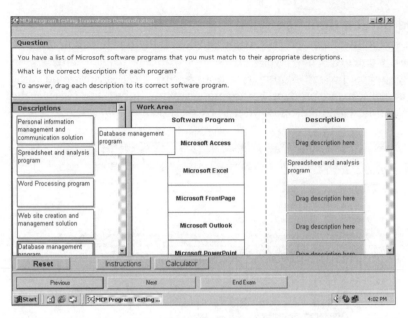

Figure 1.6 Using a drag-and-drop technique to match the correct application description to each software program listed.

Simulation Question Types

Simulation questions ask you to indicate the correct answer by performing specific tasks, such as configuring and installing network adapters or drivers, configuring and controlling access to files, or troubleshooting hardware devices. Many of the tasks that systems administrators and systems engineers perform can be presented more accurately in simulations than in most traditional exam question types (see Figure 1.7).

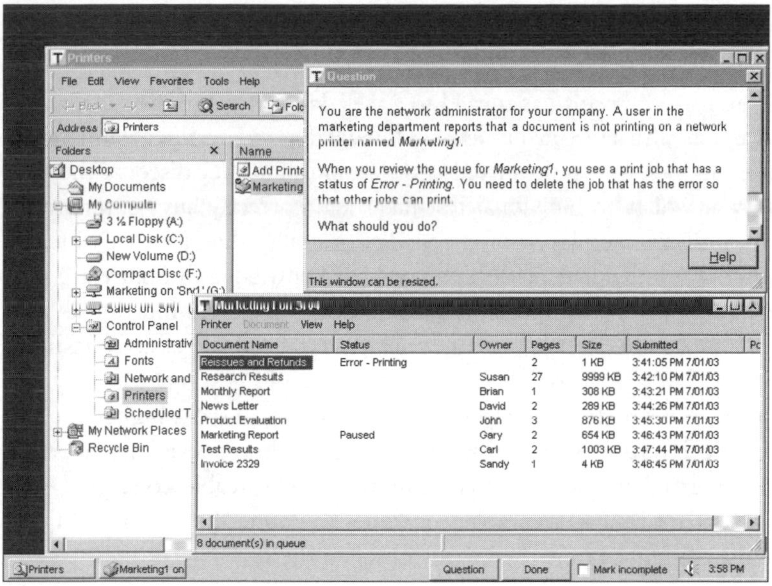

Figure 1.7   Answering a simulation question about how to troubleshoot a network printing problem.

Microsoft's Testing Formats

Currently, Microsoft uses four different testing formats:

➤ Case study   ➤ Adaptive

➤ Fixed length   ➤ Short form

As mentioned earlier, the case study approach is used with Microsoft's design exams. These exams consist of a set of case studies that you must analyze so that you can answer questions related to them. Such exams include one or more case studies (tabbed topic areas), each of which is followed by 4 to 10 questions. The question types for design exams and for the core exams are multiple-choice, build-list-and-reorder, create-a-tree, drag-and-connect, and select-and-place. Depending on the test topic, some exams are totally case based, whereas others are not.

Other Microsoft exams employ advanced testing capabilities that might not be immediately apparent. Although the questions that appear are primarily multiple-choice, the logic that drives them is more complex than that in older Microsoft tests, which use a fixed sequence of questions, called a *fixed-length test*. Some questions employ a sophisticated user interface, which Microsoft calls a *simulation*, to test your knowledge of the software and systems under consideration in a more-or-less live environment that behaves just like the real thing.

You should review the Microsoft Training and Certification Web pages at www.microsoft.com/traincert for more information.

For some exams, Microsoft has turned to a well-known technique called *adaptive testing* to establish a test-taker's level of knowledge and product competence. Adaptive exams look the same as fixed-length exams, but they discover the level of difficulty at which an individual test-taker can correctly answer questions. Test-takers with differing levels of knowledge or ability therefore see different sets of questions; individuals with high levels of knowledge or ability are presented with a smaller set of more difficult questions, whereas individuals with lower levels of knowledge are presented with a larger set of easier questions. Two individuals might answer the same percentage of questions correctly, but the test-taker with a higher knowledge or ability level will score higher because the more difficult questions are worth more. Also, the lower-level test-taker will probably answer more questions than a more-knowledgeable colleague. This explains why adaptive tests use ranges of values to define the number of questions and the amount of time it takes to complete the test.

Adaptive tests work by evaluating the test-taker's most recent answer. A correct answer leads to a more difficult question, and the test software's estimate of the test-taker's knowledge and ability level is raised. An incorrect answer leads to a less difficult question, and the test software's estimate of the test-taker's knowledge and ability level is lowered. This process continues until the test targets the test-taker's true ability level. The exam ends when the test-taker's level of accuracy meets a statistically acceptable value (in other words, when the test-taker's performance demonstrates an acceptable level of knowledge and ability) or when the maximum number of items has been presented (in which case the test-taker is almost certain to fail).

Microsoft has also introduced a short-form test for its most popular tests. This test delivers 25 to 30 questions to its takers, giving them exactly 60 minutes to complete the exam. This type of exam is similar to a fixed-length test, in that it allows readers to jump ahead or return to earlier questions and to cycle through the questions until the test is done. Microsoft does not use adaptive logic in short-form tests, but it claims that statistical analysis of the question pool is such that the 25 to 30 questions delivered during a short-form exam conclusively measure a test-taker's knowledge of the subject matter in much the same way as an adaptive test. You can think of the short-form test as a kind of "greatest hits exam" (that is, the most important questions are covered) version of an adaptive exam on the same topic.

NOTE

Microsoft certification exams use either the adaptive-question format or the more traditional fixed-length question format. Microsoft published adaptive-question format exams in the past, but currently seems to be moving away from the format.

Because you won't know in which form the Microsoft exam will be given, you should be prepared for an adaptive exam instead of a fixed-length or a short-form exam. The penalties for answering incorrectly are built in to the test itself on an adaptive exam, whereas the layout remains the same for a fixed-length or short-form test, no matter how many questions you answer incorrectly.

> The biggest difference between adaptive tests and fixed-length or short-form tests is that you can mark and revisit questions on fixed-length and short-form tests after you've read them. On an adaptive test, you must answer the question when it is presented and cannot go back to that question later.

Strategies for Different Testing Formats

Before you choose a test-taking strategy, you must determine what type of test it is—case study, fixed length, short form, or adaptive:

> ➤ Case study tests consist of a tabbed window that allows you to navigate easily through the sections of the case.

> ➤ Fixed-length tests consist of 50 to 70 questions with a check box for each question. You can return to these questions if you want.

> ➤ Short-form tests have 25 to 30 questions with a check box for each question. You can return to these questions if you want.

> ➤ Adaptive tests are identified in the introductory material of the test. Questions have no check boxes and can be visited (and answered) only once. You do not have the option of reviewing any questions once you have answered them all.

> You'll be able to tell for sure whether you're taking an adaptive, fixed-length, or short-form test by the first question. Fixed-length and short-form tests include a check box that enables you to mark the question for later review. Adaptive test questions include no such check box and can be visited (and answered) only once.

Case Study Exam Strategy

Most test-takers find that the case study type of test used for the design exams (including exams 70-297, 70-219, 70-220, 70-221, and 70-226, among others) is the most difficult to master. When it comes to studying for a case study test, your best bet is to approach each case study as a standalone test. The biggest challenge you're likely to encounter with this type of test is that you might feel you won't have enough time to get through all the cases presented.

Each case study provides a lot of material that you need to read and study before you can effectively answer the questions that follow. The trick to taking a case study exam is to first scan the case study to get the highlights. Make sure that you read the overview section of the case so that you understand the context of the problem at hand. Then you should quickly move on to scanning the questions.

As you're scanning the questions, you should make mental notes to yourself so that you'll remember which sections of the case study you should focus on. Some case studies might provide a fair amount of extra information that you don't really need to answer the questions. The goal with this scanning approach is to avoid having to study and analyze material that is not completely relevant.

When studying a case, read the tabbed information carefully. It's important to answer each and every question. You will be able to toggle back and forth from case to questions, and from question to question within a case testlet. However, after you leave the case and move on, you might not be able to return to it. We suggest you take notes while reading useful information to help you when you tackle the test questions. It's hard to go wrong with this strategy when taking any kind of Microsoft certification test.

The Fixed-Length and Short-Form Exam Strategy

A well-known principle when taking fixed-length or short-form exams is to first read through the entire exam from start to finish. Answer only those questions that you feel absolutely sure you know. On subsequent passes, you can dive into more complex questions more deeply, knowing how many such questions you have left and the amount of time remaining.

There's at least one potential benefit to reading over the exam completely before answering the trickier questions: Information supplied in later questions sometimes sheds more light on earlier questions. At other times, information you read in later questions might jog your memory about facts, figures, or behaviors that help you answer earlier questions. Either way, you'll come out ahead if you answer only those questions on the first pass that you're absolutely confident about.

Fortunately, the Microsoft exam software for fixed-length and short-form tests makes the multiple-visit approach easy to implement. At the top-left corner of each question is a check box that permits you to mark that question for a later visit.

Here are some question-handling strategies that apply to fixed-length and short-form tests. Use them if you have the chance:

➤ When returning to a question after your initial read-through, read every word again; otherwise, your mind could miss important details. Revisiting a question after turning your attention elsewhere sometimes enables you to see something you missed, but the strong tendency is to see what you've seen before. Try to avoid that tendency at all costs.

➤ If you return to a question more than twice, try to articulate to yourself what you don't understand about the question, why answers don't appear to make sense, or what appears to be missing. If you chew on the subject awhile, your subconscious might provide the missing details, or you might notice a trick that points to the right answer.

As you work your way through the exam, another counter that Microsoft provides will come in handy: the number of questions completed and questions outstanding. For fixed-length and short-form tests, it's wise to budget your time by making sure that you've completed one-quarter of the questions one-quarter of the way through the exam period and three-quarters of the questions three-quarters of the way through.

If you're not finished when only 5 minutes remain, use that time to guess your way through any remaining questions. Remember, guessing is potentially more valuable than not answering. Blank answers are always wrong, but a guess might turn out to be correct. If you don't have a clue about any of the remaining questions, pick answers at random or choose all A's, B's, and so on. Questions left unanswered are counted as answered incorrectly, so a guess is better than nothing at all.

 At the very end of your exam period, you're better off guessing than leaving questions unanswered.

The Adaptive Exam Strategy

If there's one principle that applies to taking an adaptive test, it could be summed up as "Get it right the first time." You cannot elect to skip a question and move on to the next one when taking an adaptive test because the testing software uses your answer to the current question to select the question it presents next. You also cannot return to a question after you've moved on because the software gives you only one chance to answer the question. You can, however, take notes, and sometimes information supplied in earlier questions sheds more light on later questions.

When you answer a question correctly, you're presented with a more difficult question next to help the software gauge your level of skill and ability. When you answer a question incorrectly, you're presented with a less difficult question, and the software lowers its current estimate of your skill and ability. This continues until the program settles into a reasonably accurate estimate of what you know and can do, and it takes you, on average, somewhere between 15 and 30 questions to complete the test.

The good news is that if you know your stuff, you're likely to finish most adaptive tests in 30 minutes or so. The bad news is that you must really, really know your stuff to do your best on an adaptive test. That's because some questions are so convoluted, complex, or hard to follow that you're bound to miss one or two, at a minimum, even if you do know your stuff. So, the more you know, the better you'll do on an adaptive test, even accounting for the occasional weird or unfathomable questions that appear on these exams.

Because you can't always tell in advance whether a test will be a fixed-length, short-form, or adaptive exam, you should prepare for the exam as if it were adaptive. That way, you will be prepared to pass no matter what kind of test you take. But if you do take a fixed-length or short-form test, you need to remember the tips from the preceding sections. These tips should help you perform even better on a fixed-length or short-form exam than on an adaptive test.

If you encounter a question on an adaptive test that you can't answer, you must guess an answer immediately. Because of how the software works, however, you might suffer for your guess on the next question if you guess right because you get a more difficult question next!

Question-Handling Strategies

For those questions that have only one right answer, usually two or three of the answers will be obviously incorrect, and two of the answers will be plausible. Unless the answer leaps out at you (if it does, reread the question to look for a trick; sometimes those are the ones you're most likely to get wrong), begin the process of answering by eliminating those answers that are most obviously wrong.

At least one answer out of the possible choices for a question can usually be eliminated immediately because it matches one of these conditions:

➤ The answer does not apply to the situation.

➤ The answer describes a nonexistent issue, an invalid option, or an imaginary state.

After you eliminate all answers that are obviously wrong, you can apply your retained knowledge to eliminate further answers. You should look for items that sound correct but refer to actions, commands, or features that are not present or not available in the situation that the question describes.

If you're still faced with a blind guess among two or more potentially correct answers, reread the question. Try to picture how each of the possible remaining answers would alter the situation. Be especially sensitive to terminology; sometimes the choice of words (*remove* instead of *disable*) can make the difference between a right answer and a wrong one.

You should guess at an answer only after you've exhausted your ability to eliminate answers and are still unclear about which of the remaining possibilities is correct. An unanswered question offers you no points, but guessing gives you at least some chance of getting a question right—just don't be too hasty when making a blind guess.

If you're taking a fixed-length or a short-form test, you can wait until the last round of reviewing marked questions (just as you're about to run out of time or unanswered questions) before you start making guesses. You usually have the same option within each case study testlet (but after you leave a testlet, you might not be allowed to return to it). If you're taking an adaptive test, you have to guess to move on to the next question if you can't figure out an answer some other way. Either way, guessing should be your technique of last resort!

Numerous questions assume that the default behavior of a particular utility is in effect. If you know the defaults and understand what they mean, this knowledge will help you cut through many of the trickier questions. Simple "final" actions might be critical as well. If a utility must be restarted before proposed changes take effect, a correct answer might require this step as well.

Mastering the Inner Game

In the final analysis, knowledge breeds confidence, and confidence breeds success. If you study the materials in this book carefully and review all the practice questions at the end of each chapter, you should become aware of the areas in which you need additional learning and study.

After you've worked your way through the book, take the practice exams in the back of the book. Taking these tests provides a reality check and helps you identify areas to study further. Make sure you follow up and review materials related to the questions you miss on the practice exams before you schedule a real exam. Don't schedule your exam appointment until after you've thoroughly studied the material and feel comfortable with the whole scope of the practice exams. You should score 80% or better on the practice exam before you proceed to the real thing (otherwise, obtain some additional practice tests so you can keep trying until you hit the magic number).

 If you take a practice exam and don't get at least 70% to 80% of the questions correct, keep practicing. Microsoft provides links to practice exam providers and also self-assessment exams at **www.microsoft.com/traincert/mcpexams/prepare/**.

Armed with the information in this book and with the determination to augment your knowledge, you should be able to pass the certification exam. However, you need to work at it, or you'll spend the exam fee more than once before you finally pass. If you prepare seriously, you should do well.

The next section covers other sources that you can use to prepare for Microsoft certification exams.

Additional Resources

A good source of information about Microsoft certification exams comes from Microsoft itself. Because its products and technologies and the exams that go with them change frequently, the best place to go for exam-related information is online.

If you haven't already visited the Microsoft Training and Certification Web site, you should do so right now. Microsoft's Training and Certification home page resides at www.microsoft.com/traincert (see Figure 1.8).

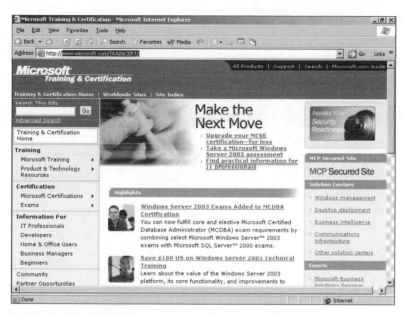

Figure 1.8   The Microsoft Training and Certification home page.

Coping with Change on the Web

Sooner or later, all the information we've shared with you about the Microsoft Certified Professional pages and the other Web-based resources mentioned throughout the rest of this book will go stale or be replaced by newer information. In some cases, the URLs you find here might lead you to their replacements; in other cases, the URLs will go nowhere, leaving you with the dreaded 404 File Not Found error message. When that happens, don't give up.

There's always a way to find what you want on the Web if you're willing to invest some time and energy. Most large or complex Web sites—and Microsoft's qualifies on both counts—offer search engines. On all of Microsoft's Web pages, a Search button appears at the top edge of the page. As long as you can get to Microsoft's site (it should stay at **www.microsoft.com** for a long time), you can use the Search button to find what you need.

The more focused you can make a search request, the more likely it is that the results will include information you can use. For example, you can search for the string:

"training and certification"

to produce a lot of data about the subject in general, but if you're looking for the preparation guide for Exam 70-297, "Designing a Microsoft Windows Server 2003 Active Directory and Network Infrastructure," you'll be more likely to get there quickly if you use a search string similar to the following:

"Exam 70-297" AND "preparation guide"

Likewise, if you want to find the Training and Certification downloads, you should try a search string such as this:

"training and certification" AND "download page"

Finally, you should feel free to use general search tools such as **www.google.com**, **www.altavista.com**, and **www.excite.com** to look for related information. Although Microsoft offers great information about its certification exams online, there are plenty of third-party sources of information and assistance that need not follow Microsoft's party line. Therefore, if you can't find something where the book says it lives, you should intensify your search.

Gathering and Analyzing Business and Technical Requirements

Terms you'll need to understand:

✓ DNS
✓ BIND
✓ Active Directory
✓ SRV records
✓ Dynamic updates
✓ Domain
✓ Forest
✓ Tree
✓ Site
✓ Organization unit

Techniques you'll need to master:

✓ Understanding the elements that make up Active Directory
✓ Analyzing the effect of Active Directory on the technical environment
✓ Analyzing DNS for Active Directory service implementation
✓ Analyzing existing network operating system implementation
✓ Analyzing security requirements for Active Directory services
✓ Identifying network topology and performance levels

This chapter begins by providing an introduction to Active Directory and its various components. The chapter also discusses the various aspects that must be analyzed when planning an Active Directory and network infrastructure. Remember that making good decisions during the planning phase is dependent on gathering the required information about the existing network.

Active Directory Overview

For experts to properly implement an Active Directory infrastructure, they must have an understanding of the Active Directory design elements and, equally important, an understanding of the business for which the Active Directory infrastructure is being designed. The process of developing an Active Directory infrastructure involves an analysis of the business's current administrative and geographic model, goals it wants to achieve, as well as any future plans. With proper business analysis, an Active Directory infrastructure can meet the current requirements while easily allowing for future growth and expansion.

Active Directory is implemented as a service that allows network administrators to centrally organize and manage objects such as users, computers, printers, applications, and profiles. That means locating and managing network resources is now much simpler.

Objects that are stored in Active Directory are accessible to users throughout an organization. Users do not need to know the physical location of the objects because they are logically grouped into a central location. The specific structure of Active Directory can be customized to meet the needs of almost any business environment. The structure of Active Directory is hierarchical and consists of five main design elements:

➤ Forests

➤ Trees

➤ Domains

➤ Organizational units

➤ Sites

The Five Main Elements

Before diving into the analysis process of Active Directory design, you need to understand the various Active Directory elements outlined in the preceding list. The following sections provide an overview of the five main Active Directory elements.

Forests

The first design element that we'll discuss is the forest. A *forest* is the boundary of the scope of an Active Directory implementation. In its simplest form, a forest is a single domain. A forest can contain multiple domains, and each new domain created with its own unique namespace establishes a new tree within the forest (trees will be discussed later in the chapter).

The first domain created within the forest is the *forest root*. It's important to plan which domain will become the forest root domain for an organization. Careful planning can help avoid the possibility of having to completely reorganize the Active Directory structure in the future. However, Windows Server 2003 makes restructuring simpler because any domain, including the forest root domain, can now be renamed (this was not the case in Windows Server 2000).

 Because the ability to rename the forest root domain is a new feature in Windows Server 2003, be prepared to encounter an exam question pertaining to this topic. You can use the Rendom.exe utility to rename a domain.

After the forest root domain has been configured, new domains can be added as child domains of the forest root or they can be established as new trees within the forest. When you are designing the forest structure, remember that simpler is usually better. It's possible to create multiple forests with Active Directory, but a single-forest environment is much easier to administer and maintain. However, it might be necessary for organizations to create more than one forest in order to meet their administrative needs.

Domains within a single forest share some common elements:

➤ Schema

➤ Configuration container

➤ Global catalog

➤ Enterprise Admins group

➤ Schema Admins group

Having common elements shared among domains within a single-forest environment makes the administration of multiple domains much simpler. Conversely, this could also be a reason why an organization would opt to create a multi-forest structure. The next two sections should clarify this statement.

Schema

The *schema* maintains a list of all objects that can be stored within Active Directory as well as the attributes associated with each object. The schema is made up of two main components:

➤ The class-schema object

➤ The attribute-schema object

An example of a class-schema object within an Active Directory would be the Users class. An attribute associated with this class may be the user's first name. Each attribute, such as the user's first name, has an attribute-schema object associated with it that defines items such as the syntax of the attribute. The default schema should meet the needs of most organizations, but components can also be added or modified within the schema if needed. For example, an organization might require that employee ID be a required field for all users. In a case such as this, the schema can be modified to include this attribute.

When planning a forest structure, the design team has to consider the schema policy. If the default schema policy does not meet the needs of the entire organization, it might be necessary to create multiple forests.

 To make changes to the schema, you must be a member of the Schema Admins group.

Configuration Container

A forest also contains a single configuration container that is copied to all domain controllers in each domain. This container stores configuration information about the entire forest, such as which subnets have been combined into sites and the site links that connect them. This information can be used for tasks such as replication. The configuration container can be examined when determining links between sites and the best route for replication if multiple links exist. The existence of a forestwide configuration container means that configuration information does not have to be created for each domain, which makes the administration of multiple domains much easier.

Global Catalog Server

All domains within a forest also share a single global catalog server. The global catalog server stores certain attributes that pertain to each object within the forest. You can query the global catalog by using an attribute of an object to determine its location. This is beneficial for clients because they do not have to search for an object in different domains.

Think of a global catalog server as analogous to the Yellow Pages, which stores certain attributes for businesses in a city. You use the Yellow Pages when you want to quickly determine the location of a business or find its phone number. When searching for an object within the forest, you can query the global catalog server to determine the object's locations instead of performing an extensive search. This is a welcome change from Windows NT 4.0, where users who wanted to locate an object within the network had to perform a search of the entire domain and any trusted domains.

Default attributes are automatically included within the global catalog. An organization has the option to add attributes and customize the information stored in the global catalog server to meet its needs (see Figure 2.1). For example, adding the employee ID attribute to the global catalog enables you to search for users based on this attribute.

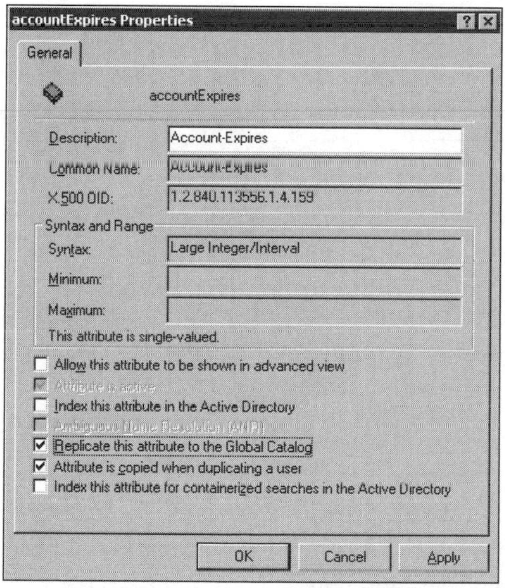

Figure 2.1   Adding an attribute to the global catalog.

During the logon process, the global catalog server is also used to determine universal group membership. If a global catalog is unavailable and the user has never logged on before, he will only be able to log on locally. However,

Windows Server 2003 allows users to log on with cached credentials. If the functional level is Windows 2000 native or Windows Server 2003 and the user has previously logged on, he will be able to log on with cached credentials if the global catalog is unavailable. Administrators, on the other hand, can log on regardless of whether or not they've logged on in the past.

By default, the first domain controller within the forest is designated as the global catalog server. An organization can thereafter designate its domain controller of choice as the global catalog server (see Figure 2.2).

NTDS Settings Properties

General | Connections | Object | Security

NTDS Settings

Description:

Query Policy:

DNS Alias: 79DF3C1A-64F3-4555-BC31-D9E21BDD94B0._msdcs.

☑ Global Catalog

The amount of time it will take to publish the Global Catalog varies depending on your replication topology.

OK | Cancel | Apply

Figure 2.2 Designating a global catalog server.

Trusts

Windows Server 2003 makes the process of providing access to resources across multiple domains and forests much simpler. In previous versions of Windows NT, for users in one domain to access resources in another domain, at a minimum, a one-way trust had to be manually set up between the two domains.

With Active Directory, two-way transitive Kerberos trusts are automatically established between all domains in the same forest. This eliminates the need for trusts to be manually created between domains.

NOTE

Trusts can be established in an organization that has a combination of Windows Server 2003 and Windows NT 4.0 domains, but they must be set up manually.

Trees

Within a forest, domains that share a contiguous namespace form a *tree*. After a tree has been established within a forest, any new domain added to an existing tree inherits a portion of its namespace from its parent domain.

A forest can also consist of multiple trees. For example, an organization that has more than one registered domain name can create multiple trees within a single forest so that the namespaces can be maintained.

Each time a new domain is created with Windows NT 4.0, an administrator must manually configure a trust with any other domains with which the new domain needs to share resources. If the environment consists of multiple domains configured in a multiple-master domain model, the administrator would have to establish several trusts. The trusts that are set up by the administrator are also not transitive, meaning that if A trusts B and B trusts C, A and C do not trust each other.

Conversely, in Active Directory, two-way transitive trusts are immediately set up between the new domain and its parent domain without the intervention of an administrator. This means that if A trusts B and B trusts C, A and C also trust each other. When a new tree is created, a two-way transitive trust is also established between the root domain of the new tree and the forest root.

Domains

The main components of the Active Directory hierarchy are domains and organizational units. *Domains* determine the administrative boundaries within the Active Directory hierarchy. Think of a domain as a container. All the objects within the container share the same administration, replication process, and security requirements. In some cases, the same security requirements can be applied to an entire business. If a business requires separate security policies, such as unique password policies, to meet its administrative structure, it might be necessary to create more than one domain. Objects would then inherit the security policy from the domain in which they are located.

Windows Server 2003 (and 2000) uses a multi-master replication model within a domain. Within a domain, all domain controllers are considered equal, meaning that they all contain a working copy of the directory and every domain controller can read and write changes to the directory. In previous versions of Windows NT, there was only one working copy of the directory database for the domain, and it was stored on the primary domain controller (PDC). The backup domain controllers (BDCs) maintained only copies, which they received from the PDC. If a PDC was taken offline, it was necessary to promote a BDC to take its place so that a working copy of the directory database was available. Within Active Directory, each domain controller can receive changes to the directory and then replicate the changes to other domain controllers in the domain.

Organizational Units

Another design element within Active Directory is the organizational unit. *Organizational units* are container objects that are used to organize objects within a domain. They are not based on the physical structure of the network. When you're planning organizational units within Active Directory, it's important to base them on the business's current administrative model. For example, a business might decide to create an organizational unit for each department (Accounting, Human Resources, and so on). Additional organizational units could then be created to organize the objects in each department.

By creating organizational units, administrators can delegate control of the objects to other users in the organization (referred to as *delegation of authority*). In this way, domain administrators don't have to remain responsible for every administrative aspect of their organization.

All domains within a forest maintain their own hierarchy of organizational units, which enables administrators in different domains to establish a hierarchy that best meets their needs. Likewise, if all domains within a forest require the same hierarchy of organizational units, they can be modeled on one another. For example, if a central IT team manages an entire corporation, this team can develop a structure of organizational units within Active Directory that could then be implemented by each domain in the forest.

Not only can organizational units be created to assign a user, group, and computer control over the objects contained within them, but they can also be used to group objects that require a similar group policy. By applying a group policy to an organizational unit, an administrator can limit the capabilities and restrict the environment of the objects contained within it. A group of users that requires a similar desktop environment can be grouped into an organizational unit, and a group policy can then be applied to that specific organizational unit.

Group policies are similar in concept to system policies in Windows NT 4.0. Group Policy is a directory-based management tool that can be used by administrators to define configurations for users and computers.

Sites

Sites are the last major design element within the Active Directory structure. A *site* is basically a collection of IP subnets that are connected by high-speed, reliable links with a lot of available bandwidth. Sites are created within the Active Directory infrastructure to optimize replication between domain controllers. A site topology is designed around the physical location of IP subnets within a domain and the type of link connecting them. As with the other design elements we've discussed, a careful analysis of the physical structure must be done to determine the number of sites needed.

When planning for sites, the first thing you must determine is where the domain controllers will be located. Clients usually prefer a quick response time; so, in most situations, at least one domain controller will be placed in each of the sites (there might be instances when it is determined that a site does not require a domain controller, such as when a site has a very small number of users). After the domain controllers have been placed, a careful examination of the type of links connecting them and how much network use each one will experience must be done. After connectivity and available bandwidth have been assessed, you can determine where site links will be established.

DNS and DNS Namespace Planning

Windows Server 2003 has adopted the DNS naming convention for naming an object within Active Directory. Each DNS name within the DNS database is derived from a root name, forming a hierarchical structure. A host's DNS name identifies its position within the hierarchy. This is the same naming structure that has now been implemented within Active Directory. The naming scheme is simple and logical for administrative purposes, but it's also descriptive of the object's location within the hierarchy. A domain within an Active Directory structure is identified by the name it has been assigned, and its domain name identifies its position within the Active Directory hierarchy. When you're choosing a DNS name for an organization, it is once again important to assess the organization's structure, needs, and future plans.

The DNS naming standards are now applicable to the objects stored within Active Directory to ensure that all names remain unique. By implementing this type of naming scheme, the names that users use on their intranet are also compatible and ready for use on the Internet. Users no longer need to remember two different names—their logon name and their email name. For example, with Active Directory, a user can log on to the network with a name such as JohnD@xyz.corp, which could also be his email address.

The naming scheme implemented by Active Directory adheres to the same naming requirements as DNS names so that all names within a hierarchy remain unique. When assigning DNS names, keep the following points in mind:

➤ A child domain can have only one parent domain.

➤ If two children share the same parent domain, each must be assigned a unique name. In other words, to keep names among domains unique, each domain within a single tree requires a unique name.

Contiguous and Disjointed Namespaces

Within the Active Directory structure, there are basically two types of namespaces:

➤ Contiguous namespace

➤ Disjointed namespace

A *contiguous namespace* is one in which a child object inherits a portion of its namespace from its parent object. For example, assume that the Bayside Corporation uses the name Bayside.net. When a new domain is added to the forest for the San Francisco location as a child domain, the new domain inherits a portion of its namespace from its parent and becomes SF.Bayside.net (see Figure 2.3).

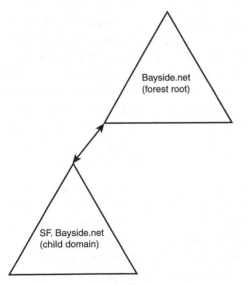

Bayside.net
(forest root)

SF. Bayside.net
(child domain)

Figure 2.3   A contiguous DNS namespace.

A *disjointed namespace* is one in which a new parent domain has a namespace that is independent from the forest root domain. If the Bayside Corporation assumes ownership of the Riverside Corporation, Riverside can maintain its existing DNS name of Riverside.net if it's added as a new tree to the existing Bayside forest (see Figure 2.4). This is an example of a disjointed namespace because it is independent of the forest root domain, bayside.net.

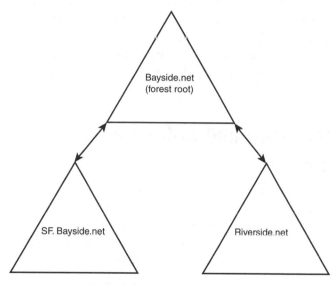

Figure 2.4 A disjointed DNS namespace.

  Here's an easy way to differentiate between the two types of namespaces within a forest: A contiguous namespace forms a tree structure, whereas a disjointed namespace establishes a new tree within the forest.

Now that you're familiar with some of the fundamental concepts of Active Directory, let's move on and take a look at the role of analysis on the design of an Active Directory infrastructure.

Analyzing the Effect of Active Directory on the Technical Environment

Before you can start implementing a technology such as Active Directory, you must understand the organization that plans to implement it. A huge and important part of implementing Active Directory is performing a thorough analysis of the existing environment. The following section and the remainder of this chapter focus on gathering the information required later in the design process.

Analyzing Hardware and Software Requirements

It's important to analyze information pertaining to the current hardware and software in use. Information about the hardware and software requirements and how the current configurations will integrate with Active Directory must be included in the initial design plans. Consider some of the following questions when analyzing hardware and software requirements:

➤ Do the current systems meet the hardware requirements?

➤ Is the hardware currently used supported by Windows Server 2003?

➤ What operating systems are currently in use? What service packs have been applied?

➤ How will the current operating systems integrate with Windows Server 2003 and Active Directory?

➤ Will any operating systems have to be upgraded to a later version before installing Windows Server 2003?

➤ Does the business have any DNS servers configured and how will they interoperate within Active Directory?

Not only must the systems be assessed but attention must also be given to the applications that the business is running on them. What applications does the business currently use? What applications do the business and its employees require to perform their job tasks? After you've determined which applications are required, test them to ensure that they are compatible with Windows Server 2003 and to see how they can integrate with Active Directory.

This might seem like an unimportant step in the design of Active Directory, but it will be much easier for you and the organization if it is known beforehand that some systems or applications need to be upgraded.

Analyzing Interoperability Requirements

Many networks consist of a number of different operating systems. For example, when new workstations are added to the network, they might be configured with the latest operating system, whereas current workstations might remain configured with older platforms. So, an important part of implementing Windows Server 2003 and Active Directory is to analyze the existing platforms and determine how they will interoperate within the new environment.

Windows Server 2003 interoperates with and supports the following platforms:

➤ Windows 2000

➤ Windows XP

➤ Windows NT 4.0

➤ Windows Me/98/95

➤ Windows 3.x

➤ Unix

➤ Macintosh

By default, Windows Server 2003 domain controllers secure communications using Server Message Block (SMB) signing and encrypting or signing of secure channel traffic. This is to prevent communications between a domain controller and a client from being intercepted and tampered with. Not all platforms have built-in support for these features. So, when assessing the interoperability of existing platforms with Windows Server 2003 Active Directory, keep the following points in mind:

➤ Windows 95 clients do not have built-in support for these features. The Active Directory client must be installed or the operating system must be upgraded.

➤ Windows for Workgroup clients must be upgraded.

➤ It is recommended that any Windows NT 4.0 clients be upgraded. They can interoperate with Windows Server 2003 Active Directory if Service Pack 4 or later has been installed.

Windows NT 4.0 can also have the Active Directory client installed as long as Service Pack 6a is installed.

Analyzing the Current Level of Service Within an Existing Technical Environment

The rollout of Windows Server 2003 is bound to have an effect on the technical support within an organization. The current technical support requirements must be assessed to determine how they will be affected. If a business currently relies on internal staff for technical support, what effect will Active Directory have on this? The skill set of the current technical support staff must be assessed and a training plan must be put into place. If you're upgrading from Windows NT 4.0, the IT staff might require highly specialized training on Active Directory features and functions that are being implemented. Upgrading from Windows 2000 may require training only on the new features included with Windows Server 2003. In any case, it's an important consideration. Imagine performing a rollout of Windows Server 2003 only to discover afterward that the IT staff cannot provide the technical support necessary to maintain the new structure.

When analyzing the current level of service, consider including end users as well as the IT staff. Providing end users with some basic training on the Active Directory infrastructure being implemented might help reduce the technical support requirements as the upgrades and rollouts occur.

If a business currently outsources all or some of its technical support to external companies, the effect that the rollout will have on these arrangements must be considered. After the business begins to migrate to Windows Server 2003, consider whether the company currently responsible for the business's technical support will still be able to meet the business's needs. If not, this job must be managed by a company that is fluent in Active Directory technologies.

 One of the jobs of the design team is to ensure that the upgrades and rollouts go as smoothly as possible for everyone. Therefore, determining the current level of service within a technical environment is crucial.

Analyzing DNS for Active Directory Service Implementation

Because Active Directory relies on DNS, DNS is an important consideration when planning an Active Directory implementation. Most organizations already have a DNS structure in place. When analyzing DNS for Active Directory, you need to determine how DNS is currently implemented within the environment as well as the current namespace. Both of these will have a major effect on the Active Directory design.

Analyzing the Current DNS Implementation

A successful DNS infrastructure design must meet both business and technical requirements. The business needs must be addressed first so that existing applications and systems are not affected by the addition of Windows Server 2003, Active Directory, and a new DNS.

When assessing the current DNS implementation, one of the things you must consider is whether there are existing DNS servers in place and how they will integrate with Windows Server 2003 DNS.

Windows Server 2003 DNS and BIND

BIND (Berkeley Internet Name Domain) is a Unix-based DNS service. It's not uncommon for many organizations to have BIND DNS servers on a Windows-based network. Because DNS plays such an important role, many organizations won't be willing to do away with their existing BIND servers for Windows Server 2003 DNS servers. In such cases, you need to be aware of how the two will interoperate.

If you're upgrading from Windows 2000 to Windows Server 2003, there's a good chance that the existing implementation of DNS won't have to be modified.

Windows Server 2003 DNS is capable of interoperating with various versions of BIND. As you will see, the later versions of BIND support many of the features not found in earlier versions. So you must consider the BIND version to determine how it will integrate with Windows Server 2003 DNS.

In Windows Server 2003, as well as Windows 2000, the DNS service locator records (SRV records) are used to locate domain controllers that run specific services. SRV records must be supported by a BIND DNS to integrate with Windows Server 2003 domain controllers. BIND version 4.9.7 and above supports SRV records.

 Although not required, it is recommended that any DNS you use support dynamic updates. Dynamic updates allow a DNS client to update its own host records with a DNS server. This is particularly useful when adding new domain controllers because several SRV records must be created. Dynamic updates eliminate the need to manually add these records to a DNS zone file. BIND version 8.2.2 and above supports dynamic updates.

Other DNS Servers

Microsoft Windows NT 4.0 DNS supports SRV records if Service Pack 4 has been applied. Windows NT 4.0 DNS does not support dynamic updates, so the Active Directory SRV records must be manually updated every time a domain controller, global catalog server, or site is added or deleted. Windows 2000 DNS servers support both SRV records and dynamic updates, and are therefore capable of functioning within a Windows Server 2003 environment. So, when analyzing the current DNS implementation, keep the following points in mind:

➤ Windows Server 2003 domain controllers must use a DNS server with SRV record support.

➤ Dynamic updates are strongly recommended because changes in the domain controllers or Active Directory might require updates to SRV record information.

 Note that only a standard primary DNS server needs to support dynamic update. Secondary DNS servers pull updates from the primary server and therefore do not need dynamic update capability.

Analyzing the Current Namespace

During your analysis of the current DNS implementation, you must also consider the current namespace. If you're upgrading from Windows 2000, the existing namespace might be sufficient. In any case, you still must determine how the current namespace has been implemented. Use the following questions as a guideline when analyzing the current namespace:

➤ Does the organization have an Internet presence? Does the organization have multiple names registered on the Internet? If the company uses multiple Internet names, does it plan to continue to do so?

➤ Does the external DNS namespace need to be separate from the internal namespace? In many cases, security considerations might require an internal name that is different from the external Internet name recognized by the public.

➤ If an organization currently uses Windows 2000 Active Directory, how is DNS currently implemented? Will the new design affect the existing DNS structure?

Evaluation of the answers to these questions helps you develop a sound naming strategy. That naming strategy must then be translated into an approach for implementing a new DNS infrastructure, enhancing existing DNS services, or interoperating with non-Microsoft DNS servers.

Analyzing Existing Network Operating System Implementation

At this point in the analysis, your focus will be on the existing network operating system implementation. Some of the things you must determine at this point include:

➤ The domain model that currently exists

➤ The number of domain controllers and where on the network they are placed

➤ The configuration details of servers on the network

Identifying the Existing Domain Model

A domain model determines how users and resources are currently organized. Determining the existing domain model will assist you in determining whether the current model can simply be upgraded or if a restructure of the existing model is required. If you're moving from Windows NT 4.0 to Windows Server 2003, there's a good chance that the existing domain model will change far more than if you're moving from Windows Server 2000 to Windows Server 2003.

Windows NT 4.0 Domains

There are four different domain models that you might come across in a Windows NT 4.0 environment:

➤ *Single domain*—In this implementation, there is a single domain with a single primary domain controller hosting both user accounts and resources.

➤ *Single master*—In this model, multiple domains exist. User accounts are contained within a master domain and resources are contained within a separate domain. This model requires the use of trust relationships in which the resource domains trust the master domain.

➤ *Multiple master*—This implementation employs two or more master domains along with resource domains. It requires the use of more trusts because two-way trusts are configured between master domains and one-way trusts are configured between resource domains and master domains.

➤ *Complete trust*—This model is the most complex of the four types and can result in many trusts having to be configured. In this model, several domains exist—each with its own user accounts and resources. Two-way trusts must be configured between each domain.

The domain model currently in use will affect the Active Directory design. For example, Active Directory eliminates the need to create resource domains because organization units can be created instead, thus reducing the number of domains required. So, if an organization currently employs two master domains and three resource domains, the resource domains may be eliminated in the Active Directory design and configured as organizational units instead. By eliminating the resource domains, you reduce the number of domains from five to two.

Windows Server 2000 Domains

Because the Active Directory structure is the same between Windows Server 2003 and Windows Server 2000, there might be little restructuring involved when it comes to deploying Windows Server 2003 Active Directory as long as the present infrastructure meets all the current requirements. However, you still must assess the domain structure so that it can be incorporated into the new design.

Identifying the Number and Location of Domain Controllers on the Network

Those responsible for assessing the various aspects of the existing network infrastructure must also determine the number and location of domain controllers on the network. Because domain controllers are required for the logon process, they perform an important role on the network and you want to ensure domain controller availability for users.

At this point, you want to determine how many domain controllers currently exist within the infrastructure. Doing so will assist in determining whether additional domain controllers are required to support the new Active Directory infrastructure.

The placement of domain controllers must also be analyzed: Look at the physical network and determine where domain controllers currently exist. For example, if there are a number of branch offices, determine whether domain controllers currently exist in each of the locations. For performance purposes, the new Active Directory design might call for the addition of a new domain controller in various locations. Or you might also determine that it would be more appropriate to move a particular domain controller. In any case, many of these decisions cannot be made without first determining where domain controllers currently exist on the network.

Identifying the Configuration Details of All Servers on the Network

If you're upgrading existing servers to Windows Server 2003, you need to document the current configuration of the servers. The servers will be configured in a way that meets the requirements of an organization. Part of the analysis process is to determine the configuration details and how they will be affected by upgrading to Windows Server 2003 (or even just by co-existing on a Windows Server 2003–based network).

Analyzing Security Requirements for Active Directory Services

The security requirements of a business have a major effect on the design of Active Directory. The security plan that's developed by the design team should be based on the security requirements of the business. Security has become a hot issue when designing a network infrastructure. As the need for enterprise networks has increased and the need to distribute internal data among employees become a necessity, businesses have implemented strict security policies to secure their network resources. When assessing a business's security requirements, you need to consider user security needs and local (geographical) security requirements.

Analyzing Current Security Policies, Standards, and Procedures

Almost all businesses implement various forms of security to protect network resources and lower the total cost of ownership (TCO). When designing Active Directory, it's crucial that the current security practices of an organization be assessed so that they can be included in the new design. For example, an organization might require some of the following security requirements for its users:

➤ Preconfigured desktop for all users

➤ Limited capability for users to modify the configurations assigned to them

➤ Secure logon (Smart card or EAP, for example)

➤ Application restrictions

➤ Sensitive data available to select groups

➤ Encrypted data for mobile users

➤ PKI infrastructure implementation

➤ RADIUS for remote connection authentication

Those in charge of the Active Directory design need to be aware of these security needs so the Active Directory infrastructure can support them.

> One of the reasons why a multiple-domain structure might be created is to meet the security requirements of a business. If the business implements decentralized administration and needs to maintain a distinct security boundary between its different business units, a multiple-domain structure has to be established. Creating a separate domain within the forest for each business unit will allow each unit to maintain its own administration.
>
> If the different locations or departments within a business have different security needs (such as password requirements) or if a single security policy for the entire organization cannot be agreed upon, multiple domains might have to be created. That way, the administrators from each domain can establish security policies that meet their specific requirements.

It's always good practice for organizations to implement security standards and procedures. Doing so ensures that the required level of security is maintained. Make sure that you're familiar with the various standards and procedures implemented within an organization so they can also be incorporated into the Active Directory design.

Another point to consider when assessing the security practices within an organization is that the security requirements and needs might vary throughout. There could be instances in which one location within an organization has very different security needs than another location. If this is the case, the design of the Active Directory infrastructure should reflect this.

For example, assume that an organization has several locations throughout the world. After completing an assessment of the local security needs, it might be determined that the offices in the United States and the offices in Europe have different security requirements.

You might be wondering how this information would affect the Active Directory design. To meet the different security needs of two different geographical locations, the design team might decide to create separate domains. Doing so would allow each office to implement its own security. The point is that a company's security requirements will have a major effect on the creation of forests, trees, domains, and organizational units. Therefore, they comprise an aspect of planning that deserves attention.

 A particularly critical aspect of domain design is understanding all the security requirements of an organization. Security policies are configured at the domain level, so if part of an organization requires specialized security, it might result in the creation of multiple domains.

Analyzing the Effect of Active Directory on the Current Security Infrastructure

The migration to Windows Server 2003 and Active Directory should affect the security infrastructure in a positive way and introduce many benefits. This is not to say that everything will remain the same because there will be expected changes.

Before you begin the implementation of Active Directory, you need to determine the effect that it will have on the existing environment. After you've assessed the security policies and procedures implemented by an organization, you know what the environment currently looks like. The next step is to take this information and determine what the environment will look like after Active Directory has been implemented. This enables you to determine how certain policies and procedures will be affected and changed with Active Directory. Some of these might remain unaffected and others might experience a complete overhaul.

Identifying the Existing Trust Relationships

After you've identified the type of domain model that is currently implemented, you need to assess the trust relationships that currently exist, if any. The trust relationships define the domain boundaries that users can cross for resource access. These boundaries will need to be maintained in the Active Directory infrastructure.

Windows NT 4.0 Trusts

For those of you who made the transition from Windows NT 4.0 to Windows 2000, one of the major differences was how trusts were implemented. In Windows NT 4.0, there was only one kind of trust relationship that could exist: one-way non-transitive trust.

In a Windows NT 4.0 environment, trusts are not automatically created. They must be established manually by an administrator. Trusts are also one way, meaning that they are not transitive like the trusts found in Windows Server 2003 and Windows 2000. For example, if A trusts B, B does not trust A. For users in two domains to share resources, two one-way trusts must be configured.

Windows Server 2003 Trusts

Three different types of trust relationships can be implemented in Windows Server 2003 to allow users to gain access to resources located in other domains: transitive, shortcut, and external trusts. Transitive trusts are automatically established, whereas shortcut and external trusts must be explicitly defined.

A transitive trust is a two-way trust that is automatically created between parent domains and child domains, as well as between the root domain of a forest and any new trees. The trust path created from a transitive trust makes resources throughout the forest accessible to all users (see Figure 2.5).

As already mentioned, when a user attempts to access a resource in another domain within the forest, the trust path must be followed. Depending on the structure of the Active Directory hierarchy, the trust path between two separate domains can be long.

In a case such as this, creating a shortcut trust can shorten the trust path. A *shortcut trust* is basically a transitive trust (a two-way trust); the difference is that it must be explicitly defined or created. Creating a shortcut trust between two separate domains within a forest can improve the authentication process discussed in the previous section.

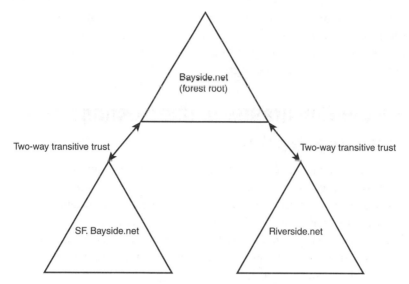

Figure 2.5   Windows Server 2003 two-way transitive trusts.

The third type of trust that can be implemented is an *external trust*. An external trust is similar to a trust set up between Windows NT 4.0 domains. It is a one-way trust and must be manually created.

Within a forest, two-way trusts are established automatically. In Windows Server 2003, two separate forests can be linked together by creating a one-way trust or a two-way transitive trust. A two-way transitive trust is created between two forest root domains to establish a transitive trust relationship between all domains in each forest.

For the most part, trusts in Windows Server 2003 and Windows 2000 are the same. However there is one difference to be aware of. Windows Server 2003 now supports a forest trust. This allows two separate forests to be linked together with a one-way or two-way transitive trust. Doing so can form a transitive trust between every domain in each forest. In Windows Server 2000, when users located in one forest needed access to resources within another forest, a one-way nontransitive trust had to be explicitly defined. This could result in several one-way trusts being established between domains.

Identifying Network Topology and Performance Levels

At this point in the analysis phase, your focus really turns to the physical aspects of the network. Now you're looking at the physical topology, such as the connections between various locations and the connection speeds as well as the performance of servers on the network. Doing so enables you to set expectations so that you know before Active Directory is implemented how well the network and servers will perform within the new infrastructure and what possible upgrades should be suggested.

Identifying Constraints in the Existing Network Infrastructure

The existing network infrastructure is bound to have a significant effect on the Active Directory design. When analyzing the existing network infrastructure, you might discover constraints that must be considered. For example, you might discover constraints in the WAN connectivity between different locations where the connections are already heavily utilized or unreliable. Because there is a good chance that the physical network will not be upgraded, constraints such as these must be considered.

LAN/WAN Connectivity

Begin the assessment of LAN/WAN connectivity by determining the physical topology of the network. Document the network topology and the size of the network. After the layout of the network has been established, you can assess the connectivity between the physical networks. Documenting the connectivity within a business will assist you in designing an Active Directory structure that complements the physical layout. Not doing so could result in things such as regular replication occurring over a slow network connection.

 A good starting point to get an overall picture of the existing network structure is to create a diagram that is representational of the physical network. The diagram should document such things as the LAN/WAN connectivity and bandwidth constraints. This provides a good reference point when planning Active Directory and the network infrastructure.

After you've documented the physical layout, you can determine the type and speed of connections within the different locations as well as the speed of the connections between them. Determining the appropriate speed of the links within an organization will depend on the amount of network traffic that is generated. Further analysis of the amount of network traffic generated throughout the business must be done to determine the amount of bandwidth that is available.

Completing these assessments will help the design team determine the best replication routes within the business and the optimum location for its servers.

Available Bandwidth

The amount of bandwidth available within an existing network environment will affect things such as the creation of Active Directory sites. A connection between two locations might be high speed and reliable, but if it is already heavily utilized, it might not have enough bandwidth available to support regular replication. This information could lead the design team to create sites on either side of the connection. Only a thorough analysis of the network traffic generated within an organization will give you a good picture of the available bandwidth. Using a network analyzer, such as Network Monitor, will help you determine the amount of traffic currently being generated.

The physical LAN and WAN infrastructure will influence not only site design but also the number of domains created and the placement of servers within a domain.

When determining the amount of traffic that is generated on the network and the available bandwidth, consider some of the following traffic-generating events and how often they occur:

➤ How often are users required to change their passwords?

➤ How many users log on to the network?

➤ When do the bulk of the logons occur?

➤ How many DNS queries are performed throughout the day?

➤ If DHCP is used, how often are users required to renew their IP addresses?

Interpreting Current Baseline Performance Requirements for Each Major Subsystem

In addition to security and availability, another aspect of the current setup that you must consider when designing Active Directory is performance. During your initial assessment of the existing network, you need to determine the current performance levels of the major subsystems (for example, memory and disk). After you've determined the current performance levels for servers on the network, you can set expectations for performance levels.

A good starting point for monitoring server performance is to use the performance tool that's included with Windows Server 2003. With the performance tool, you can monitor the real-time performance of the various subsystems. The information will help you determine what kind of performance can be expected. You can also use the information to identify any bottlenecks that currently exist on a server (and possibly address them before performing implementing Windows Server 2003 Active Directory).

Exam Prep Questions

All questions for this chapter refer to the following case study.

Case: DKP Int'l

DKP Int'l

DKP Int'l is a large produce company with locations in Canada, United States, and Europe. DKP Int'l consists of three different departments: Transportation, Cooling, and Sales. The headquarters is located in Salinas, California. The three divisions are spread out across the various locations.

Current LAN/Network

DKP Int'l currently has a Windows NT 4.0 infrastructure. It has a single user account domain. Each continent has its own resource domain. Most workstations are currently running Windows 95. Some workstations within the head office are running Windows XP Professional.

10 Mbps twisted-pair Ethernet is used at all office locations.

Proposed LAN/Network

DKP Int'l has decided to upgrade the existing infrastructure to Windows Server 2003. A DNS name has been registered. DKP.com will be used for the internal and external namespace.

Current WAN Connectivity

The company has four facilities in North America, connected by full T-1 links. The two European plants are connected to each other with a 256Kbps circuit, and the two Canadian facilities are linked with a 256Kbps Virtual Private Network (VPN). All these links are relatively underutilized.

The headquarters office in Salinas is connected to both the European and Canadian locations via a 64Kbps link. This circuit is very heavily used, especially during Salinas's business hours.

Proposed WAN Connectivity

No changes are proposed at this time, although management has recognized that the 64Kbps circuit between Europe, North America, and Canada must be upgraded eventually.

Directory Design Commentary

CIO: Divisions within each of the different continents remain fairly autonomous. IT, however, is currently centralized in Salinas. Local administrators will be granted more authority in the future. Unique password policies are required for each continent.

CEO: DKP Int'l has entered into a joint venture with ICI Produce, a grower of organic vegetables. The venture makes the organic vegetables available to buyers through DKP Int'l. DKP Int'l needs access to ICI Produce information.

Current Internet

DKP Int'l currently has no Internet presence.

Future Internet Presence

DKP Int'l plans to develop a Web site (www.dkp.com).

Questions

Question 1

> When planning for the forest root domain, which of the following DNS names should you choose?
>
> ○ A. us.DKP.com
>
> ○ B. ICI.com
>
> ○ C. dkp.com
>
> ○ D. www.DKP.com

Answer C is correct. Because DKP Int'l intends to use the same DNS name for the internal and external namespace, answer C is correct. Answer A is incorrect because it places the forest root under the dkp.com. The domain name of us.dkp.com may not be the best representation of the company. Answer B is incorrect because it is the name of another company and is not at all appropriate as the forest root. Answer D is incorrect because this is the future name of the Web site.

Question 2

An Internet presence is being created for ICI Produce. An Internet name of ici.com is registered. How should the Active Directory design be modified for this new domain?

○ A. Create a child domain of dkp.com called ici.dkp.com

○ B. Create a child domain of dkp.com called dkp.ici.com

○ C. Create a new domain tree with a root domain of ici.com

○ D. Create a new forest with a root domain of ici.com

Answer C is correct. Because ici.com is a different DNS namespace from DKP Int'l, it's best to create a new domain tree rather than use the approach suggested by answer A. Answer B is incorrect because the child and parent domain names are reversed. Because DKP Int'l management requires full access to ICI Produce data, including Active Directory contents, answer D is also incorrect.

Question 3

You're planning the number of Active Directory domains. How many child domains should be created off the forest root domain?

○ A. None

○ B. One: ici.com

○ C. Three (one for each continent)

○ D. Three (one for each division)

Answer C is correct. Because of the security requirements (separate password policies for each continent) and the WAN constraints, separate domains are required for each continent. Answer A is incorrect because of the same WAN speed and security restrictions. Finally, answer B is incorrect because ici.com is a different namespace from dkp.com.

Question 4

During the migration process, users might be required to access resources within a Windows NT 4.0 domain. If this is the case, what kind of trust can be configured?

- ○ A. No trust relationships can exist between Windows Server 2003 and Windows NT 4.0 domains.
- ○ B. A two-way transitive Kerberos trust can be created.
- ○ C. A two-way nontransitive Kerberos trust can be created.
- ○ D. A one-way nontransitive NTLM trust can be created.

Answer D is correct. Old-style NTLM trusts can be established between Windows Server 2003 domains and Windows NT domains. These trusts are nontransitive. If a two-way trust is required, two one-way trusts can be set up, just as was done under NT. Therefore, answer A is incorrect. Answers B and C are also incorrect because Windows NT does not support Kerberos authentication or trust relationships.

Question 5

What kind of trust relationship exists automatically between dkp.com and ici.com?

- ○ A. None
- ○ B. Two-way transitive Kerberos trust
- ○ C. One-way nontransitive NTLM trust
- ○ D. Shortcut trust

Answer B is correct. A two-way Kerberos trust is automatically created between root domains of a disjointed namespace in the same forest, which means that answer A must be incorrect. No one-way trusts are automatically created in Windows Server 2003, so answer C is incorrect. Answer D is also incorrect because shortcut trusts are manually created between domains that do not have a direct trust relationship between them. Shortcut trusts speed Kerberos credential validation by shortening the validation path through the forest.

Question 6

What is the first domain created in an organization's Active Directory called?

- ○ A. The root domain
- ○ B. The forest
- ○ C. The forest root
- ○ D. The schema

Answer C is correct. Answer A is incorrect because although the forest root is also a root domain, the forest root domain has special importance in Active Directory, which other root domains will not have. Answer B is incorrect even though the creation of the forest root occurs at the same time as the creation of the forest. The schema is the logical definition of Active Directory. Therefore, answer D is incorrect also.

Question 7

Which of the following are shared between all domains within a single forest? (Select all correct answers.)

- ❑ A. Global catalog
- ❑ B. Schema
- ❑ C. Sysvol
- ❑ D. Domain naming context
- ❑ E. Configuration container

Answers A, B, and E are correct. The global catalog, schema, and configuration container are shared between all domains in a single forest. The Sysvol folder is replicated only within each domain, therefore, answer C is incorrect. The domain naming context is shared only between domains that are in the same tree within a forest, but a forest can have multiple domain naming contexts, therefore answer D is incorrect.

Question 8

DKP's Active Directory design has a root domain of dkp.com, with child domains of na.dkp.com, eur.dkp.com, and ca.dkp.com. By default, can users in ca.dkp.com access resources in na.dkp.com?

- ○ A. No. A shortcut trust must be created between ca.dkp.com and eur.dkp.com.
- ○ B. No. Trusts in Active Directory are not transitive.
- ○ C. Yes. Two-way Kerberos trusts are automatically created between parent and child domains as well as between root domains in a forest.
- ○ D. Yes. Trusts are created automatically between every domain in a forest.

Answer C is correct. Two-way transitive Kerberos trusts are created automatically whenever a new domain is added to a forest. The trust goes from child domain to parent domain or between root domains in a disjointed namespace. Although you can create a cross-link trust between two domains to speed Kerberos validation, answer A is incorrect because this trust is not necessary. Answer B is incorrect because the default trusts established between domains are indeed transitive. Finally, answer D is incorrect because trusts are not created between every domain, but rather from parent to child and between root domains in the forest.

Question 9

A new office has been opened in Auckland, New Zealand, and the IT director wants to know whether a new domain should be created for the Australian continent. Business plans call for an expansion of operations to include 2000 employees at three locations within two years. What factors should the IT director consider in making her decision? (Choose two correct answers.)

❑ A. Security requirements specific to Australia

❑ B. Number of employees

❑ C. Local administration of resources

❑ D. The size of Active Directory

❑ E. Replication traffic and wide area link availability

Answers A and E are correct. Security policies are set at the domain level, so if there are requirements specific to the Australian operation, a separate domain should be considered. Also, if wide area links are slow, congested, or unreliable, a new domain will allow use of the SMTP protocol for Active Directory replication over the slow link.

Answers B and D are not correct. The tested limits of Active Directory are more than 50 million objects, so it isn't necessary to create additional domains to handle 2,000 additional employees.

Finally, answer C is not correct because administration can be delegated at the organizational unit level, thus eliminating the need to create a domain to achieve administrative granularity.

Question 10

An application being used by ICI Produce requires some modifications to the Active Directory schema. Who can perform this operation? (Choose all correct answers.)

❑ A. A member of the Domain Admins global group in the domain where the application is installed.

❑ B. A member of the Enterprise Admins global group.

❑ C. A member of the Schema Admins global group.

❑ D. Attributes cannot be added to the global catalog without permission from Microsoft.

Answers B and C are correct. Members of the Schema Admins group can modify the schema. Answer B is also correct because the initial Administrator account created in the forest root domain is a member of both the Enterprise Admins and Schema Admins groups. The Active Directory Schema MMC snap-in is used to mark an attribute as one that should be replicated to the global catalog. Answer A is incorrect on two counts: Schema modifications affect the entire forest, not a single domain, and domain administrators do not have the rights to modify the schema. Finally, answer D is incorrect because the Active Directory design allows an organization complete flexibility in modifying the schema.

Need to Know More?

 Try searching the TechNet CD or use Microsoft's online version at www.microsoft.com and search for keywords such as *Active Directory, tree, forest,* and *organizational unit.*

 The Microsoft Windows Server 2003 Deployment Kit, Microsoft Press, 2000, ISBN: 0735614865. Contains in-depth information about deploying Windows Server 2003.

 Microsoft Corporation. *Microsoft Windows Server 2003 Resource Kit.* Microsoft Press, 2003.

Creating the Active Directory and Network Services Conceptual Designs

Designing an infrastructure that will properly support Windows Active Directory requires a large amount of pre-planning. Many organizations will be upgrading their current infrastructure. With that in mind, the organization will likely have in mind certain requirements for the new infrastructure. An important part of the design phase is to identify the business and technical requirements, and then use the information to design an Active Directory hierarchy that meets these requirements.

Designing the Active Directory Infrastructure to Meet Business and Technical Requirements

You need to begin your analysis of the business and technical requirements by addressing the organization's administrative model.

Designing the Envisioned Administrative Model

During this phase of the Active Directory design, you assess the current administrative model that is being used by an organization. This information has a major effect on the Active Directory structure that will be put into place—for example, the number of domains that are created.

Determining the Administrative Model

Determining the administrative model that a business has implemented is important to the Active Directory design process. The administrative model basically determines who holds the decision-making authority within a business and who is responsible for implementing these decisions. There are basically three administrative models that can be implemented: centralized, decentralized, and mixed mode. Table 3.1 summarizes these three administrative models.

Table 3.1	The Three Administrative Models
Model	**Description**
Centralized	A central group holds all the decision-making authority within an organization.
Decentralized	Different units within a business are responsible for their own administration.
Centralized-decentralized or mixed mode	A central group maintains some level of decision-making authority, but certain administrative tasks are assigned to each business unit.

Identifying Responsibilities for Administering Resources

After the administrative model within the organization has been identified, the next step is to identify who is currently responsible for administering network resources. When determining administrative responsibilities, consider the following questions:

➤ Who is responsible for what?

Determine which individuals or groups within the business should have administrative privileges and what their responsibilities are. For example, a group of individuals might have been given the responsibility of administering user accounts, whereas another group might have administrative privileges over network printers.

➤ Where do these privileges apply?

Do the permissions apply throughout the organization or only to certain areas? For example, in an enterprise network, if a user has been given administrative authority over user accounts, should this privilege apply to all domains and organizational units (OUs) or just specific ones? In other words, what is the scope of the administrative privilege?

➤ What type of privilege is assigned?

Does the individual or group have full administrative privileges or control over only certain aspects? For example, what level of control does the individual or group have over user accounts? Does the individual or group have full control or control over only certain aspects of user accounts?

Determining the answers to these questions will help you develop a delegation plan that can easily integrate into the business's current administrative model and its current way of distributing administrative tasks among its employees.

Determining the Type of IT Organization

To effectively design an Active Directory hierarchy, the current structure of the IT organization within the business must be assessed. After the current structure has been documented, the design team can work with the company to determine whether there are any areas that need improvement or areas that can be restructured for easier administration. This information will assist in creating a design that meets the requirements of the business.

When assessing how the IT organization within a business is structured, determine the model that is currently in place. Is the network administration centralized or does the business allow for distributed administration (decentralized)? Determining this will ensure that the needs of the IT organization are identified and reflected in the administrative model that is developed.

NOTE An organization can also have decentralized management but a centralized IT function, and vice versa. Do not assume that decentralized management means decentralized IT.

The centralized model is hierarchical in structure. It is characterized by one individual or group overseeing all network development and administration to whom the IT organization would report. Some of the day-to-day administrative tasks might be assigned to select individuals or groups outside the IT organization, but most network administration remains centralized. The IT organization maintains decision-making authority as well as the responsibility for ensuring that all decisions are implemented throughout all levels within the business.

There is also a slight variation to this model in which the IT group is still centralized, but some of the day-to-day management tasks are decentralized. The central IT organization is responsible for overseeing network development and possibly implementing organization-wide policies, and the IT groups within the different business units are responsible for the day-to-day administrative tasks, such as creating user accounts.

With decentralized management, one person or group no longer holds all the decision-making and network administrative authority; in other words, no hierarchy or central IT organization oversees all network development. Each business unit maintains its own IT organization and implements its own IT model based on its needs. When it comes to technical issues affecting the entire organization, the different IT groups from each of the business units would have to work together. For example, if a business is planning a rollout of Windows Server 2003, each of the IT groups from the different business units would have to be involved.

The type of IT management structure that a business implements will not have a direct effect on the Active Directory structure. It is still crucial to characterize the current IT organization that a business has implemented because this information helps the design team determine the administrative model to use. However, the administrative model directly affects the organization of the different elements within the Active Directory structure.

Developing a Model for Administration

After you've characterized the type of IT organization that a business has in place, the next step is to develop a model for its administration. The administration model that is chosen determines the organization of the Active Directory structure. The type of model that is developed should be based on the structure of the IT organization (centralized versus decentralized). There are basically four models for administration:

➤ Geographical (location)

➤ Organizational (business unit or department)

➤ Functional (role)

➤ Hybrids (combinations of the preceding types)

> The administrational model chosen directly affects the Active Directory design—particularly the creation of top-level domains or organizational units.

Geographical (Location)

If you choose to implement an administration model that's based on geographical location, the Active Directory structure will be organized around the different locations within the business. This type of model is well suited for a business that maintains a central IT organization but decentralizes management by assigning the responsibility of performing day-to-day administrative tasks to the different IT groups within the business units.

> Before implementing this type of model, make sure that an individual or a group of individuals at the different locations is capable of performing these day-to-day tasks.

One of the positive features of an administrative model based on location is that it is fairly immune to reorganization and expansion. When a company changes its structure, it most often reorganizes departments but not the geographical locations of the business. Accommodating expansion can be as simple as creating a new domain or OU for the new location.

Organizational (Business Unit or Department)

If a business has implemented a decentralized IT organizational model and allowed the different departments to maintain localized control, a model for administration that is organizational (based on business units or departments) might be best. The organization of the Active Directory structure would be based on the different business units or departments within the company.

One of the nice features of this model is that it allows a business to maintain its departmental divisions. Each business unit maintains control over itself. However, in a model based on departments, if the departments are reorganized, it could mean a reorganization of the Active Directory structure.

Functional (Role)

This type of model is based on the different job roles within a business, without consideration of the different geographical locations and departments. For businesses that implement a decentralized IT organization and have job roles that span multiple divisions, the functional model might be more suited to their administrative needs than an organizational model.

This model is more manageable within a smaller business because users are more easily grouped into general functions. The larger the business, the more variance in job roles and the harder it is to group users. However, large organizations with many mobile users might find this model very attractive.

Because this model is based on the different roles within the business, it is essentially immune to reorganization. Reorganizations within a business most often affect departments, whereas job roles are not usually affected.

So far, we've covered three different administration models that a business could implement. The fourth model is a combination of those three models.

Hybrids

To design an Active Directory structure that meets the administrative needs of the IT organization, it might sometimes be necessary to combine several models. This type of models is known as a *hybrid*. Two of the common hybrid designs are "geographical, then organizational" and "organizational, then geographical."

In a "geographical, then organizational" model, the upper layers within the Active Directory structure are based on location, and the lower layers are organized around business units. This type of model is well suited for a business that spans geographical locations. Because the lower levels of the structure are based on business units, it also allows a business to maintain departmental independence.

Because the upper layers of the Active Directory structure are organized around the geographic locations of the business, it is immune to company reorganizations. However, a reorganization of the company might result in some restructuring of the lower layers because they are based on departments. Nonetheless, restructuring of OUs is simpler than the restructuring of domains.

The second type of hybrid model is the opposite of the one we just discussed: The upper levels of the hierarchy are based on the different business units or departments within the company, and the lower levels are based on the geographical locations. This model is ideal for businesses that need to maintain independence between the different departments for security purposes. Basing the lower levels on the physical structure (geography) also allows a business to distribute administration among the IT groups in different locations.

 You might recall the discussion about models for administration based on departments and how they are affected by reorganization. This model will be affected by any reorganization that occurs within the business and might result in an entire restructuring of the Active Directory.

Creating the Conceptual Design of the Active Directory Forest Structure

In most cases, a single-forest structure should be sufficient. You also want to keep your Active Directory design as simple as possible. With that in mind, a single-forest structure is usually recommended for administrative purposes. However, in some instances, it will be necessary to consider a multiple-forest environment to meet the requirements of a business. This type of model is one of the most difficult to design and administer, so when you're considering the forest structure, keep the following topics in mind:

➤ Business reasons

➤ Trusts relationships

➤ Schema issues

Business Reasons

Before designing an elaborate structure that includes multiple forests, be sure to assess the business to determine whether there is an actual need for more than one forest. Consider a multiple-forest structure if a business has any of the requirements discussed in the next few paragraphs.

Does the business maintain partnerships or have subsidiaries with which it needs to maintain a very limited partnership? One of the most common reasons why you would create a multiple-forest environment is to meet an organization's need to maintain a limited trust with another organization or its subsidiaries. A situation such as this might arise when a business establishes a limited partnership with another organization or when an organization includes subsidiaries gained through corporate acquisitions. Separate forests might need to be created for security purposes, and when multiple forests are established, the scope of the trust relationship can be limited and closely monitored.

Does the business need multiple global directories? The global directory maintains a listing of all objects within the forest as well as certain attributes pertaining to each object, and all domains within a forest have access to a common global directory. If a business does not want one global directory for its entire organization, a multiple-forest structure must be implemented.

You'll recall from Chapter 2, "Gathering and Analyzing Business and Technical Requirements," that the schema maintains a list for the entire forest of all objects that can be stored within Active Directory as well as the attributes associated with each object (see Figure 3.1). A default schema policy comes with Windows Server 2003, but it can be modified if it does not meet your business's requirements. If an organization requires different schema policies for its various business units or if the administrators from the different business units cannot agree on a schema policy, multiple forests must be created.

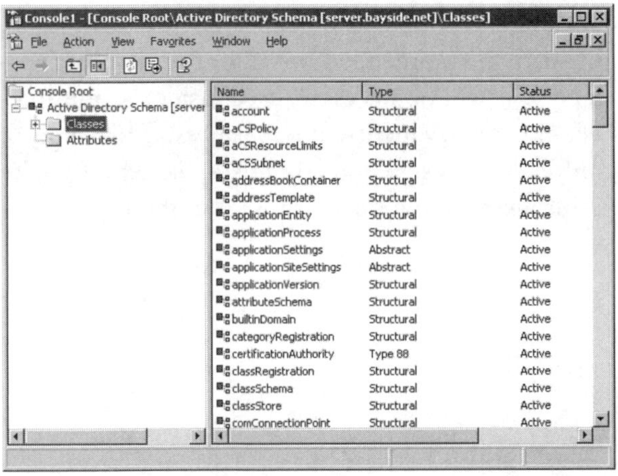

Figure 3.1   The Active Directory schema.

Partitions are applied at the forest level, so all domains within a forest will be affected by the same partition. If a business plans to make changes to the default schema but does not want its entire organization to be affected by changes, a multiple-forest structure should be considered. An appropriate partition could then be implemented for each forest. Because partitions are not replicated between forests, schema changes in one forest do not affect other forests.

Make sure you understand the circumstances under which it is appropriate to create multiple forests. Be prepared to encounter exam questions in which you must determine whether multiple forests are necessary based on a given scenario.

Creating the Conceptual Design of the Active Directory Domain Structure

As you've probably already noticed, assessing the needs of the business is crucial in all aspects of designing an Active Directory infrastructure. The needs of the business should also be the first thing considered when designing a domain. The infrastructure created by the design team should reflect the current structure of the business. When assessing the business, you need to detail the administrative requirements as well as the security requirements. Both of these requirements have a major effect on the domain and OU structure that will be planned for the business.

Administrative and Security Requirements

When designing a domain, the first thing that should be documented (or reviewed, if it has already been determined) is the administrative strategy that the business has implemented. The type of administrative structure that a business has in place determines the creation and organization of domains within the Active Directory. Does the business implement a centralized or decentralized strategy for administration? Knowing how the administrative tasks are distributed throughout the business helps determine the model for administration that will best meet the needs of the business. The administration model implemented should allow the business to distribute administrative tasks in a way that meets its administrative requirements. The administration model will also determine the organization of domains and OUs in the Active Directory hierarchy.

Recall that there are essentially four models that can be implemented for administration: geographical (location), organizational (business unit), functional (role), and hybrid models. The domain design should be based on the administrative model.

After you've determined the administrative requirements of the business, the security requirements have to be assessed. (Security within a business is usually crucial, so be sure that the assessment is thorough.) When assessing the security requirements, you need to determine who is responsible for administration within the business (delegation of authority). Documenting this information ensures that the proper permissions are assigned to the proper individuals. Use the following questions as a guide when performing the assessment:

➤ Who in the business requires administrative privileges?

➤ What are they responsible for?

➤ What type of administrative privileges do they require to do their jobs?

➤ What is the scope of their responsibilities?

➤ Will their privileges apply at the site, domain, or OU level?

After the administrative and security requirements of the business have been determined, you should have a good understanding of the domain structure that best meets the business's needs. Your next step is to plan the creation of the first domain within the Active Directory structure.

Creating the First Domain in Active Directory

The first domain created within Active Directory becomes the forest root domain. This is the domain that represents the entire business. It is important to plan which domain will become the forest root domain because it can be difficult to restructure the Active Directory hierarchy if this domain must be renamed.

Careful planning is required when choosing a name for the forest root domain because other domains added to the structure might inherit a portion of their namespace from the root domain.

When deciding what to name the first domain in Active Directory, keep the following points in mind:

➤ Choose a name that will not change in the near future; that is, choose a name that is static. Changing the name of the forest root domain is not easy, so try to choose a name that will not be change in the next 3 to 5 years.

➤ Choose a name that is meaningful to the business, its employees, and its clients. When naming the forest root, consider using the name of the business.

➤ Make sure that the name is available for use on the Internet. Even if the business has no intention of using its name on the Internet, make sure that the name is registered in case the business changes its mind in the future.

➤ The internal namespace can be, and often is, different from the company's external namespace, but it can still cause problems if it is the same as a name already being used on the Internet.

When creating the forest root domain, the design team might determine that the business's name is an appropriate choice (as long as the business has no intention of changing the company name in the near future). The company name provides a general representation of the business and an appropriate namespace for child domains within the forest. The company name is meaningful to employees and clients and makes the domain easily identifiable.

Several elements make up an Active Directory infrastructure. When you're planning for each element, different aspects of the business must be assessed to ensure that each element is implemented in a way that meets these business requirements. When you're designing a domain tree, one of the first things that must be done is an assessment of the business. When you're designing a domain structure, keep in mind that a single-domain model is simpler to implement and easier to administer than a multiple-domain model. There will definitely be times when a single-domain model is not suitable for a business, but only a thorough assessment of the business can determine whether a multiple-domain model is necessary.

Requirements for Multiple Domains

There are some instances in which a single domain will not meet the requirements of an organization. In other words, certain situations might result in the creation of multiple domains. If one of the requirements discussed in this section is met, consider implementing multiple domains.

Does the business want to maintain decentralized administration among its business units or geographical locations? If the business requires each division or geographical location to be responsible for its own administration, multiple domains might need to be created.

Is there a need to maintain a distinct administrative boundary between different areas within the business? If so, multiple domains should be considered. Domains determine both the security and administrative boundaries within an Active Directory hierarchy. When multiple domains are created in a forest, the Domain Admins group within each domain has privileges only within its own domain unless permissions to another domain are explicitly granted.

Does the business require multiple security policies? Remember that in an Active Directory hierarchy, the domain is the security boundary. In some cases, a single security policy can meet the security needs of an entire business. For cases in which a company has to create multiple security policies for different areas within the business, a multiple-domain structure is needed.

Does the business have subsidiaries that need to maintain separate and distinct namespaces? For those businesses that have established partnerships and need to be included in the Active Directory structure, a multiple-domain structure is necessary, especially if a separate namespace is required.

Does the physical structure of the current network present a need for multiple domains? Replication within a domain occurs between all domain controllers. If there are locations within a business that are connected by physical links that are slow or unreliable, multiple domains can be created to optimize replication.

 Be sure that you understand when to create multiple domains. You're likely to encounter exams questions in which you must decide whether to implement a single domain or multiple domains based on a specific scenario.

Planning Domain Trees

So far, we've been talking about creating a single forest with a single tree. However, there could also be instances in which you need to create multiple trees within a single forest. To create a domain structure that meets the business requirements, it's crucial that you first have a thorough understanding of how certain operations occur between domains (certain operations that occur within a domain might occur differently between domains). When you're planning domain trees, an understanding of the following topics is necessary:

➤ Accessing resources between domains

➤ Authentication across domains

➤ Types of trust relationships

➤ Creating an empty root domain

Accessing Resources Between Domains

Windows Server 2003 provides support for the Kerberos version 5 protocol (an industry-supported authentication protocol), which is responsible for the authentication of users across domains. One of the features of the Kerberos version 5 protocol is transitive trusts. In a multiple-domain structure, two-way transitive trusts are automatically configured between parent and child domains within a forest. This enables users to be granted permissions to resources throughout the forest. When a user attempts to access a resource located within another domain in the forest, the transitive trust path is followed.

Authentication Across Domains

Authentication is the process of confirming the identity of the user attempting to gain access to network resources. Before a user in one domain can access resources in another domain within the forest, that user must be authenticated. As already mentioned, the Kerberos version 5 protocol is responsible for authentication across domains. Because support is included for this industry-standard security protocol, users need only provide a single username and password at logon to gain access to resources throughout the forest.

Before a user is granted access to resources in another domain, the key distribution center (KDC) from each domain in the trust path must first authenticate the user. The KDC has two roles: It is responsible for authenticating users and for issuing session tickets to users so that they can identify themselves to other domains.

Types of Trust Relationships

Three types of trust relationships can be implemented in Windows Server 2003 to enable users to gain access to resources located in other domains: transitive, shortcut, and external trusts. Transitive trusts are automatically established, whereas shortcut and external trusts must be explicitly defined. Within a single forest, no trust relationships have to be explicitly defined. This is due to the fact that two-way transitive trusts are automatically established between parent domains and child domains, thereby creating a trust path throughout the forest. Shortcut trusts can be established between two domains to shorten the trust path. However, the trust exists between only the specified domains.

Creating an Empty Root Domain

In an Active Directory hierarchy where there are multiple domains, the design team might choose to create an empty forest root domain. That domain would not contain any OUs, and the only users in the domain would be the members of the Enterprise Admins group. The empty forest root domain establishes the namespace that will be inherited by child domains (see Figure 3.2). Creating an empty forest root domain would be appropriate for a business that wants to maintain a contiguous namespace throughout the organization and allow for decentralized administration.

Now that you've familiarized yourself with how some of the operations occur within a multiple-domain structure, let's take a look at some of the guidelines that you must consider when designing multiple domains.

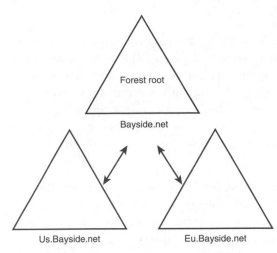

Figure 3.2 A forest root domain with its child domains.

Domain Design Issues

When planning a multiple-domain structure, keep the following design issues in mind:

➤ Security

➤ WAN or LAN bandwidth constraints

➤ Legal issues

➤ Domain-wide policies

Security

One of the reasons why a multiple-domain structure might be created is to meet the security requirements of a business. If the business implements decentralized administration and needs to maintain a distinct security boundary between its different business units, a multiple-domain structure should be established. Creating a separate domain within the forest for each business unit allows each business unit to maintain its own administration.

If the different locations or departments within a business have different security needs (such as password requirements) or if a single security policy for the entire organization cannot be agreed upon, multiple domains might have to be created. That way, the administrators from each domain can establish security policies that meet their specific requirements.

Also keep in mind that the more domains you create, the more Domain Admins groups there are to monitor. This adds administrative overhead and might become difficult to track (especially for security purposes).

WAN or LAN Constraints

Replication is based on the multi-master replication model. All domain controllers within a domain are equal and all maintain an up-to-date working copy of the directory database. That means there will be more replication traffic *within* a domain (as opposed to *between* domains) because any changes made to the directory will be replicated throughout the domain to all domain controllers.

Also keep in mind that every attribute associated with an object is replicated throughout the domain, which adds to network traffic. On the other hand, only certain attributes are replicated to Global Catalog servers in other domains.

The point of this discussion is that if there are LAN or WAN links within the organization that are slow, unreliable, or already heavily used, they might not be able to support the amount of replication traffic that will be generated within a domain. In cases such as this, multiple domains must be created to optimize replication.

 The use of site links within a single domain can also provide the same control over replication as creating multiple domains.

Legal Issues

In today's world of enterprise networks that span different countries, there might be legal issues to consider when planning domains that could result in the implementation of a multiple-domain structure. For example, a business that has an international presence might be required to maintain separate domains for its overseas locations. An organization might need to keep employee information for its European subsidiaries separate from U.S. employees because the European Union has much more stringent confidentiality requirements than the United States. To meet the security requirements of different countries, separate domains would have to be created.

Domain-Wide Policies

If there is a need to create different security configurations for different groups of users and computers throughout the business, it might be necessary to create more than one domain. Only a thorough assessment of a business's security requirements can determine whether more than one domain will be needed. The following are some security options set on a domain basis:

➤ *Password policy*—Password policies determine the requirements for user passwords, such as a minimum password length.

➤ *Account lockout policy*—An account lockout policy determines the guideline for locking a user account out of the system.

> ➤ *Kerberos policy*—A Kerberos policy determines the settings pertaining to Kerberos security, such as session ticket expiration time.

Multiple-Tree Forests

A *forest* is established when the first Active Directory domain is created; this domain is known as the *forest root*. Within a forest, any domains that share a contiguous namespace form a *tree* (see Figure 3.3). After a tree has been established within a forest, any new domain added to an existing tree inherits a portion of its namespace from its parent domain. Any domain that is added to the forest and maintains a unique namespace forms a new tree. Therefore, it's possible to have more than one tree within a single forest, and there might be instances in which multiple trees are required to meet the needs of a business.

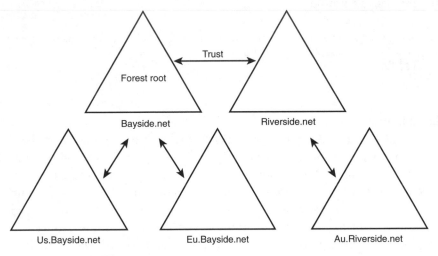

Figure 3.3   A multiple tree forest.

Business Requirements

Remember that when you're planning a domain structure, simplicity is always best. If a business does not require multiple trees, don't make things more difficult by creating an elaborate multiple-tree structure. However, there will be instances when multiple trees are required. Again, only a thorough assessment of the business can determine whether this is necessary. When considering a multiple-tree structure, keep the requirements discussed in the following subsections in mind. If a business requires any one of the following, you might need to design a multiple-tree structure.

DNS Names

If a business is comprised of different subsidiaries or has partnered with other businesses that need to maintain their distinct public identities as well as separate (noncontiguous) DNS names, multiple trees might have to be created within a single forest.

 If an organization has subsidiaries with unique DNS domain names, the organization can create a domain tree for each namespace to maintain the subsidiaries' individual DNS identification.

Central Directory Information

All trees within a single forest share the same schema, configuration container, and Global Catalog. If an organization wants to have centralized administration of these and maintain a single schema, configuration container, and Global Catalog for the entire organization and all its business units, a single forest with multiple trees can be implemented.

One of the nice features of being able to create a distinction between business units while keeping them within the same forest is that users within different trees can still easily search for objects forest-wide because all objects share a common Global Catalog.

Trusts Between Trees

When a new tree is established within a forest, a two-way transitive trust is automatically established between the two root domains. This two-way trust creates a trust path that enables users from one tree to access resources located within another tree in the same forest. The really nice thing about this is that a path is created throughout the Active Directory hierarchy without any administrative effort.

Creating the Conceptual Design of the Organizational Unit Structure

The OU structure that is designed should reflect the administrative needs of the business. The OU structure is irrelevant to the regular users within the business—it is created for the purpose of administration. The design should enable administrators to easily delegate control over groups of objects to the appropriate user or group. The OU hierarchy should also allow for the linking of group policies. The following topics are covered in this section:

➤ Starting with administrative requirements

➤ Tailoring for group policy application

Starting with Administrative Requirements

When you're creating an OU structure, remember that it must meet the needs of administration (this cannot be emphasized enough). The structure you design should be based on the administrative model that the business implements. The OU structure should allow the business to continue to delegate authority and distribute administrative tasks in a way that meets its needs.

As the OU structure is being designed, keep in mind that the upper layers of the hierarchy are based on the model for administration. If the design team determines that a model based on geographical location is needed for administration, the upper layers of the OU hierarchy will reflect this model.

 Be sure to base the structure of the upper layers of the OU hierarchy on something that will remain static (for example, geographic location as opposed to department or business unit). Doing so will help to avoid a reorganization of the Active Directory hierarchy in the future.

The lower levels within the OU hierarchy should be created with specific administrative tasks in mind; in other words, what types of objects will users and groups be responsible for administering? How can these objects be grouped to allow for this administration? For example, if a group is to be responsible for printer administration within its location, an OU could be created for printer objects and delegation of authority can be assigned to that group. By nesting OUs within one another, you can create an OU structure that meets the specific administrative requirements of the business.

 Although nesting OUs is a good thing, the hierarchy can become difficult to administer and troubleshoot if it is too deep.

After you've determined that the administrative requirements have been met by the OU structure, you also need to determine how it will be affected by the application of group policies.

Tailoring for Group Policy

Group Policy is used to administer the computing environment of users and computers within a business (which is further discussed in Chapter 4, "Creating the Logical Design for an Active Directory Infrastructure"). A Group Policy object can be linked to different levels within the Active Directory hierarchy, and the level at which it is linked determines the scope of the policy. Group policies are most commonly linked to the OU level because doing so provides administrators with the most control over the computing environment and allows for the delegation of authority to users and groups, thus eliminating the need to give them administrative privileges at the domain level.

The lower levels of the OU hierarchy should enable administrators to apply specific group policies to the necessary objects. For example, if a group policy needs to be applied to a group of specific users, a lower-level OU could be created for this group and linked to the appropriate group policy.

Remember that GPOs are applied from the top level down, and if the OU structure is too deep with GPOs at different levels, it might result in poor network performance. However, it is the number of GPOs, not the OU depth, that affects logon times.

Designing the Network Services Infrastructure to Meet Business and Technical Requirements

When all the required information has been gathered, you're ready to begin designing the network infrastructure. This includes designing how the various network services, such as WINS, DHCP, and DNS, will be used in the new infrastructure.

Creating the Conceptual Design of the DNS Infrastructure

When creating the conceptual design, consider things such as the DNS namespace, DNS server placement, as well as any interoperability issues.

DNS Namespace

One of the most important points when designing a DNS infrastructure is the DNS namespace that will be used. This is essentially the foundation of the Active Directory hierarchy. When the DNS name has been chosen, it should be registered on the Internet, regardless of whether the company has an Internet presence. That way, if the company decides to implement an Internet presence in the future, you won't have to reorganize the current Active Directory hierarchy.

 NOTE

The Internal and external namespaces are frequently different, so you would not have to change the internal namespace when implementing an Internet presence or presences.

Server Placement

When you design a DNS infrastructure, you need to consider where on the network your DNS servers should be located. The main goal is to provide clients with optimal response time when resolving hostnames (of course, you also want to consider network traffic as well).

In a network that's routed, you have two options. Ideally, you want to be able to place a DNS server on each subnet. Or, if the subnets are connected via high-speed links, you can place all the DNS servers in a central location (which might be more ideal for administrators). However, in choosing the second option, the loss of a connection could mean that clients are temporarily without name resolution services.

If zones aren't integrated within Active Directory, secondary servers should be used for fault tolerance and increased availability. The primary DNS servers should ideally be located near those who are responsible for administering them. Consider placing the secondary servers on subnets that contain the most hosts or on those that generate the most name resolution traffic. For those subnets that generate a large amount of traffic, you might want to place both a primary and secondary server for load balancing purposes.

You also need to consider whether any remote sites are connected to the main sites via slow WAN connections. In these situations, caching-only servers are ideal. When the cache is built up, there will not be as much need to resolve queries over the WAN connection. The WAN link will also not be used for zone transfers (which can generate a large amount of network traffic) because the server does not store any zone information. On the other hand, if the remote location has enough clients, it would be prudent to have a domain controller placed locally, therefore using a full DNS implementation.

Interoperability Issues

When planning a DNS infrastructure, one of the important things to consider is that the version of DNS included with Windows Server 2003 will integrate with other DNS servers. In some cases, a network will already have a DNS implementation and you might be required to add a Windows Server 2003 DNS server to the infrastructure. Before you do, it's critical that you know how DNS will integrate with these existing versions. For example, if you were installing a Windows Server 2003 domain, how would an existing BIND DNS server function within the domain? Identifying any interoperability issues during the design phase can help ensure that any interoperability issues are corrected before the plan is rolled out.

You also need to consider the existing name service used for resolution. Many networks today still implement WINS servers to support legacy clients such as Windows NT 4.0 or clients that still use NetBIOS names. Because Active Directory requires the use of DNS, you must be aware how Windows Server 2003 DNS can integrate with WINS servers.

Many networks already have a DNS infrastructure in place. As the old saying goes, "If it ain't broke, don't fix it." So, many administrators may be reluctant to switch over to another DNS server when the infrastructure currently in place is fine. In such cases, you should be aware of how Windows Server 2003 DNS will interoperate with other versions of DNS.

Creating the Conceptual Design of the WINS Infrastructure

In a network environment that supports only Windows 2000, Windows XP, and Windows Server 2003 clients, WINS is not required because the primary namespace used is DNS. When NetBIOS over TCP/IP is enabled, traditional name resolution techniques are still used depending on the manner is which a request is made.

Pre–Windows 2000 clients require NetBIOS for such things as locating domain controllers. If any legacy clients such as Windows NT 4.0, Windows 95, and Windows 98 are on the network, WINS might be required for NetBIOS name resolution services. Otherwise, if all workstations can support DNS, WINS does not have to be implemented.

You also need to look at the physical network. If there is a single subnet with a small number of clients, WINS might not be necessary and you can rely on LMHOSTS files or broadcasts for name resolution. However, if there are a large number of hosts on the subnet or if there are multiple subnets, WINS should be implemented. In terms of the number of clients, the performance of a physical network can suffer if broadcasts are relied on for name resolution. Implementing WINS can reduce the number of broadcasts on a subnet. Also, because routers do not forward broadcasts between subnets, WINS should be used to facilitate network access between different subnets. WINS servers on different subnets can be configured for replication so that clients on one subnet can resolve the names of clients on other subnets.

A single WINS server is capable of handling a large number of requests. The number of WINS servers you implement on a network is dependent on several things, such as the hardware installed on the WINS server, whether or not the network is routed, as well as the number of clients on each subnet.

When determining the number of WINS servers required, keep the following points in mind:

➤ The number of NetBIOS names typically registered by a WINS client

➤ The frequency of name registrations and releases due to workstations being rebooted

➤ The speed and availability of the physical links connecting the various networks

A single WINS server is capable of handling approximately 10,000 clients; of course, this is dependent on the amount of NetBIOS traffic that is generated. It is always recommended that two WINS servers be configured for fault tolerance. So, when you're planning the number of WINS servers, a good guideline is to install two WINS servers for every 10,000 WINS clients. You can then configure the two WINS servers as replication partners.

When implementing multiple WINS servers, you also need to decide where they should be located. The speed and available bandwidth of the existing network connections have a major effect on where WINS servers are placed.

Creating the Conceptual Design of the DHCP Infrastructure

Certain factors will affect your DHCP implementation. When designing a DHCP infrastructure, you need to consider the following points:

➤ The number of DHCP servers

➤ The placement of DHCP servers

➤ DHCP in a routed network

Number of DHCP Servers

There really is no limit to the number of clients that a single DHCP server can service. Therefore, the main factors that will influence the number of servers you implement will be the existing network infrastructure and the server hardware. If your network consists of a single subnet, a single DHCP server is sufficient, although you might choose to implement more than one for a high level of availability. Implementing a single DHCP server creates a single point of failure, although clients can use APIPA in the event that the DHCP server is unavailable. You can also use the Alternate Configuration option, and manually specify the IP address parameters that a client should use if a DHCP server is not available.

In terms of the network infrastructure, if the network consists of multiple subnets, routers can be configured to forward DHCP broadcasts between subnets. Or you might choose to place DHCP servers on each of the subnets. Another option is to configure a DHCP relay agent on those subnets that do not host DHCP servers (see Figure 3.4). The DHCP relay agent can forward IP address requests to DHCP servers on other subnets on behalf of clients.

Figure 3.4   Enabling the DHCP relay agent.

In any case, before you implement any DHCP servers on the network, consider the following points:

➤ DHCP servers should be configured with fast disk subsystems and as much RAM as possible. If your DHCP server lacks the hardware (and depending on the number of clients), you might need to implement more than one DHCP server to improve response time for clients.

➤ Implementing a single DHCP server creates a single point of failure.

➤ If there are multiple subnets, you can extend the functionality of a DHCP server across subnets using the DHCP relay agent. Other solutions include placing a DHCP server on each subnet or enabling forwarding of DHCP requests via the routers.

Consider the speed of the links connecting various networks and segments. If a DHCP server is on the far side of a slow WAN link or a dial-up connection, you might choose to place DHCP servers on either side for increased performance. Because DHCP servers do not share any information, there would be no increase in network traffic. Network traffic on the slow link would actually be reduced because clients can obtain leases locally as opposed to using a remote DHCP server.

Placement of DHCP Servers

When it comes time to determine where on the network DHCP servers should be placed, keep in mind that your overall goals are to provide high levels of client performance and server availability. Placement of the DHCP servers depends on the routing configuration, how the network is configured, and the hardware installed on the DHCP servers.

If you're implementing a single DHCP server, it should be placed on the subnet that contains the highest number of clients. All other subnets will have a DHCP relay agent installed or the routers will be configured to forward DHCP broadcasts. Also keep in mind that with a single-server implementation, the network connections should be high speed and the server should be configured with the appropriate hardware.

There are a number of reasons why you might choose to use multiple DHCP servers. Some obvious reasons are high availability and redundancy. When you're determining where to place the DHCP servers, remember that they should be located on the subnets that contain the most clients. Also assess the connections between networks: If certain subnets or segments are connected with slow WAN links, such as a dial-up connection, a DHCP server should be placed at these locations so that clients do not have to use the slow connection when attempting to lease or renew an IP address. Having clients obtain IP addresses across slow unreliable links creates another point of failure if the link becomes unavailable.

Routed Networks

Networks can be subdivided into smaller networks known as *subnets*. Those subnets are connected using routers. To reduce network traffic, most routers do not forward broadcasts from one subnet to another. This poses a problem with DHCP because clients initially send out a broadcast when leasing an IP address—the client does not yet have an IP address. One solution to this problem is to use DHCP relay agents.

A relay agent is responsible for relaying DHCP messages between DHCP clients and DHCP servers that are located on different subnets. If routers are RFC 1542–compliant, they can forward the DHCP-related messages between subnets. If not, a computer running Windows Server 2003 (Windows NT 4.0 and Windows 2000 as well) can be configured as a relay agent by installing the DHCP relay agent component. Configuring a DHCP relay agent is done through the Routing and Remote Access console.

Centralized Versus Decentralized

Another aspect you need to consider when planning for DHCP is whether you will implement a centralized or a decentralized model in a subnetted environment. For example, you could choose to have all the DHCP servers in a single location servicing requests from clients on different subnets. Or you might choose to place the DHCP servers on each of the different subnets instead. Before you make your decision, you should be aware of the advantages and disadvantages associated with each option.

A decentralized approach would result in DHCP servers being placed in each of the different subnets. Doing so offers the following advantages and disadvantages:

➤ Local administrators can administer their own DHCP servers and configure them in a way that meets their own needs.

➤ Clients do not have to rely on WAN links to obtain an IP address.

➤ Placing a DHCP server at each location will obviously result in an increase in cost due to the fact that multiple servers are required.

A centralized approach would result in all DHCP servers being located in a specific location. This approach offers the following advantages and disadvantages:

➤ Administration of DHCP might be simpler because there will be fewer servers and having them in a single location where technical support is on-hand makes problems easier to troubleshoot.

➤ If fewer DHCP servers are required, the cost associated with implementing DHCP will obviously be reduced.

➤ Clients in remote sites might have to rely on WAN links to obtain an IP address. That means if the WAN link is down, clients will not be able to contact a DHCP server. This creates a single point of failure.

➤ Administration could be more difficult because it is hard for an administrator to know the configuration requirements of a remote site.

Creating the Conceptual Design of the Remote Access Infrastructure

When creating the conceptual design for remote access, you need to determine the remote access method. Windows Server 2003 supports two different remote access methods, dial-up and VPN. You need to evaluate the advantages and disadvantages of each remote access method to determine which one best suits your needs.

With a dial-up solution, remote access clients connect to a remote access server using a telephone line. The remote access server requires at least one modem or multi-port adapter as well as a telephone line or another form of connectivity. If the remote access clients require access to resources on the private network, the remote access server must also be configured with a LAN connection. The remote access client simply requires a modem and telephone connection.

The second option for remote access connectivity is to implement a VPN remote access solution. To provide users with remote access via the Internet, the remote access VPN server is normally configured with a permanent Internet connection. Again, if users require access to the private network, the server must also have a LAN connection. The VPN client must have a modem or network adapter as well as Internet connectivity using the phone line or another WAN connectivity method. A VPN solution also requires the use of a tunneling protocol. The remote access client and the remote access server must be configured to use PPTP or L2TP (keeping in mind that the client and the server must be configured to use the same tunneling protocol).

Analyzing the Effect of the Infrastructure Design on the Existing Technical Environment

After you have established the Active Directory design, you need to examine the effect that the new design will have on the existing environment. For example, will the existing hardware and software be able to support the new Active Directory infrastructure? In any case, these issues must be identified before rolling out the new design so that they can be addressed before the Active Directory infrastructure is in place.

Analyzing Hardware and Software Requirements

It's important to gather and document information pertaining to the current systems in use. Information about the existing systems and how they will integrate with Active Directory needs to be included in the initial design plans. Use the following questions as a guide when documenting this information:

➤ Do the current systems meet the hardware requirements?

➤ Is the hardware currently in use supported by Windows 2000?

➤ What operating systems are currently in use? What service packs have been applied?

➤ How will these operating systems integrate with Active Directory?

➤ Will any operating systems have to be upgraded to another version (NT 4.0) before installing Windows Server 2003?

➤ Does the business have any DNS servers configured? How will they interoperate within Active Directory?

Not only do the systems have to be assessed, but attention must also be given to the applications running on them. What applications does the business currently use? What applications do the business and its employees require when performing their job tasks? After you've determined which applications are required, be sure to test them to see how they will integrate within Active Directory.

 This might seem like an unimportant step in the design of Active Directory, but it will be much easier for you and the organization if it is known beforehand that some systems or applications need to be upgraded.

Analyzing Interoperability Requirements

Interoperability issues can pertain to hardware, operating systems, and applications. All three of these components will already exist within a network infrastructure. One of the important steps before performing a rollout is to determine how these components will interoperate with Windows Server 2003. For example, is the server hardware supported by Windows Server 2003? If existing operating systems are being used, how will they interoperate within the new environment? Interoperability issues should be identified before rolling out the new infrastructure so they can be addressed in the design plan.

Analyzing the Current Level of Service Within the Existing Technical Environment

The rollout of Windows Server 2003 is bound to have an effect on the technical support within an organization. The current technical support requirements must be assessed to determine how they will be affected. If a business currently relies on internal staff for technical support, what effect will Active Directory have on this? The skill set of the current technical support staff should be assessed and a training plan put into place. The IT staff might require highly specialized training on the Active Directory features and functions that are being implemented. Imagine performing a rollout of Windows Server 2003 only to discover afterward that the IT staff is unable to provide the technical support necessary to maintain the new structure.

When designing the training plan, consider including end users as well as the IT staff. Providing end users with some basic training on the Active Directory infrastructure being implemented might help reduce the technical support requirements as the upgrades and rollouts occur.

If a business currently outsources all or some of the technical support requirements to external companies, the effect that the rollout will have on these arrangements must be considered. When the business begins to migrate to Windows Server 2003, consider whether the company currently responsible for the business's technical support can still meet the business's needs. If not, this job will need to be managed by a company that is fluent in the Active Directory technologies.

Analyzing Network Requirements

The new infrastructure also will have specific network requirements; for example, LAN/WAN connectivity, available bandwidth, and server distribution. After you've analyzed the existing network, you can determine whether it is capable of supporting the new infrastructure. If not, certain areas of the network might need to be upgraded before performing the rollout.

Exam Prep Questions

Question 1

> You're planning the Active Directory design for FKP International. One of the requirements is that all members of the Finance department have a more stringent password policy than users in all other departments. What should you do?
>
> ○ A. Configure an OU for the Finance department. Configure a stringent password policy and apply it to the OU.
>
> ○ B. Configure a Finance domain and configure a domain-wide password policy.
>
> ○ C. Configure a new forest for the Finance department. Configure a domain-wide password policy.
>
> ○ D. Create a new universal group called finance. Configure a stringent password policy and apply it to the finance group.

Answer B is correct. Password policies are configured at the domain level. There can be only one password policy per domain. To apply a different password policy for the Finance department, two domains must be configured. Answer A is incorrect because password policies are not configured at the OU level. Answer C is incorrect because creating a new forest is unnecessary. Answer D is incorrect because a password policy cannot be specifically applied to a group.

Question 2

> Which of the following administrative models organizes the Active Directory hierarchy around the different business units or departments?
>
> ○ A. Geographical
>
> ○ B. Functional
>
> ○ C. Organizational
>
> ○ D. Hybrids

Answer C is correct. An organizational model organizes the Active Directory hierarchy around the various business units or departments within a company. Answer A is incorrect because the model organizes Active Directory components around the various geographical locations. Answer B is incorrect because this model organizes the Active Directory hierarchy around the various job roles defined within a business. Answer D is incorrect because this model uses a combination of the other models.

Question 3

FKP International has recently bought out another company. The new company already has its own network infrastructure. While assessing the requirements of both companies, you determine that each company will require separate partitions. What should you do?

- ○ A. Configure two forests
- ○ B. Establish the new company as a new domain tree within the FKP International forest
- ○ C. Configure a child domain under the FKP International forest root domain for the new company
- ○ D. Configure an OU for the new company

Answer A is correct. Partitions are applied at the forest level. Therefore, if a company requires unique schema policies, multiple forests are required. Answers B, C, and D are incorrect because partitions are configured only at the forest root level.

Question 4

You are designing the Active Directory infrastructure for DKP International. DKP International was recently bought by FKP International. You're trying to determine how the new company will fit within the FKP International Active Directory hierarchy. During your assessment, you determine that DKP International already has an Internet presence that needs to be maintained. The organization also wants to use this namespace internally. What should you do?

- ○ A. Configure two separate forests, one for each company
- ○ B. Configure DKP International as a new tree within the forest
- ○ C. Configure a child domain under the forest root for DKP International
- ○ D. Configure an OU for DKP International

Answer B is correct. By configuring a new tree within an existing forest, DKP International can maintain its Internet presence while still being part of the FKP International Active Directory infrastructure. Answer A is incorrect because creating two separate forests is unnecessary. Answer C and D are incorrect because these solutions would not allow the new company to maintain its current DNS name.

Question 5

You're planning the WINS design for FKP International. Approximately 5,000 clients are on the network. The network is also routed. How many WINS servers are required?

○ A. 1

○ B. 2

○ C. 3

○ D. 4

Answer A is correct. There is no requirement for the number of WINS server that must be implemented. Because WINS is required for name resolution, one server must be used, although two WINS servers would be recommended for fault tolerance. Therefore, answers B, C, and D are incorrect.

Question 6

FKP International consists of a routed network. The company wants the new network infrastructure to include DHCP to automate the assignment of IP addresses to workstations. All routers do not support DHCP broadcasts. Which of the following would meet this requirement?

❏ A. Install a single DHCP server to be used by all workstations

❏ B. Install a single DHCP server and place a DHCP relay agent on each subnet without a DHCP server

❏ C. Place a DHCP server on each subnet

❏ D. Install the DHCP relay agent

Answers B and C are correct. Because the network is routed, you have two options. First, a DHCP server can be placed on each subnet or you can place a DHCP server on one subnet and enable the DHCP relay agent on the remaining subnets. Therefore, answers A and D are incorrect. A single DHCP server will not work because the routers do not support DHCP broadcasts. A DHCP server is required and therefore implementing only a relay agent is incorrect.

Question 7

FKP International has offices throughout North America. The corporate head-quarters is located in Chicago. The NYC and Boston locations are connected to the head office via T1 connections. The office in San Francisco is connected to the head office via a 56kbps frame relay connection that is already heavily utilized. How many sites are required?

- ○ A. 1
- ○ B. 2
- ○ C. 3
- ○ D. 4

Answer B is correct. Because the WAN connection between San Francisco and the head office is slow and already heavily utilized, at least two separate sites should be required. Answer A is incorrect because replication will not occur correctly. Answers C and D are incorrect because only the minimum number of sites that are required should be created.

Question 8

FKP International has offices throughout North America. The corporate head-quarters is located in Chicago. The NYC and Boston locations are connected to the head office via T1 connections. The office in San Francisco is connected to the head office via a 56kbps frame relay connection that is already heavily utilized. The NYC location currently has its own Internet presence which should be maintained. The Active Directory DNS name for NYC should be the same as its Internet domain name. How many domains will be required?

- ○ A. One domain for the entire company
- ○ B. Two domains: a forest root domain and a child domain for the NYC location
- ○ C. Three domains: A root domain, and two geographical domains for San Francisco and NYC
- ○ D. Five domains: A root domain, and four geographical domains

Answer C is correct. A forest root domain is required. Two geographical domains should be created: one for San Francisco because the link is not capable of sustaining Sysvol replication and one for the NYC location because it needs to maintain an Internet presence. Therefore answers A, B, and D are incorrect.

Question 9

When creating the Active Directory design for DKP international, four domains are required. Each domain will be configured as a child under the root domain. What must be done so that users in one domain can access resources in another domain within the forest?

○ A. Configure two-way transitive trusts between all domains.

○ B. Nothing. Two-way transitive trusts are automatically configured.

○ C. Configure shortcut trusts between all domains in the forest.

○ D. Configure two one-way trusts between each domain.

Answer B is correct. Within a forest, two-way transitive trusts are automatically configured between parent and child domains, thereby creating a trust path throughout the forest. Therefore, answers A and D are incorrect. Answer C is incorrect because shortcut trusts are required only if you want to shorten the trust path between two domains.

Question 10

FKP International is expanding and a new office is being opened in Europe. The number of users in the new location will be close to 3,000 within the next two years. The IT director for the company wants to know whether a new domain is required for the new location. Which of the following should be considered?

❑ A. Security requirements

❑ B. Number of users

❑ C. Number of local resources

❑ D. WAN connectivity

❑ E. Operating systems in use

Answers A and D are correct. When assessing the requirements for a new domain, you should consider the security requirements and WAN connectivity. Both of these could warrant the creation of additional domains. Therefore answers B, C, and E are incorrect.

Need to Know More?

 Try searching the TechNet CD or use Microsoft's online version at www.microsoft.com and search for keywords such as *Active Directory*, *network services*, *domain*, *organizational unit*, and *forests*.

 The Microsoft Windows Server 2003 Deployment Kit, Microsoft Press, 2003. Contains in-depth information about deploying Windows Server 2003.

 Microsoft Corporation. *Microsoft Windows Server 2003 Resource Kit*. Microsoft Press, 2003.

4

Creating the Logical Design for an Active Directory Infrastructure

. . . .

Terms you'll need to understand:

✓ Delegation
✓ Group Policy Object
✓ Filtering
✓ Global Group
✓ Universal Group
✓ Domain Local Group
✓ Kerberos

Techniques you'll need to master:

✓ Designing an OU structure
✓ Designing a strategy for Group Policy implementation
✓ Designing a security group strategy
✓ Designing a user and computer authentication strategy
✓ Designing an Active Directory naming strategy
✓ Designing migration paths to Active Directory
✓ Designing an Active Directory services site topology

Designing an OU Structure

Organizational units (OUs) are created within a domain to logically group objects for administrative purposes. More specifically, they are created for applying group policy objects (GPOs) and delegating authority. After an OU hierarchy has been established, GPOs can be applied to the various containers based on the requirements of the organization, and specific users or groups can be assigned the task of administering the objects contained within the OUs.

Creating OUs enables a fine granularity for configuring the user and computer environments. It enables you to limit the scope of an administrator's privileges through delegation and provides a fine granularity of control when assigning administrative rights and permissions to other individuals and groups. The following section looks at how the group policy requirements and delegation of authority affect an OU design.

Designing an OU Structure for the Purpose of Delegating Authority

Delegation is the process of decentralizing network administration by assigning some of the administrative duties to individuals or groups within the business. Individuals or groups can be assigned specific administrative privileges to certain objects within the Active Directory structure without having control over all objects within a domain. For example, assume that OUs are created based on the geographical locations of various branch offices. The local administrator within each office could be granted authority over the appropriate OU, giving that person administrative control over the objects within the container, while at the same time limiting the scope of the administrative permission to a single OU.

Delegation of authority was introduced in Windows 2000 and was a welcome change from Windows NT 4.0, where a user who was given privileges to administer user accounts could administer all user accounts within the domain. In other words, there was no way to limit which user accounts could be administered or what attributes could be changed on a per-user basis.

A strategy for delegation determines the level in the Active Directory structure at which administrative permissions should be assigned: site, domain, or organizational unit. The level at which the permissions are applied will be determined by the scope of the administrative duties. It is most common to delegate authority at the organizational unit level because this level is much easier to manage and provides a finer granularity of control.

Before you begin developing a strategy for delegation, make sure you've determined the answers to the following questions:

➤ Who will be assigned administrative privileges?

➤ What will they be administering?

➤ What will be the scope of their administrative duties?

The OU structure that's designed should be relative to the way administration is currently dispersed throughout the business, and is dependent on how the administrative tasks are currently delegated. Here are some questions to keep in mind when you're designing an OU structure for delegation:

➤ Is the delegation of administration based on location? Are there individuals in each geographical location who are responsible for performing administrative tasks?

➤ Are the administrative tasks divided into different roles, such as user account administration and printer administration?

➤ Is the delegation of administrative tasks based on department? Are there individuals or groups within each department who are responsible for performing administrative tasks?

The OU structure should be designed around the way that administrative tasks are currently dispersed. Doing so will allow the organization to continue with its current strategy of distributing administrative authority.

Design Guidelines

When designing an OU hierarchy for delegation, keep the following guidelines in mind:

➤ Perform a thorough assessment of the business and its internal IT organization so that their needs are identified.

➤ Make sure the model you create allows for flexibility and growth within the business. Growth or reorganization within a business should not have a major effect on the Active Directory structure.

➤ The OU hierarchy should reflect the structure of the organization.

➤ When at all possible, delegate authority at the OU level and use inheritance. Doing so makes it much simpler to tracking permissions.

➤ If an individual needs authority over an OU, assign the appropriate administrative permissions. Avoid putting the individual into the Domain Admins group because doing so gives that person privileges throughout the domain. Assign the most restrictive permissions that allow the user (or group) to perform the required tasks. In other words, follow the principle of least privileges.

Each OU is assigned an owner that is responsible for that object and all objects contained within it. The OU owner is responsible for delegating administrative tasks over the object.

Identifying the Group Policy Requirements for the OU Structure

Before you implement a group policy, you should perform an assessment of the organization's needs to determine where in the business the management is required and the level of management that needs to be implemented. Use the following questions as guidelines when assessing the needs of the business:

➤ What areas of the client's computing environment need to be controlled?

➤ What areas within the business require administration?

➤ Do all areas within the business require the same level of management? Are there some areas that require a high level of management and other areas that require minimal management?

Determining the different levels of management required throughout the business is important because they will have an effect on the creation of lower-level OUs in the Active Directory hierarchy. Because group policies can be linked to different levels within the Active Directory hierarchy, using the preceding questions as guides will also help the design team determine where in the hierarchy the policies should be linked to best serve the needs of the IT organization.

Designing a Strategy for Group Policy Implementation

When designing a strategy for Group Policy, you need to consider several issues. The planning issues that require consideration are the delegation of administration, the application of GPOs (or at what levels of the Active Directory hierarchy), the use of security for filtering, and the modification of inheritance.

Designing the Administration of Group Policy Objects

One of the most important factors to consider when designing a group policy implementation is the delegation of administration. In other words, who will be responsible for administering the various GPOs and what that person's scope of authority will be.

It's important to design the GPOs in a way that enables the current IT organization to manage them easily. Some sort of standard should be set in place so that the creation and organization of GPOs can remain consistent throughout the network. When you design group policies, you need to consider how administration is distributed throughout the network (centralized versus decentralized). You also need to determine who will be responsible for administering the GPOs and the scope of that person's administrative permission.

When organizing GPOs, you have basically three options: single policy, multiple policy, and dedicated policy. Keep in mind that the implementation you choose will affect a number of things, including the maintainability of the GPO, the logon times as Group Policy is processed, and the ability to delegate GPO maintenance tasks.

➤ In a single-policy implementation, a separate policy is created for each of the different policy options. Separate group policies could be created for applications settings, security settings, and desktop settings. With this type of implementation, different users or groups can be given authority over different areas of Group Policy. If this type of option were implemented within an organization, several GPOs would be applied to a single organizational unit, and each GPO could have different settings. This implementation would best meet the needs of a business that distributes the administrative tasks among different users or groups (that is, one that has a decentralized administrative model).

➤ A second option is to implement a multiple-policy structure. In this type of implementation, one GPO contains all the settings that must be applied to a container. One GPO contains all the application, security, Windows, and administrative settings. This option is best suited to a business that implements a centralized administrative model.

➤ A dedicated policy structure contains settings that are divided into two general categories. One GPO would be created to hold the computer settings, and another GPO would contain the user settings.

When designing group policy, also take into consideration which users or groups will be assigned delegation of control over the GPOs and the type of permissions they will require. Will the users or groups be given the right to create new GPOs, modify existing policies, and link policies between sites and domains, or will they be given full control? The type of permissions assigned to users will again be determined by how the business currently distributes administrative tasks.

Administrative tasks for GPOs can be grouped into three different general categories: creating, modifying, and linking. Here are some questions to keep in mind when planning the administration of GPOs:

➤ Should the user or group have the ability to create new GPOs (specifying his or her own policy settings) for an organizational unit?

➤ Should the user or group have the ability to modify an existing GPO?

➤ Should the user or group have the ability to link a GPO to an organizational unit?

Obviously, the permissions that a user is assigned over a GPO determine the scope of that user's administrative control. Remember to follow the principle of least privileges and assign only the necessary permissions for a user or group to carry out a job.

Designing the Deployment Strategy of GPOs

Group policy objects can be linked to any of the three levels within the Active Directory hierarchy. The level at which a GPO is linked determines its scope. In other words, where in the hierarchy the GPO is linked determines the number of users and computers that are affected by the policy settings. For example, linking a GPO to a domain affects more users and computers than linking it to an OU within the domain.

To deploy group policies effectively, it's important to understand the effect that a GPO has when it is linked to a certain level in the Active Directory hierarchy. Linking a group policy at the site level would have a different effect than linking a group policy at the OU level. The needs of the business will determine where group policies should be linked in the hierarchy.

Site Level

The first level at which a GPO can be linked is the site level. A GPO linked at the site level affects all users and computers within those particular IP subnets. You might be asking yourself why you would ever want to link a GPO at this level instead of applying it at the domain or OU level. Linking a GPO at this level allows a business to take advantage of the physical connections within and between groups of subnets.

To take advantage of the high-speed connections within a site, administrators can choose to create a GPO for publishing applications and link it at this level. For example, a GPO can be linked to specific sites so that users do not have to install applications over a relatively slow WAN link and the high-speed connections within the site can be utilized.

 Keep in mind that to link a GPO at the site level, you must be a member of the Enterprise Admins group.

Domain Level

The next level in the Active Directory hierarchy to which a GPO can be linked is the domain level. When a GPO is linked at this level, it affects all the users and computers that belong to that particular domain. For example, if an organization requires that all computers within a domain have the same specific type of background on their workstations that included the company logo, a GPO could be linked at the domain level.

When applying a GPO at this level in the Active Directory hierarchy, you need to be aware of a couple of issues. One of the reasons that OUs are created is to delegate control over their contents to another user or group. When a GPO is linked at the domain level, all the OUs within the domain inherit the policy settings. The policy has to be administered at the domain level, and authority over the policy cannot be delegated to administrators responsible for administering the OUs. In other words, the delegation of authority has to be done at the domain level. The administrators of the different OUs will have no administrative control over the policy.

Also keep in mind that when a policy is linked to a parent domain, the child domains are not affected by the policy. Policy settings are not inherited from parent domain to child domain.

 Domains are security boundaries, so no Group Policy settings are inherited by child domains. That means if you want to create a group policy at the domain level, you must link a GPO to each domain in a forest. Likewise, settings from a GPO linked to an organizational unit in a parent domain are not inherited by the OUs in a child domain.

If the child domains require the same Group Policy settings, you have two options. The first is to link the GPO to the child domains. The only problem with linking GPOs across domain boundaries is that doing so increases traffic because the policy must be retrieved from another domain. This becomes a major concern if the link between the domains is slow. The preferred method is to create another GPO with the same settings and apply it to the child domain.

You can use the Group Policy Management Console to copy or import Group Policy settings.

OU Level

The third level at which a GPO can be linked within the Active Directory structure is the OU level. Linking GPOs at this level provides administrators with the most control. Users and computers can be grouped together into an OU, and a GPO can be created and linked to that OU.

GPOs cannot be linked to the Users and Computers containers that are created by default when Active Directory is installed. Neither can GPOs be applied at the forest level.

One advantage of linking a GPO at this level is that delegation of authority over the GPO is still possible without giving the user or group privileges throughout the domain. This allows an organization to maintain a decentralized administrative model.

Keep in mind that GPOs don't have to be linked at a single level only. They can be linked at all three levels within the Active Directory hierarchy. It's important to understand how GPOs are processed when multiple policies are linked throughout the hierarchy: The GPO that is processed last overwrites settings applied by the other GPOs. Here are some key points to remember:

➤ Each computer running Windows Server 2003 (as well as Windows 2000 and Windows XP) has a GPO stored on the local computer (Local Group Policy Object). This is the policy that is processed first.

➤ Any policies that have been linked to the site level are processed after the local policy.

➤ GPOs linked to the domain level are processed next.

➤ The last GPOs to be processed are those linked to the OU level.

If multiple policies are linked at each level, the administrator can specify the order in which they should be processed.

Other Group Policy Design Issues

By using filtering and inheritance modification, you can change the way in which a GPO is applied. By default, all objects within a container are affected by a group policy that has been applied. However, there might be instances in which not all objects should be affected by the group policy settings. In such cases, filtering can be used. *Filtering* enables an administrator to exclude certain groups from being affected by a group policy by limiting the scope of the policy. When you filter a GPO, you exempt a group from the settings within the policy.

GPOs are linked to the site, domain, and OU objects within Active Directory. Filters, on the other hand, are applied to users or groups through discretionary access control lists (DACLs).

The group policies that are linked to an Active Directory object affect all users who have the Apply Group Policy permission for the GPO. This is the default permission given to all users for a GPO. That means all users are, by default, affected by the policy. To change the scope of the GPO and exclude certain users from being affected, simply create a security group that contains the users who need to be excluded and remove the Apply Group Policy permission to the GPO.

If the policy applies restrictions to the users' computing environment, some of the restrictions might not be required for administrative purposes. In that case, a filter could be applied to exempt those users responsible for administration of the OU from the policy. To filter by using security groups, do the following:

1. Click Start, point to Administrative Tools, and select Active Directory User and Computers (or Active Directory Sites and Services, if GPOs are configured at the site level).

2. Right-click the appropriate object and click Properties.

3. Select the Group Policy tab. From the list of GPOs, select the appropriate one and click the Properties button.

4. Click the Security tab. To exempt a group or user from the policy settings, highlight the appropriate account and clear the Apply Group Policy permission (see Figure 4.1).

In some instances, a GPO linked to a parent object should not be linked to its child objects (remember that a GPO linked at the OU level is inherited from parent object to child object). In such a case, blocking inheritance can prevent the GPO settings applied to a parent OU from being applied to a child OU.

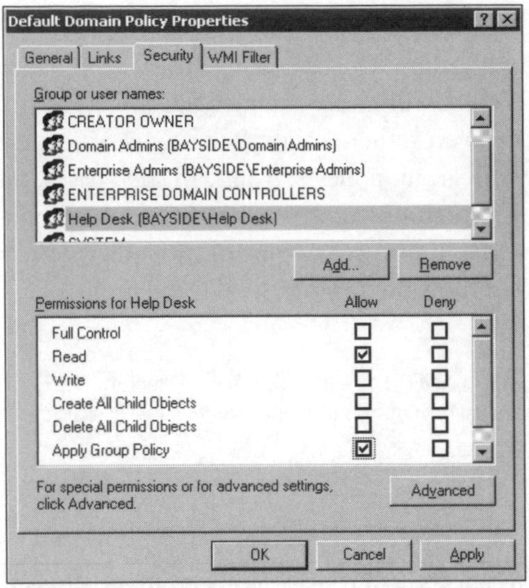

Figure 4.1 Filtering using security groups.

Using a feature called *block policy inheritance*, the inheritance of a GPO can be modified so that it is not passed on from parent container to child container. Any policy applied at the domain or OU level can be blocked.

The Block Policy Inheritance setting is not applied to the GPO itself but rather to the domain or OU that should be exempt from the policy settings. All policy settings are blocked, not just those from a single GPO. Use the following steps to block the inheritance of a GPO:

1. Open the Active Directory Users and Computers MMC snap-in.

2. Right-click the domain or OU that should be exempt from the policy and choose Properties.

3. Select the Group Policy tab and select the Block Policy Inheritance check box (see Figure 4.2).

The only time that the Block Policy Inheritance option will be ignored and the policy will still be applied is when the No Override option is set. *No Override* means exactly that. If the No Override option is set, any group policies linked to a parent object will be applied to the child objects regardless of whether the Block Policy Inheritance option is set. This option prevents any other GPO from overwriting the settings contained within it. Any GPO link that has the No Override option set will not be overwritten by another policy.

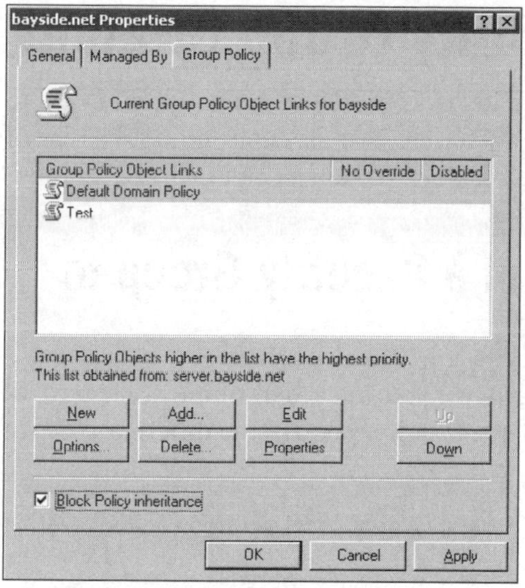

Figure 4.2   Using the Block Policy Inheritance option.

Use the following steps to specify the No Override option:

1. Open the Active Directory Users and Computers MMC snap-in or the Active Directory Sites and Services MMC snap-in. If you're setting the No Override option at the site level, use the Sites and Services snap-in. Use the Users and Computers snap-in to set No Override at the domain and OU level.

2. Right-click the site, domain, or OU that the GPO is linked to and choose Properties.

3. Choose the Group Policy tab, select the GPO you want to set the No Override option to apply to, and choose Options.

4. From the dialog box that appears, check the No Override check box (see Figure 4.3).

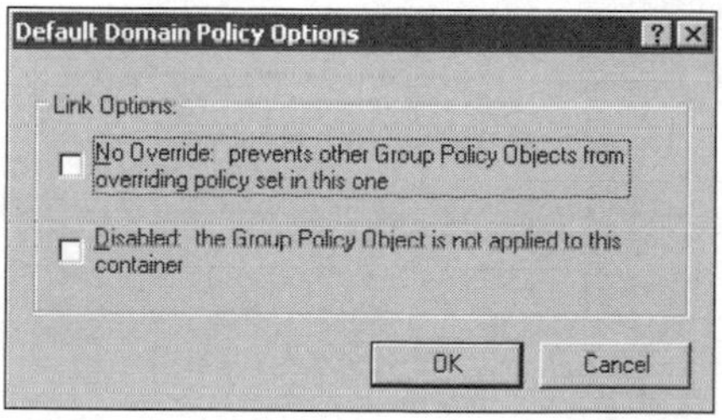

Figure 4.3   Using the No Override option.

Designing a Security Group Strategy

Security groups enable an organization to control and define users' access to resources. Designing a security group strategy entails determining the type of security group to implement as well as how to manage and maintain groups.

Defining the Scope of a Security Group to Meet Requirements

When you're planning security groups, you must determine what type of security group to use. Windows Server 2003 supports four different types of security groups:

➤ Local groups   ➤ Domain local groups

➤ Global groups   ➤ Universal groups

Local groups are found on computers running Windows XP Professional and those running Windows Server 2003 and configured as member servers. Local groups can contain user accounts only on the local computer. They're used to assign permissions to a group of users for resources on the computer where the group has been created. The difference between a local group and a domain local group is that a domain local group can be used to grant users permissions to resources throughout a domain. On the other hand, a local group provides access to only resources on a local computer.

You'll select the type of group when creating a new group using the Active Directory Users and Computers MMC snap-in. You can also change the group type for existing groups using the same interface (see Figure 4.4).

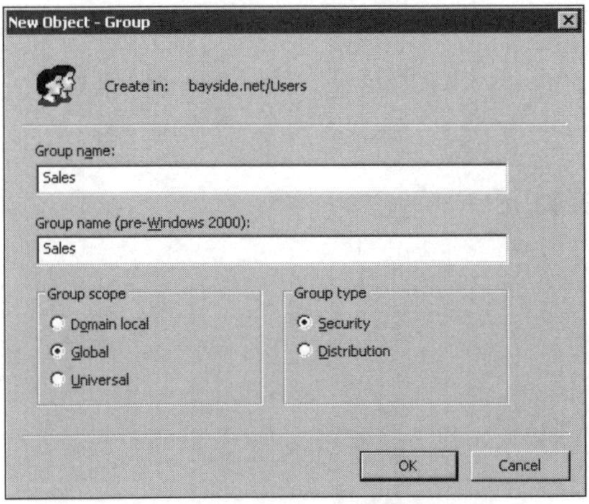

Figure 4.4   Selecting the type of group to create.

The option to create a universal group is not available if the domain functional level is Windows 2000 Mixed.

Global Groups

The first type of security group created in a domain is the *global group*. Global groups are used to logically organize users within a domain who have common needs and to assign them permissions to network resources. When deciding whether to use global groups, keep the following characteristics in mind:

➤ A global group can contain other global groups or user accounts only from the domain in which the group was created.

➤ After the group has been created, it can be assigned permissions to resources throughout the forest. The group name will appear in the global catalog so that trusted domains can assign the group permissions to their resources.

➤ If network traffic is a concern, consider using global groups. Because only the name of the group is replicated to the global catalog server, not the actual membership list, network traffic is less than for universal groups.

Group membership will still be replicated within the domain but not to other domains.

Domain Local Groups

Like global groups, domain local groups are also used to assign permissions to resources on the network. Domain local groups are used to organize users throughout the forest to assign them permissions to resources in the local domain. Domain local groups have the following characteristics:

➤ Domain local groups can contain global groups and user accounts from any domain in the forest.

➤ A domain local group can be used to assign permissions to resources only within the domain where the group has been created.

Unlike a global group, a domain local group is not replicated to global catalog servers within the forest because other domains cannot use it. The group name and membership are still replicated between domain controllers within the domain where the group is created.

Universal Groups

The third type of security group in a domain is the universal group. This type of group is used to assign a group of users from different domains permission to network resources throughout the forest.

Universal groups are also used to combine groups from multiple domains. For example, if there is a Managers group within each domain, you can create a Managers group with a universal scope and add each of the Managers groups from the various domains. This group can then be used throughout the enterprise.

Here are some points to keep in mind concerning universal groups:

➤ Universal groups can contain other universal groups (nesting), global groups, and also user accounts from any domain.

➤ A universal group can be assigned permissions to resources throughout the forest.

When deciding whether to use universal groups, keep in mind that they are available only when the functional level is set to Windows 2000 Native or Windows Server 2003.

Any universal groups you create will be replicated to all global catalog servers in the forest, as well as to their membership lists, so be sure to keep membership static and to a minimum. Doing so will help reduce replication traffic. Restricting universal group membership to only global groups is good practice. It minimizes the number and frequency of changes, thus reducing global catalog replication traffic.

Defining Resource Access Requirements

Now that you're familiar with the different security groups in Windows Server 2003, let's take a look at resource access requirements. Access to network resources can be managed using several different methods. For example, permissions to network resources can be granted to individual user accounts or to security groups. You obviously must take an organization's resource access requirements under consideration when you determine which strategy to use.

Resource Access Methods

Because each user requires a user account to log on to a domain, you can use these accounts to grant access to network resources. That means permission to a resource must be granted to each user account that requires access. This method might be ideal for small organizations with few user accounts and network resources. But in larger environments, it can be very difficult to track what resources a particular user has been granted access to. For individual resources, you might need to assign permissions to specific user accounts.

Another option, which is more ideal in terms of administration as well as scalability, is to place users into global groups and grant permissions to the groups as opposed to individual user accounts. However, keep in mind that if different groups require different access to a resource, each group must be added to the access control list (ACL) for the resource and granted permission.

Finally, you can also grant access to network resources using resource groups. With this method, user accounts are still placed in global groups, but groups are also created for network resources. For example, if you have a printer on the network, you could create a resource group called PrtSrv. Permissions would then be assigned to the resource groups. To grant users access to a network resource, the appropriate global groups would be added to the resource group. This difference between this method and the method outlined earlier is that permission to a resource needs to be set only once on the resource group.

Defining User Roles

Part of the Active Directory design process entails defining user roles for access control. Roles should be based on the organization structure of a company. Roles will most often be based on job categories (such as sales) or on responsibility. For example, you might choose to create a role called Help Desk. In any case, a thorough assessment of the current structure and goals of a company must be performed to ensure that the roles defined meet all the necessary requirements.

Designing a User and Computer Authentication Strategy

Authentication is the process of verifying one's identity. Designing an authentication strategy prevents unauthorized users and computers from gaining access to a private network, accessing sensitive information, consuming network resources, and impersonating other users.

Designing a computer and user authentication strategy entails creating user accounts, establishing secure authentication methods, and establishing network authentication standards.

Identifying Common Authentication Requirements

Before you can implement an authentication strategy, you must first identify the authentication requirements for an organization. Consider the following points when assessing the current environment:

➤ *The number of domain controllers and where they are located*—Ensure that the current environment has enough domain controllers to service all the authentication requests. Also consider where the domain controllers are located and network connectivity. Slow network connections could result in the need for additional domain controllers.

➤ *The number of users and computers on the network*—This will affect the amount of authentication requests and the number of domain controllers required.

➤ *The operating systems and applications affect the authentication methods used*—Some operating systems and applications do not support Kerberos and therefore another methods of authentication will be required.

➤ *If a public key infrastructure is being used, determine the number of CAs*—Ensure that sufficient CAs are available to handle the amount of client requests.

Selecting Authentication Methods

Before a user can gain access to resources within a domain, he must first be authenticated by Active Directory. After he has been authenticated, a user can access resources on the network for which he has been granted permissions. In terms of authentication, Windows Server 2003 provides support for a number of different authentication methods, including

➤ Kerberos

➤ Public Key Infrastructure (PKI)

➤ Smart Cards

The operating systems and application running on a network influence the authentication methods used. For example, pre–Windows 2000 and non-Windows operating systems might not support the Kerberos authentication protocol and therefore another mechanism must be deployed as well.

Kerberos

Kerberos version 5 protocol is responsible for authentication within and between domains. That means users need provide only a single username and password at logon to gain access to resources throughout the forest.

Before a user is granted access to resources in another domain, the key distribution center (KDC) from each domain in the trust path must first authenticate the user.

 The KDC has two roles: authenticating users and issuing session tickets to users so that they can identify themselves to other domains.

1. When a user attempts to access a resource in another domain, the KDC within the user's own domain issues the user a session ticket. The session ticket simply identifies the user to other servers in the forest.

2. Following the trust path, the user presents his session ticket to the KDC in the parent or child domain.

3. The user is then issued another session ticket from the KDC in this domain that identifies the user to the next domain in the trust path.

4. The user presents the session ticket to the KDC in the next domain in the trust path and is issued a session ticket for the server that contains the resource.

5. When the user presents his or her session ticket to the server with the desired resource, he is granted the appropriate access to that resource.

PKI Infrastructure

A public key certificate is the most secure authentication method and is ideal for nontrusted environments, remote access, access involving the Internet, and those computers that do not support Kerberos V5. This method requires a public key infrastructure (PKI) because each computer requires two keys: a public key and a private key.

Smart Cards

Windows Server 2003 supports smart cards for authentication. With this type of authentication, a user's credentials are stored on a card that is inserted into a smart card reader. To access the information stored on the card, the user must provide the correct PIN number. After the user has provided the correct PIN number, she can be the certificate stored on the smart card and authenticate to Active Directory. This method of authentication is more secure than Kerberos because a smart card and certificates are required to log on to the network.

LAN Manager Authentication

To remain backward compatible with earlier Windows operating systems, Windows Server 2003 supports LAN Manager authentication. However, due to the fact that LAN Manager is highly susceptible to attack, it should be enabled only if necessary.

Optimizing Authentication Using Shortcut Trust Relationships

When a user attempts to access a resource in another domain within the forest, the trust path must be followed. Depending on the structure of the Active Directory hierarchy, the trust path between two separate domains can be long.

In such cases, creating a shortcut trust can shorten the trust path. A *shortcut trust* is basically a transitive trust (a two-way trust); the difference is that it must be explicitly defined or created. Creating a shortcut trust between two separate domains within a forest can improve the authentication process.

Designing a User and Computer Account Strategy

User and computer accounts represent physical entities within a network infrastructure. Some user accounts also represent specific services that are running on computers. In any case, user and computer accounts play an important role and serve the following purposes:

➤ Accounts are used to authenticate entities on a network. Users log on to a domain with a user name and password that verifies their identity.

➤ Accounts are used to grant and deny access to network resources. After an individual has been authenticated, access to network resources can be explicitly granted or denied by granting permissions to an account for a resource.

➤ Accounts are used to audit actions performed on a network.

When designing a user and computer account strategy, one of the first things that must be determined is who will be responsible for creating and managing user and computer accounts.

At least one trusted individual should be granted the right to create user and computer accounts. You can do this be granting the User Account Creation right to a user. Because creating user and computer accounts poses a security threat, make sure that only trusted individuals are granted this right. Because unused user accounts also pose a security threat, a plan needs to be established that outlines how and when user accounts can be disabled. For example, a policy can be put in place to state that when an employee leaves the organization, that employee's user account is deleted.

Specifying Account Policy Requirements

Account policies contain various settings that control how users can interact on a local computer or on a network. Account policies consist of the following three components (see Figure 4.5):

➤ *Password policy*—The password policy determines such things as how often users are required to change their password and the password history.

➤ *Account Lockout policy*—The account lockout policy defines how the system monitors failed log on attempts and the action to take when a certain number of failed log on requests is reached.

➤ *Kerberos policy*—The Kerberos policy configures settings such as the maximum lifetime for user and service tickets.

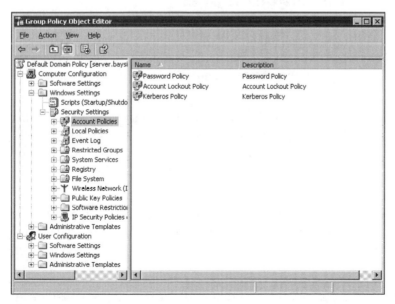

Figure 4.5 Components of an account policy.

Account policies can be applied locally or through a GPO. Within a domain, only one account policy can exist and it must be configured at the domain level (using the default domain policy). Therefore, careful planning as to the account policy settings is required because they affect all computers and user accounts within a domain.

 Because account policies are configured at the domain level, this could affect the Active Directory design. If a business requires separate account policies, multiple domains might be required.

Designing an Active Directory Naming Strategy

Becaus Active Directory relies on DNS, a DNS infrastructure is required. When designing an Active Directory naming strategy, you must consider the existing DNS infrastructure, the company's Internet presence, the external and internal namespaces, and any NetBIOS naming requirements.

Identifying Internet Domain Name Registration Requirements

To avoid conflicts with other organizations on the Internet, the root domain for an Active Directory tree should be registered with an Internet authority when planning the DNS names. This holds true if you're planning to publish the domain name on the Internet. If not, the internal root domain name can be anything you want.

This includes the forest root domain as well as other root domains that might exist. You'll be able to determine which domain names need to be registered after you've designed the DNS infrastructure. Chapter 5, "Creating the Logical Design for a Network Services Infrastructure," looks at the different DNS strategies that can be implemented.

In some instances, you might not be required to register any domain names; for example, if a company already has an existing Internet presence that it wants to maintain.

 The Active Directory root domain names must be unique within a DNS hierarchy. So, if you're planning to have an Internet presence and interact with other Internet domains, the root domain must be registered. If the Active Directory namespace is internal only, this is not necessary.

Specifying the Use of Hierarchical Namespace Within Active Directory

The first domain created within Active Directory becomes the forest root domain. This is the domain that represents the entire business. It is important to plan which domain becomes the forest root domain; after it has been established, it can be difficult to rename because doing so might affect existing child domains.

Careful planning is required when choosing a name for the forest root domain. Choosing an appropriate name for the forest root domain is important because all other domains created under the forest root (child domains) derive a portion of their namespace from it.

When deciding what to name the first domain in Active Directory, keep the following points in mind:

➤ Choose a name that won't change in the near future—a name that is static. Changing the name of the forest root domain might not be easy, so choose a name that won't change in the next 3 to 5 years.

➤ Choose a name that is meaningful to the business, its employees, and its clients. When naming the forest root, consider using the name of the business.

➤ If the internal and external namespace will be the same, make sure that the name is available for use on the Internet.

When creating the forest root domain, the design team might determine that the business's name would be an appropriate choice (as long as the business has no intention of changing the company name in the near future). The business's name provides a general representation of the business and an appropriate namespace for child domains within the forest. The company name is meaningful to employees and clients and makes the domain easily identifiable.

 Be prepared to encounter exam questions that require you to select an Active Directory namespace based on a given scenario.

Identifying NetBIOS Naming Requirements

In a pure Windows 2000 or Windows Server 2003 environment, NetBIOS is not required. However, you might still need to support it for backward compatibility with pre–Windows 2000 operating systems.

Operating systems earlier than Windows 2000 use NetBIOS names to identify computers on the network and the network services those computers are running. Computers running Windows 2000 and Windows Server 2003 can be identified by a NetBIOS name to remain backward compatible with legacy clients, by the full computer name, or by a fully qualified domain name. The NetBIOS name for a Windows 2000 or Windows Server 2003 computer is the first 15 characters of the full computer name.

Windows NT 4.0 also uses NetBIOS names as domain names. If you're upgrading a domain from Windows NT 4.0 to Windows Server 2003, you must also then consider the NetBIOS name and the DNS prefix to be used. You must decide whether the current NetBIOS name is suitable for the DNS prefix. If the current name is suitable, meaning that it appropriately represents the company and meets all naming requirements, it can be retained as the DNS prefix as well. If not, the NetBIOS name can be different from that of the DNS prefix.

When deploying new domains, it is recommended that the NetBIOS name for the domain be the same as the DNS prefix.

Designing Migration Paths to Active Directory

When an Active Directory design is in place, you can begin planning the migration. Various migration strategies can be used, depending on the existing network infrastructure. During this phase of Active Directory design, you need to assess the current infrastructure and determine the best way to migrate to Active Directory (more specifically, the best way to migrate to the Active Directory infrastructure that has been designed). Three different migration paths are available:

➤ In-place upgrade

➤ Domain restructuring

➤ New Active Directory environment

In-place Upgrade

With an in-place upgrade, the existing domain infrastructure is maintained. One of the advantages of choosing this migration path is that a business can maintain its current administrative and IT structures. Also, because there is little change, the effect on users is minimized.

Planning for an in-place upgrade includes the following:

➤ Documenting the existing network infrastructure.

➤ Determining the order in which domains will be upgraded. User accounts domains should be upgraded first.

➤ Determining the upgrade paths for the various operating systems. Table 4.1 and Table 4.2 outline the various operating systems that can be upgraded to Windows Server 2003.

Table 4.1 Windows NT 4.0–Supported Upgrade Paths			
Operating System	**Windows Server 2003 Standard Edition**	**Windows Server 2003 Enterprise Edition**	**Windows Server 2003 Datacenter Edition**
Windows NT Server 4.0	Yes	Yes	No
Windows NT Server 4.0 Enterprise Edition	No	Yes	No
Windows NT Server 4.0 Terminal Server	Yes	Yes	No

All versions of Windows NT Server 4.0 must be running Service Pack 5 or later before they can be upgraded to Windows Server 2003.

Table 4.2 Windows 2000–Supported Upgrade Paths			
Operating System	**Windows Server 2003 Standard Edition**	**Windows Server 2003 Enterprise Edition**	**Windows Server 2003 Datacenter Edition**
Windows 2000 Professional	No	No	No
Windows 2000 Server	Yes	Yes	No
Windows 2000 Advanced Server	No	Yes	No
Windows 2000 Datacenter Server	No	No	Yes

Domain Restructuring

The difference between an in-place upgrade and domain restructuring is that an in-place upgrade maintains the existing domain infrastructure. In domain restructuring, the existing domain infrastructure is altered to meet the business requirements. For example, existing resource domains might be consolidated into organizational units. One of the benefits of choosing to restructure the existing domain infrastructure is that it provides an opportunity to fix any problems that exist with the current model.

Domain restructuring usually involves migrating user accounts from a Windows NT 4.0 or a Windows 2000 domain to a Windows Server 2003 domain. You can use the Active Directory Migration Tool (ADMT) to migrate objects between domains.

New Active Directory Environment

The third option for migration is to create a new Active Directory environment. You'll need to determine the costs and effects associated with domain restructuring or an in-place upgrade when deciding whether to create a new Active Directory environment. You'll also need to compare the existing domain structure with the new proposed Active Directory infrastructure. Plan to create new Active Directory domains for those domains that cannot be upgraded or restructured.

Designing an Active Directory Services Site Topology

An *Active Directory site* is basically a collection of well-connected IP subnets. The links between the subnets within a site are generally fast, reliable, and capable of supporting replication.

Because the creation of sites is based on the physical topology, a site can contain IP subnets from multiple domains.

Creating sites enables you to control and optimize the following events:

➤ *User authentication*—When a user logs on to the network, a domain controller within the same site is contacted to authenticate the user. This means the logon process is more efficient because the user does not have to log on over a slow, unreliable link.

➤ *Controlled replication*—Creating multiple sites allows replication across slow, unreliable links to be controlled by specifying a schedule, frequency, and cost.

➤ *Site-aware applications*—An application that is site-aware, such as the Distributed File System (DFS), can take advantage of the site topology by attempting to connect to a domain controller within the same site before attempting to connect to a domain controller in another site.

Active Directory sites are created to optimize replication. Replication within a site occurs differently than it does between two separate sites. *Intrasite replication* is designed to take advantage of the fact that the IP subnets within a site are connected by fast, reliable links. Replication between sites (*intersite replication*) is designed to occur differently because it is assumed that the links connecting two sites are slow, unreliable, and possibly already heavily utilized. Table 4.3 summarizes the differences between intrasite and intersite replication.

Table 4.3 Intrasite Versus Intersite Replication	
Intrasite Replication	**Intersite Replication**
Information replicated within a site is uncompressed.	Information replicated between sites is compressed to optimize bandwidth.
Domain controllers within a site notify each other when a change occurs, which reduces the time for changes to appear throughout a site.	To optimize bandwidth, there is no notification process between sites, which means that information on domain controllers might not always be up to date.
Domain controllers within a site poll each other for changes on a regular basis.	Domain controllers between sites poll each other at a preconfigured interval during scheduled times.
Replication occurs between multiple domain controllers.	Replication between sites occurs between specific domain controllers only.

Designing Sites

Creating sites gives an administrator the ability to control workstation logons and replication throughout a network infrastructure. When planning and defining the site boundaries, your main focus will be on the physical topology of the network. At this point, it would be a good idea to refer to the diagram you created when performing an assessment of WAN links and available bandwidth. When planning site boundaries, use the following guidelines:

➤ Create a site for each group of IP subnets connected by fast, available, and reliable links.

➤ For a network compromised of a single LAN, a single site is usually sufficient.

➤ Create a separate site for those IP subnets connected by slow, unreliable, and heavily utilized links.

➤ For sites that don't have a domain controller located within them, consider merging them with another nearby site.

These are just some basic guidelines to follow when determining how many sites to create.

Identifying Site Links

Site links are similar in concept to trust relationships. A *trust* is the link between two domains; a *site link* is the connection between two Active Directory sites. The site link that is established between two sites is used to control replication across the physical link.

Site links are transitive by default. That means if a site is defined between sites A and B, and another is defined between sites B and C, it is automatically assumed that sites A and C can communicate. These transitive site links basically establish a replication path so that information can be replicated throughout the organization. When you're defining a site link, certain options are used to control replication over the link (see Figure 4.6).

This can be used to allow remote sites with poor connectivity access through a nearby site with better connectivity; on the other hand it could cause replication overload on the intermediate site.

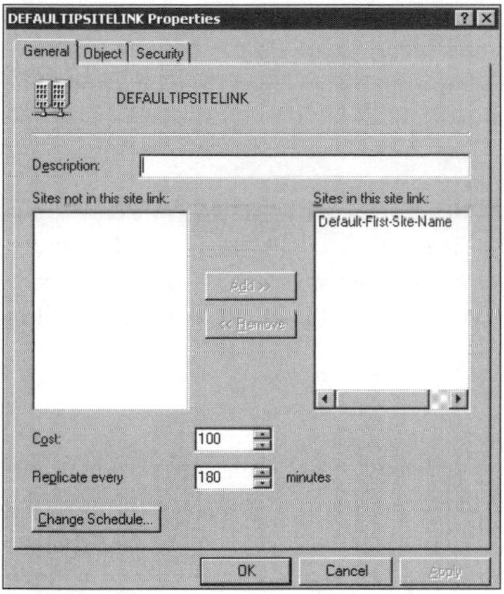

Figure 4.6   Properties of a site link.

A site link is defined by the following characteristics, each of which is discussed in detail later in this chapter:

➤ *Schedule*—The schedule defined for a site link specifies the times when replication can occur over the link.

➤ *Interval*—The frequency that intersite replication occurs across a link. The default is every 180 minutes (every 3 hours).

➤ *Link cost*—The value assigned to the site link. If there are multiple site links, the one with the lowest cost is tried first.

➤ *Replication protocol*—The protocol used to transfer data between two sites. You can use one of two methods: RPC over IP or SMTP.

Schedule

Another option an administrator has in controlling replication between sites is scheduling when site links are available. Intersite replication does not use the process of notification. If changes occur within one site, the other sites are not notified. Instead, a domain controller in one site periodically checks for changes by contacting a domain controller in another site.

To optimize this process, an administrator can schedule certain times when the site link can be used for intersite replication. Doing so ensures that replication does not occur when the link is already heavily utilized.

One of the drawbacks of placing a schedule on a site link is that it can increase replication latency. *Replication latency* is the time it takes for changes made on one domain controller to appear on another domain controller. Placing a schedule on a link obviously implies that information between sites might not always be up to date.

However, if a link used for RPC replication is saturated when a replication cycle begins, the replication might fail with an RPC timeout. Therefore, although latency can be a problem in a multiple-master environment such as Active Directory, setting site link schedules could actually improve replication performance.

Interval

As already mentioned, the interval indicates how often replication occurs during the times when replication is allowed to occur. The default interval is 180 minutes. Lowering this value reduces latency and keeps the domain directory partitions up-to-date, but doing so increases the amount of replication traffic.

Link Cost

One of the advantages of using site links is that they can be assigned a site cost. A *site cost* is basically a number that is assigned by an administrator to a site link. By assigning a cost to a site link, an administrator can basically define a preferred route for replication when multiple routes exist (similar to the metrics used in routing tables).

When assigning a cost to a site link, keep in mind that a site link with a lower value is preferred to a site link with a higher value. However, the route used is ultimately up to the route path defined in the routing tables.

Replication Protocol

When planning for sites and site links, you also need to decide on the protocol to use to replicate information. You can use RPC over IP or SMTP.

The default transport that can be used for intersite replication is RPC over TCP/IP. This transport can be used for intersite as well as intrasite replication. RPC uses synchronous transfer, meaning there must be a direct connection with the destination server before any information will be replicated. This poses a problem for WAN links that are unreliable because if a connection cannot be established, replication does not occur. Also, if the WAN link is slow or congested, RPC timeouts can occur, causing replication to fail. RPC is inadvisable for link speeds under 128Kbps. RPC timeouts and replication failures can also occur when using VPN connections, even at 128Kbps or higher. The reason for the timeouts is the unpredictable latency of VPN circuits, which depend on the Internet to transmit data from one location to another.

One of the main advantages of using RPC over IP is that it can support inter-site replication traffic between all servers, including domain controllers from the same domain. RPC is also more efficient as an intersite transport.

SMTP basically sends information to be replicated between sites as email messages. Unlike RPC, it provides asynchronous data transfer, meaning that a direct connection with the remote server is not required. It also uses the store-and-forward method of sending information, meaning that if the destination host is not available, the message can be stored. This transport is an ideal choice if the link between two sites is unreliable. For example, when the link is not available, the message can be stored and sent when the destination server is available. However, note that the schedules set on a site link by an administrator are ignored when the SMTP protocol is used.

Using SMTP as an intersite transport has some limitations because it can be used to replicate only the configuration, schema, and application directory partitions. It cannot be used to replicate the domain directory partition, and therefore cannot be used to replicate information between domain controllers in the same domain. In such cases, RPC must be used. The primary reason is that Sysvol replication, which is required to replicate part of a group policy object, must use RPC. Even if no GPOs are configured, Windows Server 2003 will not replicate the domain naming context via SMTP.

Exam Prep Questions

Question 1

John is designing a group policy strategy. One of the GPOs that will be created and linked to the Employees OU will be used to distribute a company application. Members of the In-Training group should not receive the application until they have completed the company training program. How can this be achieved?

○ A. Configure another OU within the Employees OU for the In-Training group

○ B. Deny the In-Training group permission to the GPO

○ C. Enable the Block Inheritance option for the GPO at the Employees OU

○ D. Enable the No Override option for the GPO

Answer B is correct. By filtering using security groups and denying the In-Training group permission to the GPO, you can control which groups are affected by the policy settings. Answer A is incorrect because the policy settings would be inherited from parent container to child. Answer C is incorrect because enabling this option means that the settings configured within the OU cannot be overwritten by policies applied to parent containers. Answer D is incorrect because the No Override option ensures that the security settings configured within a GPO are not overwritten by a policy applied at a lower level in the Active Directory hierarchy.

Question 2

Group policies can be applied to different levels of the Active Directory hierarchy. Place the following in the correct order in which group policies are applied:

Domain

Organizational Unit

Site

Local

Forest

The correct answer is

Local

Site

Domain

Organization Unit

Group policies cannot be applied at the forest level.

Question 3

FKP Consulting consists of a forest root domain (fkp.com) and three child domains. Executives from each domain require access to financial data throughout the forest. How should access be granted? (Select two answers.)

❑ A. Assign permissions to the appropriate resources throughout the forest to each executive account.

❑ B. Create a global group called Executives within each domain and add the appropriate user accounts. Create a universal group and add the Executives global groups to this universal group.

❑ C. Create the necessary domain local groups and add the universal group.

❑ D. Create a single global group. Add the executive user accounts from each domain to the global group.

Answers B and C are correct. By creating a single universal group, permissions to resources has to be granted only once. This makes it easier to assign users from different domains access to network resources. Answer A is incorrect because this approach would drastically increase the administrative overhead. Answer D is incorrect because a global group can contain user accounts only from the domain in which it was created.

Question 4

John is designing an Active Directory infrastructure for FKP Consulting. The company needs to have two separate password policies. a more stringent policy for the Financial department and another policy for all other users. How can this be accomplished?

○ A. Create a separate domain for the Financial department

○ B. Create two separate password policies at the domain level

○ C. Configure an OU for the Financial department, and apply the password policy at the OU level

○ D. Configure a password policy at the domain level, and deny users in the Financial department permission to the GPO.

Answer A is correct. Only one password policy can exist for an entire domain, so another domain must be configured for the Financial department. Answer B is incorrect because only one password policy can exist per domain. Answer C is incorrect because password policies are configured at the domain level. Answer D is incorrect because users in the Financial department would be exempt from the domainwide password policy.

Question 5

Mike has finished planning the OU hierarchy. There is a top-level OU and three child OUs for three different departments. Group policies will be used for software distribution. However, the OU hierarchy is not granular enough to control which users have which applications. What feature can he use to solve this problem?

- ○ A. Inheritance blocking
- ○ B. No Override
- ○ C. Delegation
- ○ D. Filtering

Answer D is correct. Filtering with security groups enables you to control which groups of users are affected by a group policy object. Answers A and B are incorrect because these features are used to change the default behavior of group policy inheritance between parent and child containers. Answer C is incorrect because delegation is used to assign a user or group administrative rights over a container.

Question 6

Don is planning the replication topology for FKP Consulting. Two sites are connected to the corporate headquarters using 56kbps links that are already heavily saturated. Which of the following is the best way to manage replication?

- ○ A. Create site links using RPC over IP, and allow replication to occur any time
- ○ B. Create site links using SMTP, and configure the replication schedule so that replication can occur only during off-hours
- ○ C. Create a site link using RPC over IP, and configure the replication schedule so that replication can occur only during off-hours
- ○ D. Create site links using SMTP

Answer D is correct. Because RPC replication is unreliable over 56kbps links, SMTP should be used. SMTP ignores replication schedules; therefore, answers A, B, and C are incorrect.

Question 7

Which of the following groups can cross domain boundaries? (Select two answers.)

❑ A. Local groups

❑ B. Domain local groups

❑ C. Global groups

❑ D. Universal groups

Answers C and D are correct. Global groups and universal groups can cross domain boundaries. Answer A is incorrect because local groups are used only to assign rights and permissions on a local computer. Answer B is incorrect because domain local groups can be used to assign permissions only to resources in the domain which the group was created.

Question 8

Which of the following operating systems can be upgraded to Windows Server 2003 Standard Edition? (Choose all correct answers.)

❑ A. Windows 2000 Professional

❑ B. Windows NT Server 4.0

❑ C. Windows 2000 Server

❑ D. Windows 2000 Advanced Server

Answers B and C are correct. Windows NT Server 4.0 and Windows 2000 Server can be upgraded to Windows Server 2003 Standard Edition; therefore, answers A and D are incorrect. Windows 2000 Professional and Windows 2000 Advanced Server cannot be upgraded to Windows Server 2003 Standard Edition.

Question 9

Dan is planning for delegation of authority. A help desk employee will be given the right to change passwords for user accounts. There are two top-level OUs, Employees and Managers; and two child OUs created under Employees, Sales and Manufacturing. The help desk employee is granted the right to change passwords in the Employees OU. By default, in which OUs can he change passwords?

- ○ A. Employees
- ○ B. Employees and Managers
- ○ C. Employees, Sales, and Manufacturing
- ○ D. Employees, Managers, Sales, and Manufacturing
- ○ E. Managers

Answer C is correct. Rights and permissions are inherited from parent container to child container. Permissions and rights assigned to the Employees OU are also applicable to the child OUs, which in this case are Sales and Manufacturing. Therefore, answers A, B, D, and E are incorrect.

Question 10

Dan is planning the migration strategy for his company. One of the backup domain controllers is running Windows NT Server 3.51. How should this domain controller be upgraded?

- ○ A. Upgrade to Windows NT Server 4.0 first, install the latest Service Pack, and then upgrade to Windows Server 2003
- ○ B. Install the latest Service Pack and upgrade to Windows Server 2003
- ○ C. Upgrade directly to Windows Server 2003
- ○ D. Format the hard drive and perform a clean installation of Windows Server 2003

Answer A is correct. Because there is no direct upgrade path from Windows NT Server 3.51 to Windows Server 2003, you must first upgrade the operating system to one that supports an upgrade path. After you've upgraded to Windows NT Server 4.0, Service Pack 5 or later is required to continue the upgrade to Windows Server 2003. Therefore, answers B, C, and D are incorrect.

Need to Know More?

 Try searching the TechNet CD or use Microsoft's online version at www.microsoft.com and search for keywords such as *Active Directory*, *Group Policy*, *migration*, *organizational units*, and *sites*.

 The Microsoft Windows Server 2003 Deployment Kit, Microsoft Press, 2000. Contains in-depth information about deploying Windows Server 2003.

 Microsoft Corporation. *Microsoft Windows Server 2003 Resource Kit*. Microsoft Press, 2003.

5

Creating the Logical Design for a Network Services Infrastructure

Terms you'll need to understand:

✓ DNS name resolution
✓ Zones
✓ NetBIOS name resolution
✓ WINS
✓ RAS
✓ Remote access policies
✓ Dynamic DNS
✓ DHCP

Techniques you'll need to master:

✓ Designing a DNS name resolution strategy
✓ Designing a DNS services implementation
✓ Designing a NetBIOS name resolution strategy
✓ Designing security for remote access servers
✓ Designing a remote access strategy
✓ Designing an IP address assignment strategy

Clients on a network have to be able to find each other in order to share information and hardware resources. This requires the correct logical and physical infrastructure. In this chapter, we focus on the logical infrastructure of a Windows Server 2003 network. This includes its IP addressing systems, name resolution services, remote access services, and security features. A sound logical structure is an essential element of all networks.

Designing a DNS Name Resolution Strategy

Windows Server 2003 requires a sound DNS infrastructure in order to operate at all. This was not true of Windows NT, which could function without DNS by using NetBIOS. Windows Server 2003 and Windows 2000 replace NetBIOS name resolution with DNS name resolution and SRV records. SRV records are service records that are stored in the DNS database and indicate which service each server brings to the network. Without SRV records, the network would not know its own members and each one's function in the network. Because these SRV records are proprietary to each network, they should never be exposed to the Internet. This requires a firewall and a functional and secure DNS namespace design.

The DNS namespace typically comes from the name of the organization, but administrators have three basic choices in regard to namespace design:

➤ Use the same name on the outside of the firewall as on the inside

➤ Delegate a subdomain for the inside of the firewall

➤ Use a completely different name on the inside and the outside of the firewall

Each of these choices has its advantages and disadvantages. For example, let's consider a company named widgetsinc.com. We'll examine each of its options and highlight the advantages and disadvantages of each choice.

First, if the administrators choose to use widgetsinc.com on the inside and the outside of the firewall, there would be no confusion about the name and no training would be necessary. On the other hand, the administrators would need to make sure that they kept only the public records on the DNS servers that are on the outside of the firewall, and *never* let the servers replicate the SRV records from the inside to the outside.

As an alternative, the administrators could use a delegated subdomain on the inside of the firewall. In that case, they might use ad.widgetsinc.com. This would in effect separate the records so that the inside of the firewall and the outside were two different, yet connected, databases. This would require less concern for security, but might require a little training to explain to users the small difference in the names if they are accessing the network from inside the firewall as opposed to from the outside.

The third option would be to use a completely different name. In this case, the administrators might use gadgets.com on the inside and widgets.com on the outside. This would be the most secure because none of the records associated with gadgets.com would ever be exposed to the Internet. It would also require the most training and explanation to make sure that the users can access the information that they need from inside the network as well as from outside. Table 5.1 illustrates each choice and its advantages and disadvantages.

Table 5.1 Namespace Design Choices		
Design Choice	**Advantages**	**Disadvantages**
Same name	No training necessary	Low security
		Needs constant firewall
Delegated subdomain	Higher security	Some training for users
	Familiar name for users	Not most secure method
Completely different name	Highest security	Most training required
		Confusing to users
		Potentially more DNS servers required

DNS is extremely important to a network, but it is only one of the services in the network. There are many other services with which DNS must interoperate. These include Active Directory, WINS (Windows Internet Name Service), and DHCP (Dynamic Host Configuration Protocol). All Windows 2003 and Windows 2000 DNS servers can interoperate with Active Directory, but not all DNS servers can. Some BIND servers do not support Active Directory. This must be addressed as part of an overall DNS strategy.

 A DNS server must be able to use SRV records to interoperate with Active Directory. This leaves out any version of BIND (Berkeley Internet Name Domain) server earlier than 4.9.7. In addition, BIND servers should be at least version 8.2.1 to take advantage of incremental zone transfers and dynamic updates.

DNS will continue to work with WINS as well. WINS is still necessary as long as the network has any legacy clients and/or applications—these will still register with and use WINS. DNS can be configured to use WINS lookup when a hostname is not found in the DNS database. The underlying premise is that the hostname computer1.widgets.com should have the same IP address as the computer with the NetBIOS name computer1. You can configure DNS for WINS lookup as shown in Figure 5.1.

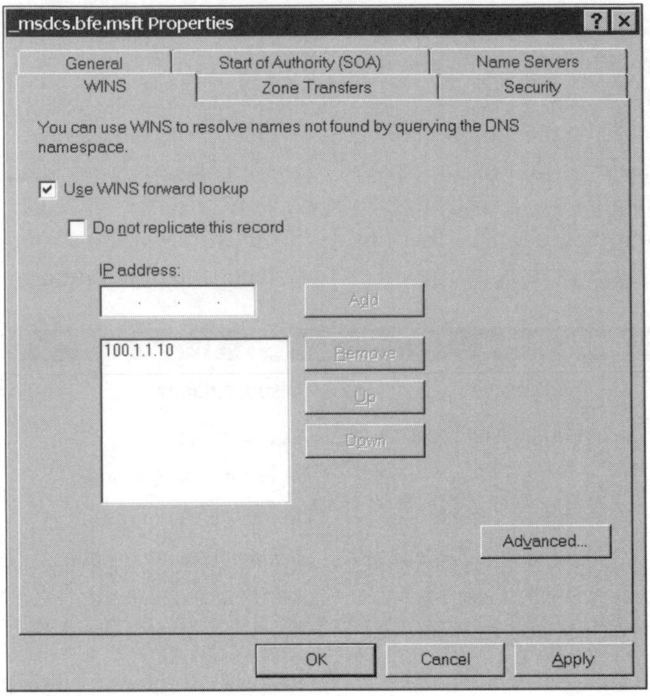

Figure 5.1 You can configure DNS for WINS lookup.

DHCP will also interoperate with DNS. When a client comes on to a network and receives an IP address from the DHCP server, that client and the DHCP server both know the address that was just given out. Therefore, either one can give this information to the DNS server.

Not all clients can register their own addresses; only clients that are Windows 2000 Professional and later can. You can set the DHCP server to register addresses for the clients that cannot register their own or for all clients. This design choice will depend on the types of clients in your network. Figure 5.2 shows the configuration settings in DHCP server for dynamic DNS. You must also enable dynamic DNS in the properties of the zone, as illustrated in Figure 5.3.

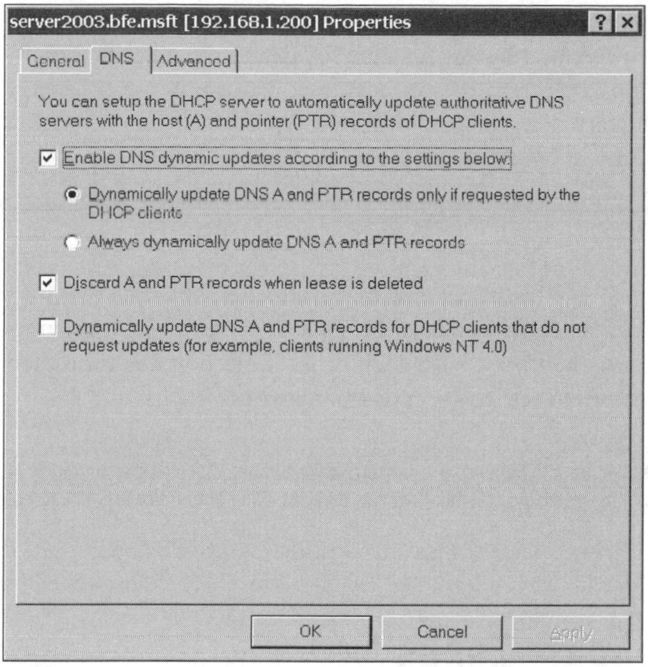

Figure 5.2   You can configure the DHCP server for dynamic DNS.

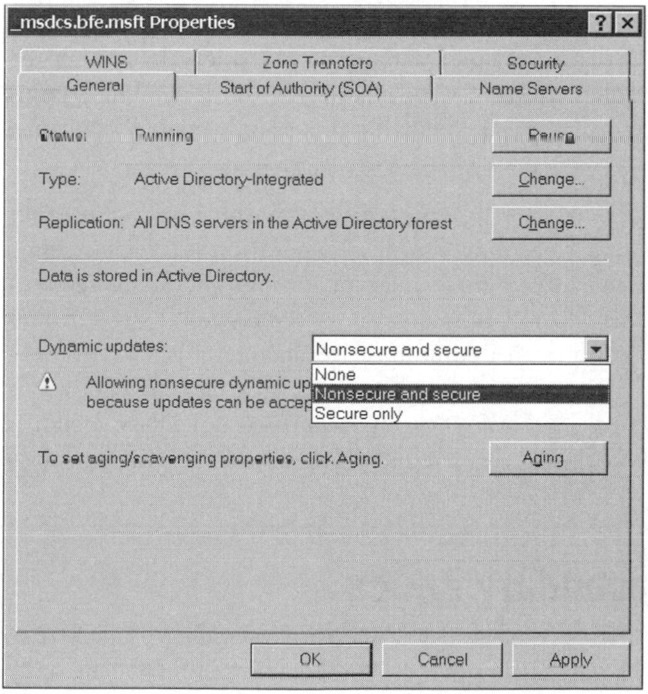

Figure 5.3   You can configure DNS zones for dynamic DNS.

DNS databases are organized in zones. A *zone* is a discrete, contiguous portion of a DNS namespace. In other words, it is set apart from all other zones, but it is a continuous hierarchy of an intranet or Internet namespace. Windows Server 2003 provides for four different types of zones:

➤ Standard primary

➤ Active Directory integrated

➤ Standard secondary

➤ Stub

Each type of zone has its advantages and disadvantages. For effective network design, it's important to understand how all of these types work individually as well has how they work with each other. Let's now examine each of these types of zones and their relation to the network.

 Adding the words *database file* to the word *zone* sometimes helps tremendously in the overall understanding of zones. We use this technique during our examination of zones.

Standard Primary Zones

A standard primary zone database file is the original database of a zone. It can be read from and written to as well. The word *standard* indicates that it is not an Active Directory–integrated zone. The zone database file contains a Start of Authority (SOA) record that sets the interval at which the standard secondary zones contacts it for changes in the zone. The administrator can make these changes manually or they can be made by dynamic DNS.

Servers that host standard primary zones can be master servers for other servers that host standard secondary zones. In addition, server hosting a standard primary zone can be a master server for many standard secondary zones. Servers that do not host a primary zone cannot be a master server. Standard primary zones communicate changes to standard secondary zones through zone transfer. Zone transfer can be bandwidth intensive, especially on slow links. An important part of DNS design is understanding and working within bandwidth limitations in regard to zones.

Standard Secondary Zones

A standard secondary zone database file is a copy of a standard primary zone database file. It can be read from, but it cannot be written to manually or by dynamic DNS. The only way that a standard secondary zone database file receives changes is by zone transfer.

The primary purpose of a standard secondary zone database file is to provide for load balancing in a network with many clients. Some clients can be set to the IP address of the server with the standard primary zone database file, and others can be set to the IP address of the server with the standard secondary zone database file.

A standard secondary zone database file provides some short-term fault tolerance for name resolution, but it cannot be considered a long-term option for fault tolerance. The SOA record on the master server with the standard primary zone controls the period of time that a standard secondary zone can still resolve queries if the master has failed. This is typically set no higher than one day.

Standard secondary zones do not provide fault tolerance and should not be used if fault tolerance is a key concern. Active Directory–integrated zones would likely be used in this situation.

Active Directory–Integrated Zones

An Active Directory–integrated zone database file has many advantages over a standard zone database file, but it cannot be used on all servers. Changes to an Active Directory–integrated zone database file are replicated to all other DNS servers that host the same zone database file by piggy-backing on normal Active Directory replication. To make this possible, all DNS servers that host Active Directory–integrated zones (zone database files) must also be domain controllers. This eliminates zone transfer between Active Directory–integrated zones. An argument can be made that the zone transfer information is contained in the Active Directory replication; however, this is not technically referred to as *zone transfer*.

Active Directory–integrated zones provide long-term fault tolerance. This is because all Active Directory–integrated zones are primary zones. In other words, they can be written to and read from as well. In addition, Active Directory–integrated zones can be secured. You can set Active Directory–integrated zones to accept updates from only specific users and computers. This is referred to as *setting Secure Only* updates. Figure 5.4 illustrates how to configure a zone for Secure Only updates.

Active Directory–integrated zones are preferred when minimizing zone transfer is a key concern. Because the replication between Active Directory–integrated zones occurs with Active Directory replication, there is said to be no zone transfer at all with Active Directory–integrated zones.

_msdcs.bfe.msft Properties	? X

WINS	Zone Transfers	Security
General	Start of Authority (SOA)	Name Servers

Status: Running   [Pause]

Type: Active Directory-Integrated   [Change...]

Replication: All DNS servers in the Active Directory forest   [Change...]

Data is stored in Active Directory.

Dynamic updates: [Secure only ▼]

⚠ Allowing nonsecure dynamic updates is a significant security vulnerability because updates can be accepted from untrusted sources.

To set aging/scavenging properties, click Aging.   [Aging...]

[OK]   [Cancel]   [Apply]

Figure 5.4   You can configure a zone for Secure Only updates.

Stub Zones

A stub zone database file is a special type of zone that is new to Windows Server 2003. It is a read-only copy of a zone database file. The major difference between a stub zone database file and a standard secondary zone database file is that the stub zone's database file contains only the records that are necessary to define the server itself. A stub zone database file keeps the servers that are hosting parent zones aware of the servers that are hosting child zones (delegated sub-domains). It does this without replicating all the records in the zone database file, thereby maintaining both name resolution efficiency and bandwidth efficiency.

Designing a DNS Services Implementation

A DNS design might include a mixture of the four types of zone database files. You should use Active Directory–integrated zones wherever possible; in other words, wherever there are domain controllers. Primary and secondary zones will always have some zone transfer. This should be taken into consideration when designing a DNS infrastructure. Remember that secondary zones are used for load balancing and not for fault tolerance. They should therefore be located near the users who are configured to use them.

If a large company has a small remote office with very few users, it might be advantageous to use a caching-only server. To create a caching-only server, first install DNS on a server without creating any zones, and then configure forwarders for the server. Because the server is not authoritative for a zone, no zone transfer takes place. All queries are resolved from the server's cache or from the forwarders that are configured. A caching-only server thereby saves bandwidth because there is no zone transfer at all. As a caching-only server learns the patterns of its users, it forwards less and less traffic as well.

Designing a NetBIOS Name Resolution Strategy

NetBIOS name resolution will still be necessary in a network as long as there are any clients and/or applications that use it. All Microsoft clients prior to Windows 2000 Professional use NetBIOS name resolution. Many legacy types of applications are written to use NetBIOS name resolution as well. NetBIOS names can be resolved within a single subnet by broadcasting, although this is certainly not the preferred method.

A well-designed network has a NetBIOS name resolution system that eliminates broadcasts within subnets and allows NetBIOS names to be resolved across routers. This could include the use of an LMHosts file that is replicated to all servers and clients.

A more efficient method in a Windows Server 2003 design would be the use of WINS. Clients can be configured to use a WINS server for NetBIOS name resolution. This configuration can be set manually by administrators or automatically by a DHCP server as part of the IP address lease process. Clients can be configured with one primary WINS server and up to 11 secondary WINS servers.

WINS servers in the same network can replicate their databases so that all WINS server databases are the same. This improves the efficiency of the NetBIOS name resolution process in a network. If one WINS server fails, the clients can use a secondary (or many secondaries) to resolve NetBIOS names. WINS servers can be configured to replicate their databases at a particular time, after a certain number of changes, or both. There are basically three settings for WINS replication as illustrated in Figure 5.5.

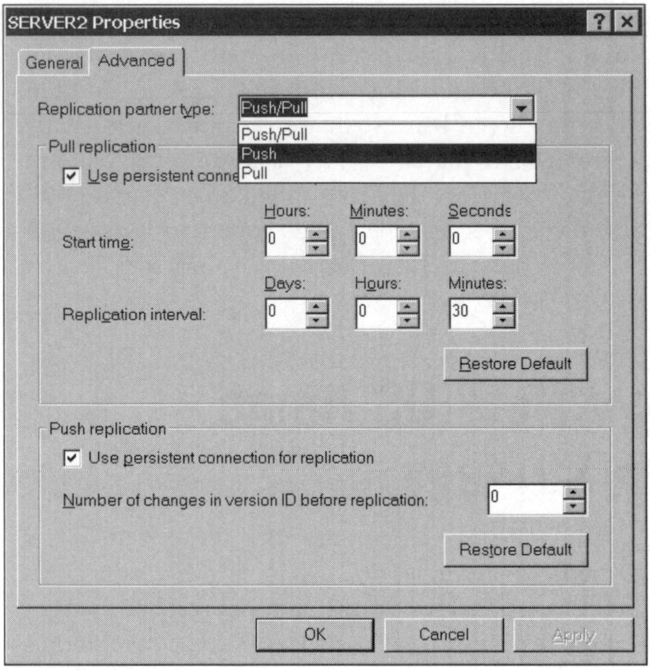

Figure 5.5 You can configure replication for WINS servers.

The WINS replication settings include the following:

➤ Push

➤ Pull

➤ Push/pull

Each option has advantages and disadvantages. It's important for proper network design to understand these differences. We will now examine each method and discuss how each relates to an efficient network design.

Push Replication

Push replication occurs after a specified number of changes on a database. The database changes are *pushed out* to all the specified partners. Push replication is the right choice if one of the key goals is to minimize the use of a link between the servers to conserve bandwidth. Push replication does not guarantee that the databases will replicate within any particular period of time. Push replication should not be used alone when one of the goals is to maintain a high degree of accuracy between WINS servers. Figure 5.6 illustrates WINS configured to push after 50 changes to the database.

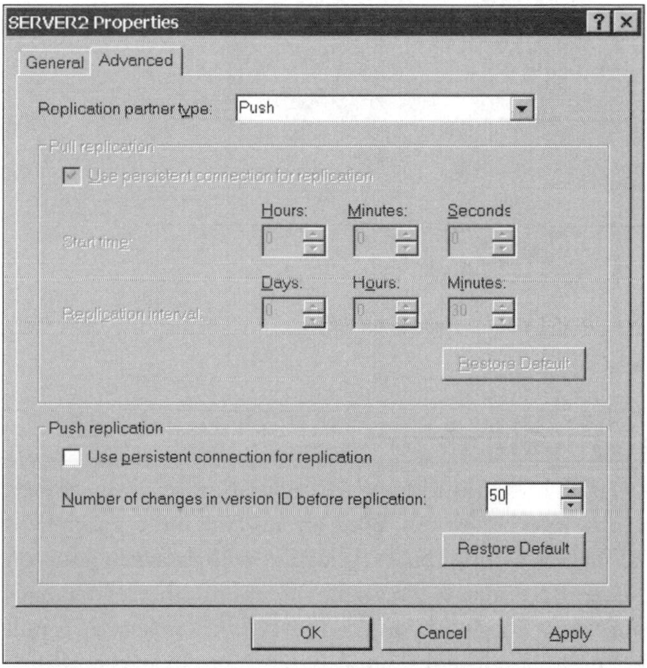

Figure 5.6   You can configure WINS for push replication after 50 changes to the database.

Pull Replication

Pull replication occurs at the specific interval set by the administrator. It should be used to force the WINS servers to replicate at a certain time. Pull replication is often used to conserve bandwidth by setting the servers to replicate at a time when the network is not busy. For example, if you want to make sure that the WINS servers replicate once per night at midnight, you could configure the server for pull replication, as shown in Figure 5.7. In this example, the current time is 6:00 p.m.

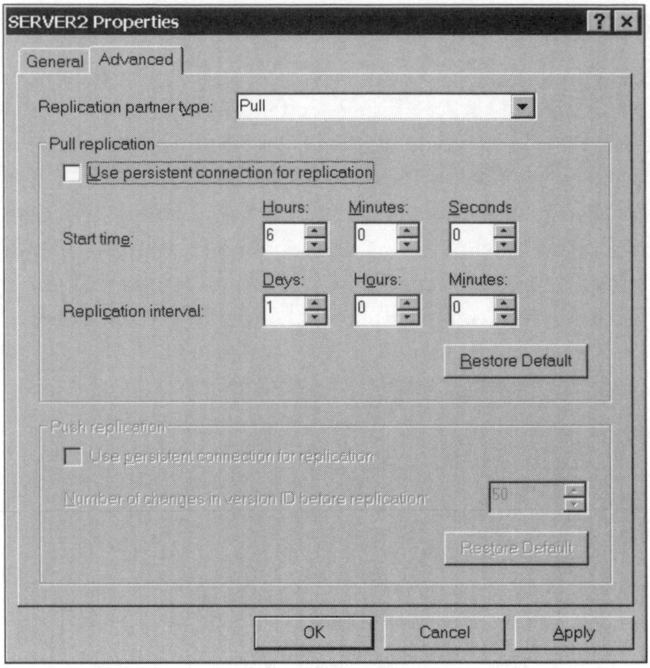

Figure 5.7 You can configure WINS for pull replication at midnight.

Push/Pull Replication

As its name implies, push/pull replication is a combination of push replication and pull replication. In other words, both an interval and a number of changes can be set. With this setting, pull replication will always happen on the interval, but push replication will also occur if the number of changes exceeds the set number. For example, you could configure a server to pull from its partners every night at midnight but also to push to its partners after 50 changes to the database, as illustrated in Figure 5.8.

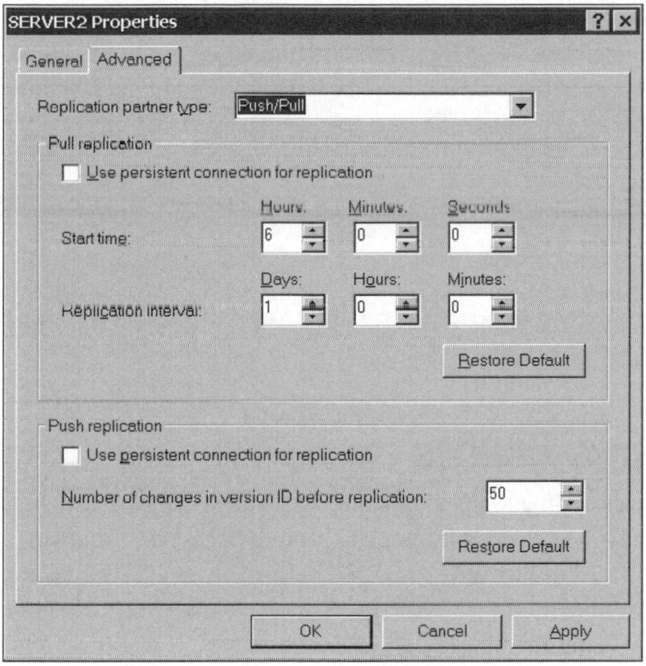

Figure 5.8   You can configure WINS for push/pull replication.

Designing Security for Remote Access Users

Today's networks don't stop at the walls of buildings. Many users work outside the office from home or other locations. Users might need access to resources in their intranet from anywhere in the world. A modern network would not be complete without a way to provide this access.

Providing Remote Access creates new challenges for administrators in regard to the design and maintenance of a network. Challenges include security, connectivity, and availability. An effective Remote Access network design must include a method of access that's transparent to the user but secure for the organization's needs.

Microsoft server operating systems prior to Windows 2000 offered very little security for Remote Access. Windows 2000 increased Remote Access security tremendously over that of Windows NT. Windows Server 2003 has new features that make it the most flexible and secure system for Remote Access to date:

➤ Remote Access policies

➤ Internet authentication services

We now move on to examine these systems in light of the security that they provide to a Remote Access network design.

Remote Access Polices

Remote Access policies are made up of flexible rules and settings that define when, where, and how a user is able to gain remote access to a network. These policies give an administrator granular control over a user's access while keeping the administrator totally transparent to the user. Remote Access policies are actually made up of three components. A well-designed network uses a combination of these three components to determine who can gain remote access to a network, when they can get in, and what authentication and encryption protocols they have to use.

These components are the following:

➤ Conditions

➤ Permissions

➤ Profile

Each of these components plays a key role in Remote Access policies. They are processed in the order listed: conditions, permissions, and profile. Let's take a closer look at each of these components and their relation to a secure design of a Windows Server 2003 Remote Access server.

Conditions

Conditions are parameters that must be met for a user to gain access to a network. Conditions are looked at only at the time of initial access to the network. These could include the requirement that a user is a member of a security group, that the user is using a certain type of connection, or that it is a certain time of day. These are only a few examples of conditions that can be applied to a Remote Access policy. Figure 5.9 illustrates the many types of conditions that can be applied to a Remote Access policy.

Name	Description
Authentication-Ty...	Specifies the authentication scheme that is used to verif
Called-Station-Id	Specifies the phone number dialed by the user.
Calling-Station-Id	Specifies the phone number from which the call originate
Client-Friendly-N...	Specifies the friendly name for the RADIUS client (IAS o
Client-IP-Address	Specifies the IP address of the RADIUS client (IAS only)
Client-Vendor	Specifies the manufacturer of the RADIUS proxy or NAS
Day-And-Time-R...	Specifies the time periods and days of week during whi
Framed-Protocol	Specifies the protocol that is used.
MS-RAS-Vendor	Description not yet defined
NAS-Identifier	Specifies the string that identifies the NAS that originate
NAS-IP-Address	Specifies the IP address of the NAS where the request
NAS-Port-Type	Specifies the type of physical port that is used by the N/
Service-Type	Specifies the type of service that the user has requeste
Tunnel-Type	Specifies the tunneling protocols used.
Windows-Groups	Specifies the Windows groups that the user belongs to.

Figure 5.9   You can configure Remote Access policy conditions.

Permissions

Permissions are set on the user's account properties on the Dial-In tab. The default Dial-In permissions for users varies depending on whether the domain is in mixed mode or native mode. In mixed mode, the default dial-in permissions for all users is Deny. This keeps the Remote Access server secure until the administrator changes the permissions. In native mode, the default permissions is Control Access Through Remote Access Policy, but the only default policy is a deny for everyone at all times. This has the same effect as the Deny permissions in mixed mode; the users cannot use the Remote Access server until the administrator changes the permissions. If this policy is deleted and no other policies are added, all attempts will be denied. Figure 5.10 illustrates the options of permissions in native mode. The third option, Control Access Through Remote Access Policy, would be grayed out in mixed mode.

You should know the default permissions for Remote Access for each mode of Windows Server 2003. Also, know that if the domain is in native mode and there are no policies at all (the default has been deleted), all attempts will be denied.

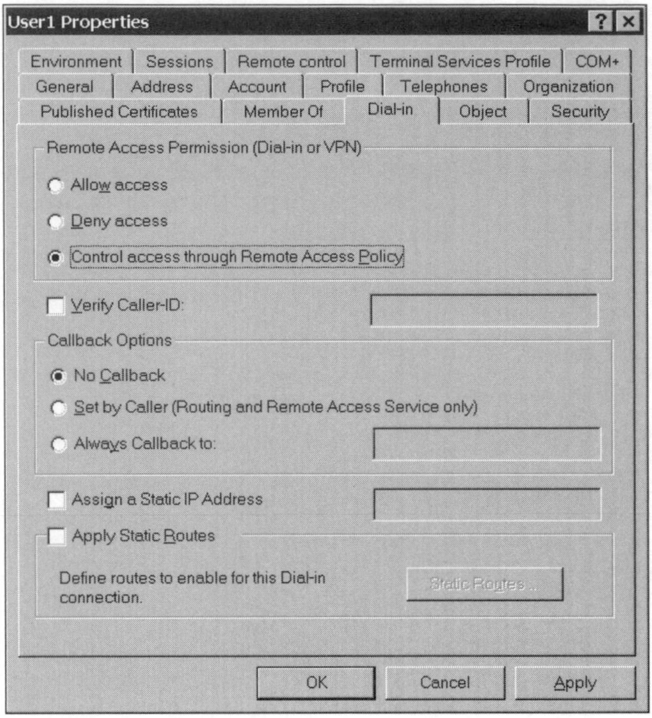

Figure 5.10 You can configure Remote Access permission settings for an account.

Profile

A *profile* is a set of rules that must be met to maintain a connection with a Remote Access server. Whereas the user's conditions are checked only once, the user's profile is continually checked by the system when he tries to gain access to a network. Elements of a profile could include a requirement that a specific encryption protocol or authentication protocol must be used. Other settings include Idle Time Out and Session Time Out. Profiles give Windows Server 2003 administrators very granular control over Remote Access services. Figure 5.11 illustrates the settings available for profiles in Remote Access policies.

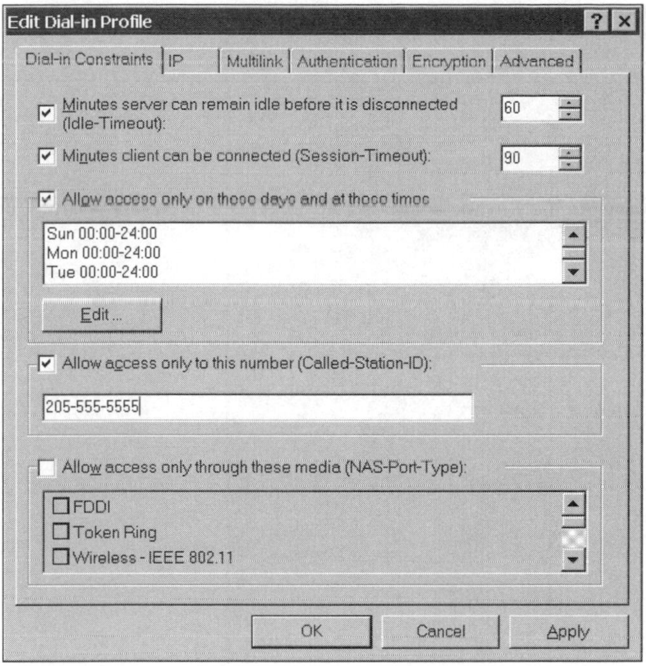

Figure 5.11   You can configure Remote Access policy profile settings.

Internet Authentication Services

In large networks containing multiple Remote Access servers, Remote Access policies can become very complex. Different servers might contain completely different policies, which could result in confusion for users as well as administrators. Internet Authentication Services is a system that takes charge of the Remote Access policies and centralizes them on one server. In addition, use of the servers can be centrally logged so that a large company can track bandwidth usage for different departments or organizations within the company.

The server that contains Internet Authentication Services is called the *RADIUS (remote authentication dial-in user service) server*. RADIUS clients are therefore RAS (Remote Access Service) servers. You can set a RAS server to provide its own authentication and logging or give these over to a RADIUS server. A RADIUS server can be configured to accept the clients (RAS servers) and provide a central store for all Remote Access policies and logged information. Figure 5.12 illustrates these settings on a RAS server.

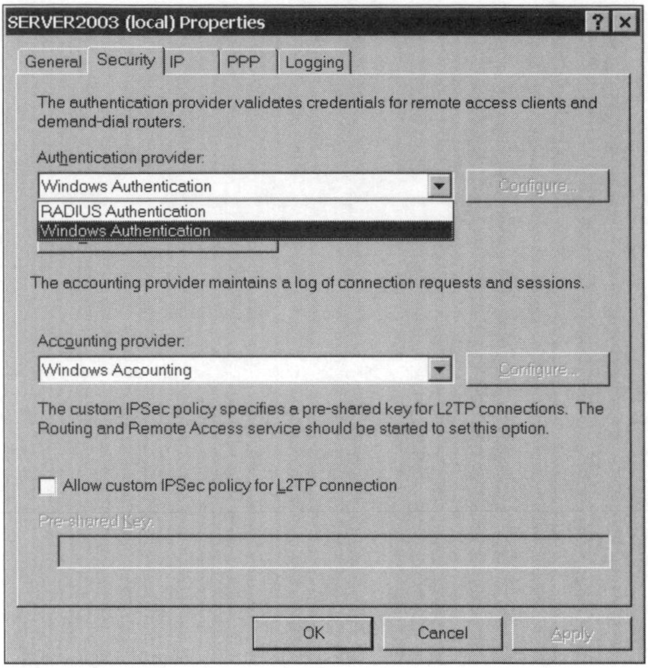

Figure 5.12   You can configure RAS server authentication and logging settings.

Designing an IP Address Assignment Strategy

Every host on a TCP/IP-based network must have an IP address to communicate on the network. Servers, network printers, and router interfaces should always have statically assigned IP addresses. Clients, on the other hand, should be assigned an IP address from a DHCP server whenever possible.

Automatically assigning IP addresses using DHCP servers saves time and is more accurate than using static address assignments for clients. In addition, an administrator can exercise granular control over the addresses that are available. Administrators can also make changes to the network topology, which affects multiple clients without the need to physically visit each client. This can save a tremendous amount of time and money in medium- and large-size companies. Finally, assigning IP addresses using DHCP servers facilitates integration of DHCP servers with DNS servers, as we discussed earlier in this chapter.

Exam Prep Questions

Question 1

Abbot.com is considering a name for its DNS structure on the inside of its firewall. The company's main goal is maximum security, even if new training for users is required. Which of these names should Abbot.com use?

- ⊙ A. abbot.com
- ○ B. abbot.com.ad
- ○ C. ad.abbot.com
- ○ D. abbot.ad

Answer D is correct. To maximize security, the company should use a name on the inside of the firewall that is totally different from its public name; therefore, answers A, B, and C are incorrect because they contain the abbott name.

Question 2

You are the enterprise admin for BFE, Inc. You have a mixture of clients and are concerned with name resolution. Which of your clients can use only NetBIOS to obtain information about servers and services in a network? (Choose all that apply.)

- ❏ A. Windows 98
- ❏ B. Windows 2000
- ❏ C. Windows XP
- ❏ D. Windows NT Workstation
- ❏ E. Windows Server 2003

Answers A and D are correct. Clients prior to Windows 2000 Professional cannot use DNS to resolve a server role such as Domain Controller or Global Catalog Server and use only NetBIOS to obtain this information about servers and services in a network; therefore, answers B, C, and E are incorrect because Windows 2000, Windows Server 2003, and Windows XP can also use SRV records.

Question 3

You are the domain admin of a Windows Server 2003 network. To improve accuracy on several WINS servers while conserving available bandwidth, you've decided to replicate WINS servers only at night. Which type of WINS replication can be configured only for an interval?

- ○ A. Push/pull
- ○ B. Push
- ○ C. Pull
- ○ D. Pull/push

Answer C is correct. WINS replication can be pulled on an interval or pushed after a set number of changes to the database. Therefore, answers A and B are incorrect because they can be set to push after a number of changes. Answer D is incorrect because it is not a valid type of WINS replication.

Question 4

Dave is a network administrator in charge of hostname resolution. He has a mixture of clients in his network and is concerned with their registration with the DNS servers. He wants to use only clients that can register their own A (host) records on the DNS servers. Which types of clients should he use? (Choose all that apply.)

- ❏ A. Windows NT Workstation
- ❏ B. Windows XP
- ❏ C. Windows 2000 Professional
- ❏ D. Windows 98
- ❏ E. Windows 95

Answers B and C are correct. Clients prior to Windows 2000 Professional cannot register their A (host) records in the DNS zone. Therefore, answers A, D, and E are incorrect because Windows NT, Windows 98, and Windows 95 cannot register their own A (host) records.

Question 5

Sandra is a network administrator for a large company. She is concerned with security in regard to DNS zones. She wants to use a type of zone that can provide secure dynamic updates. Which type of zone should she use?

- ○ A. Active Directory integrated
- ○ B. Standard primary
- ○ C. Standard secondary
- ○ D. Caching Only

Answer A is correct. Only Active Directory–integrated zones can provide secure dynamic updates. Therefore, answers B and C are incorrect because they cannot provide secure dynamic updates. Answer D is incorrect because Caching Only is a type of server and not a type of zone.

Question 6

Don is a new network administrator. He asks you to explain your choices for your current DNS design. You explain that some zones are written to directly and others are written to only through zone transfer. Which types of zones can be written to only by zone transfer?

- ❏ A. Stub
- ❏ B. Active Directory integrated
- ❏ C. Standard primary
- ❏ D. Standard secondary
- ❏ E. Caching Only

Answers A and D are correct. Standard secondary zones and stub zones are actually replicas (or partial replicas, in the case of a stub zone) of a zone and can be written to only by zone transfer. Therefore, answers B and C are incorrect because both are a primary type of zone that can be written to by an administrator or by dynamic DNS. Caching Only is not a type of zone but rather a type of server that does not host a zone; therefore, answer E is incorrect.

Question 7

> If a domain is in native mode and the users are set to the default dial-in permissions, what will happen when users attempt to connect when all Remote Access policies have been removed?
>
> ○ A. All attempts to access the server will succeed.
>
> ○ B. All attempts to access the server will fail.
>
> ○ C. Conditions will decide what happens.
>
> ○ D. Some attempts will succeed and some will fail.

Answer B is correct. When a domain is in native mode, the default dial-in permissions are Control Access Through Remote Access Policy. A policy must exist, or all attempts will be denied. Therefore, answer A is incorrect because all attempts to connect will not succeed. Answer B is incorrect because conditions are not a determining factor. Answer D is incorrect because all attempts will fail.

Question 8

> Jack is a user in a mixed mode domain. His dial-in permissions are set to the default setting. When Jack attempts to access the network through the Remote Access Services server, all attempts are denied. What could you do to allow Jack access to the network through the RAS?
>
> ○ A. Change his permissions to Allow
>
> ○ B. Change his profile to Allow
>
> ○ C. Change his permissions to Control Access Through Remote Access Policy
>
> ○ D. Change the domain to native mode

Answer A is correct. The default dial-in permission for a user in a mixed mode domain is Deny. The only way to allow Jack to use the RAS server is to change his permissions to Allow. Therefore, answers B and C are incorrect because you cannot use Control Access Through Remote Access Policy in mixed mode. Answer D is incorrect because even if the domain were changed to native mode, Jack would still be denied admission by the default Remote Access policy.

Question 9

John is an administrator in a very large network with many RAS servers. Remote Access policies have become very confusing because the same user can obtain different permissions depending on which RAS is used. John would like to use a service to centralize the authentication provided by all RAS servers. Which service should he use?

○ A. RAS

○ B. IAS

○ C. ISA

○ D. IIS

Answer B is correct. Internet Authentication Services (IAS) provides a means for centralizing authentication and accounting in a network with multiple RAS servers. Therefore, answer A is incorrect because another RAS server would only further complicate the issue. Answer C is incorrect because it is a term used for one of Microsoft's latest firewalls. Answer D is incorrect because it stands for Internet Information Services, which would not be of use in this scenario.

Question 10

Bill is a user on a Windows Server 2003 native mode domain. His dial-in permissions are set to the default. The domain has a Remote Access policy with the following:

Conditions: All users are allowed to connect on all days between 8:00 a.m. and 5:00 p.m.

Profile: All users are allowed to connect on all days between 9:00 a.m. and 4:00 p.m. and all users have a maximum session time of 2 hours.

Bill connects at 3:00 p.m. Which of the following will happen? (Choose all that apply.)

❑ A. Bill will be disconnected at 5:00 p.m.

❑ B. Bill can reconnect at 8:00 a.m. on the next day.

❑ C. Bill will be disconnected at 4:00 p.m.

❑ D. Bill can reconnect at 9:00 a.m. on the next day.

❑ E. It depends on Bill's idle session time-out setting

Answers C and D are correct. Because Bill's permissions are set to the default of Control Access Through Remote Access Policy, the connection to the network will depend on a combination of conditions and profile. Conditions are considered only at the time of the connection, but the profile must be maintained during the entire connection. Bill's profile schedule setting will disconnect him before the maximum time expires. He will then be able to reconnect only after 9:00 a.m. the next morning. At 8:00 a.m., he meets the conditions, but not the Profile. Therefore, answers A and B are incorrect because the profile will disconnect Bill at 4:00 p.m. (not 5:00 p.m.) and allow him to reconnect at 9:00 a.m. (not 8:00 a.m.). Answer E is incorrect because the idle session time-out is not a factor in this case.

Need to Know More?

 TechNet Windows 2003 Resources: www.microsoft.com/technet/ treeview/default.asp?url=/technet/prodtechnol/windows2000serv/ default.asp

 Microsoft Training and Certifications: Exams: www.microsoft.com/ traincert/mcpexams/default.asp

 Microsoft Training and Certifications: View New and Upcoming Exams: www.microsoft.com/traincert/mcpexams/status/new.asp

Creating the Physical Design for an Active Directory and Network Infrastructure

Terms you'll need to understand:

✓ Site
✓ Global Catalog server
✓ Flexible operations master
✓ IP subnet
✓ Active Directory replication
✓ Router
✓ Firewall

Techniques you'll need to master:

✓ Designing DNS service placement
✓ Designing an Active Directory implementation plan
✓ Specifying a server specification to meet system requirements
✓ Designing Internet connectivity for a company
✓ Designing a network and routing topology for a company
✓ Designing a remote access infrastructure

The physical design of a Windows Server 2003 network controls and balances two important functions: authentication and replication. In addition, Active Directory provides all users and administrators with the tools to see and use all the objects within it. An effective physical design balances the needs of the users and administrators to quickly access information against the capabilities of the network to provide this access. Concerns and challenges include the security, bandwidth, capacity, and fault tolerance of the entire network. In this section, we examine the tools that are used to create this balance and the methods you can employ to design a network that takes advantage of the inherent strengths of Windows Server 2003.

Designing DNS Service Placement

Active Directory cannot function without DNS (Domain Name Services). For this reason, it's important to have a sound DNS service before you implement Active Directory. This should include DNS servers that are located as close as possible to the domain controllers and client computers they serve. Because DNS zones must be replicated when changes occur, you must balance the need for timely replication of the DNS zones with the need for quick name resolution for clients and servers. Windows Server 2003 provides many features that can be used to create this balance. Those features include the following:

➤ Active Directory–integrated zones

➤ Stub zones

➤ Incremental zone transfer

➤ Caching-only DNS servers

➤ Conditional forwarding

In the previous chapter, we discussed these features and their relation to the logical infrastructure. We now examine how each feature relates to the physical infrastructure of a Windows Server 2003 network.

Active Directory–Integrated Zones

Active Directory–integrated zones were first implemented with Windows 2000 Server. These zones provide significant benefits to a network's physical infrastructure over and above those of standard DNS zones. Because they must be located on domain controllers, they are (by default) as close to the domain controller as they can get! In addition, Active Directory–integrated zones conserve bandwidth for clients and servers by attaching their zone transfer process to the normal replication of Active Directory. For these reasons, Active Directory–integrated zones should be used whenever possible.

It isn't always possible to use Active Directory–integrated zones because the server that hosts the integrated zone must be a domain controller as well as a DNS server. Some organizations have smaller remote offices that do not contain a domain controller. In this case, a different type of zone is required.

 You should know that Active Directory–integrated zones can be located only on domain controllers.

In addition, Active Directory–integrated zones should be used only by administrators who understand the risks associated with their use. All Active Directory–integrated zones are primary zones. This means they can be read from and written to as well. These zones can be secured, and administrators should take great care to make sure they are secure to prevent spoofing of IP addresses. *Spoofing* occurs when a hacker can collect enough information about your network to fool the system into thinking that he belongs in it. This significant security risk should be avoided. Spoofing can be prevented using Active Directory–integrated zones with secure dynamic updates.

Stub Zones

Stub zones are new to Windows 2003 DNS servers. Prior to the use of stub zones, all DNS servers in a domain always replicated all the records for each zone to the replica servers for that zone. Stub zones improve DNS efficiency for networks that are at the edge of the topology. These zones replicate only the information about the other DNS servers inside the topology. The assumption is that they will have to use these servers to gain information about the domain. In other words, they are not the name resolution severs for our domain as much as they are the name resolution servers to help other domains discover our domain.

Stub zone database files improve DNS efficiency because they do not replicate all the records for a zone. In fact, they contain and manage only the following types of records:

➤ Start of authority (SOA) resource record

➤ Named server (NS) resource records

➤ Glue host (A) resource records

We now examine each of these records and their purpose in a stub zone database.

Start of Authority Resource Record

The start of authority (SOA) resource record is an essential element in any DNS database. It is said to be the *first record* of the database and it establishes the fact that this database is a DNS database. The SOA record usually contains instructions to the database as to its role (primary or secondary) and how it maintains contact with the other DNS servers that host the replica database files. The SOA sets the schedule for how often a secondary server contacts the primary servers for database updates. SOA records on secondary servers respond to settings in the SOA record on primary servers. Figure 6.1 illustrates the settings that SOA records can communicate.

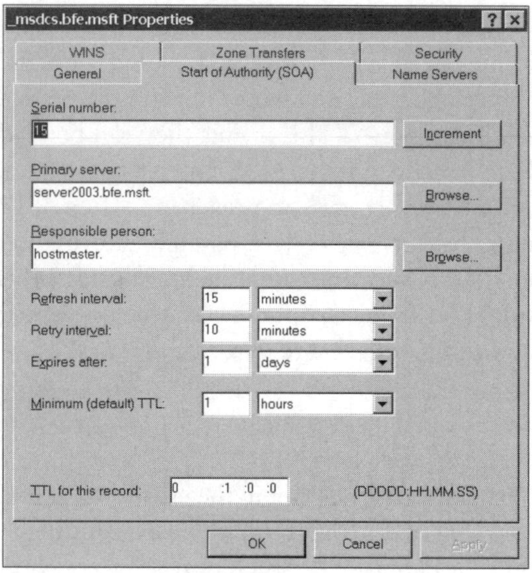

Figure 6.1 Start of authority records control communication between primary and secondary servers.

Named Server Records

Named server (NS) records identify a particular server as hosting a zone. Servers can host multiple zones and one server can be a primary for one zone and a secondary for another. Named server records allow servers and clients to locate a server by its fully qualified domain name (FQDN).

Glue Host Records

Glue host (A) records are used for locating the authoritative DNS servers for a delegated zone. In effect, they glue zones together by providing an efficient path for other DNS servers to follow when resolving a name.

Incremental Zone Transfer

Prior to the release of Windows 2000 Server, DNS databases shared "all or nothing at all." In other words, the whole database had to be replicated when replication occurred. For example, suppose a server had 2,000 records on it and you added another 2 records to the database. The entire database had to be copied (replicated) to each of the replica servers. This is referred to as AXFR (all zone transfer). The ultimate disadvantage of this type of replication was a lack of accuracy because the administrators did not want to replicate the servers as often as it was in this case.

Windows Server 2003, as well as Windows 2000 Server, provides for incremental zone transfer (IXFR). With IXFR, only the records that have changed since the last zone transfer are transferred. So, if you have 2,000 records and add 2 more, only the additional 2 records have to be replicated. This is accomplished using an additional table, which contains each record and the status of its last update. The information in the table is referred to as the *up-to-datedness vector*. The ultimate benefit of this type of zone transfer is greater accuracy because administrators are more willing to let servers replicate more often.

Caching-Only DNS Servers

The key word in caching-only DNS is *only*. All DNS servers keep a cache in addition to any DNS zones that they host. The cache includes records that have been recently resolved. You can set the cache to control how long the resolved queries remain cached. The cache is always checked before databases are checked.

However, a caching-only DNS server does not host a DNS database. It can resolve a query on its own only if the query happens to be in its cache. In other words, it can resolve a query on its own only if it has resolved it before. You might be asking how it resolved the query in the first place. Well, a caching-only DNS server is set with forwarders that allow it to ask another server to resolve the query and tell the caching-only DNS server. It then caches that information for the next time.

The main benefit of caching-only DNS servers is that they do not host a DNS zone and therefore do not need zone transfer at all. All zone transfers rob from the available bandwidth of the network; therefore, this type of zone is useful when you have a small office that is connected to the home office with a relatively slow link (low bandwidth). Caching-only DNS servers will, of course, have to use the link until they learn the addresses that are most used, but the use of the link for name resolution will decrease when the most used names are in the cache. Because there is no zone transfer at all, there is no zone transfer bandwidth use issue.

You should be aware that caching-only DNS servers do not need zone transfer and are therefore likely to be part of a solution on the test if minimizing zone transfer is a goal.

Conditional Forwarding

Conditional forwarding is new to Windows Server 2003. A *forwarder* is a designated DNS server that forwards queries to resolve external domain names for another DNS server. Forwarders can be used to reduce the amount of name resolution traffic across a WAN (Wide Area Network). Prior to Windows Server 2003, servers that were set with forwarders would forward all queries they could not resolve to all forwarders based on their position in a list. This was less than efficient because some servers that were set as forwarders did not have the best logical route to resolve the query.

Conditional forwarding allows all queries for a particular namespace to be forwarded to a particular server's IP address. This server should be logically close to the namespace listed. For example, a conditional forwarder could be used to forward all queries ending with examcram2.com to a specific IP address of a DNS server or to multiple IP addresses of DNS servers that can resolve the query. In the same way, conditional forwarders can also be used to manage name resolution between different namespaces in a network. Figure 6.2 illustrates the settings for conditional forwarding.

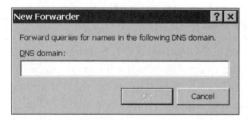

Figure 6.2   We can set DNS servers for conditional forwarding.

Designing an Active Directory Implementation Plan

In Windows Server 2003, Active Directory replication is essential to proper functioning of the network. Active Directory replication is based on a multiple-master model rather than the single-master model used in Windows NT Server. That means each domain controller is a peer domain controller and each must have an almost identical copy of the latest database.

The reason we have to use the word *almost* is that each domain controller's copy is only as accurate as its latest replication. This is referred to as *loose convergence*. With loose convergence, even though all domain controllers have a readable and writeable copy of the database, they are not alike in every way. Each has its own latest changes that the others will not have until the next replication.

Windows Server 2003 domain controllers can have many roles in the forest and in their own domain. These roles determine the additional information the domain controllers contain and transfer and the information for which they are responsible. Those roles include the following:

➤ Global Catalog servers

➤ Flexible Single Master Operation

We now discuss each of these roles and their effect on the physical design of Active Directory.

Global Catalog Servers

Servers designated as Global Catalog servers replicate a database containing all the objects in the Active Directory and a subset of the attributes of the objects. These servers are used when a person or an application performs a search of the Active Directory. Global Catalog servers contain only the attributes that are most likely to be used in a search of the Active Directory performed by a user, an administrator, or an application. You can control the list of attributes in the Global Catalog servers by modifying the attribute's properties in the schema.

By default, the first domain controller in the forest becomes a Global Catalog server. You can set any domain controller to be a Global Catalog server by using the Active Directory Sites and Services tool. Figure 6.3 illustrates the setting for the Global Catalog server in the NTDS Settings Properties dialog of a server using the Active Directory Sites and Services tool.

A *site* is a group of IP subnets that are connected by a fast and reliable link. Because Global Catalog servers are used for searches, at least one Global Catalog server should exist in each site in an Active Directory forest. This enables users to perform searches without using the relatively slower links between sites.

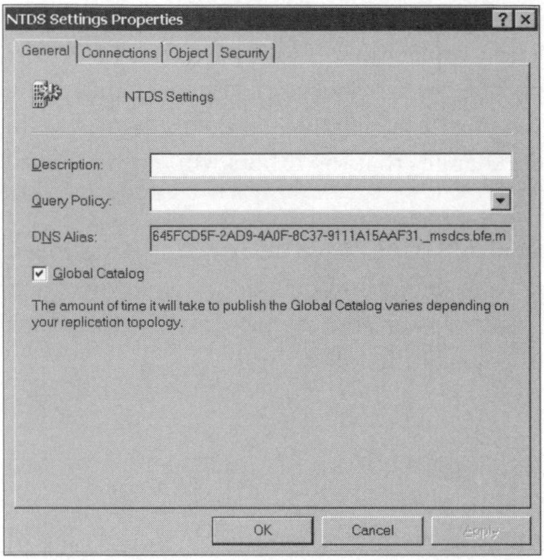

Figure 6.3 You can set any domain controller to be a Global Catalog server.

You should be aware that each site should contain at least one Global Catalog server to facilitate searches over faster links.

You should take great care when modifying the schema because modifying one object can potentially affect others.

Flexible Single Master Operation

Although most of the Windows Server 2003 Active Directory operates in a multi-master model, some functions require that one server be in charge. The Flexible Single Master Operation (FSMO) roles establish a particular server that has to be contacted when certain changes are made in the Active Directory. These roles include the following:

> Schema Master

> RID Master

> Domain Naming Master

> Infrastructure Master

> PDC Emulator

Let's now discuss each of these roles and their effect on the physical design of the Active Directory.

Schema Master

By default, the first domain controller in the forest takes on the role of the schema master. The *schema master* is the authority on changes to the schema. The schema admin must have connectivity to the schema master to make changes to the schema.

This role can be moved to another domain controller, but there can be only one schema master per forest. If the domain controller performing the role of Schema Master fails, the role can be seized and moved to another domain controller, but this should be done only as a last resort. It's better to fix the original server if it's possible to do so.

Because the schema is rarely changed, the location of the schema master is not critical to the design of the Active Directory. It is acceptable and common practice to leave the schema master in its default location.

Domain Naming Master

The first domain controller in the forest also takes on the role of the domain naming master. The *domain naming master* makes sure that all the domains in a forest are uniquely named. The enterprise admin must have connectivity with this server before a domain can be added to or deleted from a forest. Because the domain naming master needs to know all the domains in the forest, it should therefore also be a Global Catalog server.

This role can also be moved to another domain controller, but there can only be one domain naming master per forest. If the domain controller performing the role of domain naming master fails, the role can be seized and moved to another domain controller, but this should be done only as a last resort. It's better to fix the original server if it's possible to do so.

Because the addition or removal of a domain happens infrequently, the location of the domain naming master is not critical to the physical design of the Active Directory. It's acceptable to leave the domain naming master at its default location.

PDC Emulator

There is one PDC emulator per domain. The PDC emulator provides many functions to the Windows Server 2003 network design. By default, the first domain controller in each domain takes on the role of the PDC emulator. The functions it provides depend on which functional level the domain is in and whether Windows NT domain controllers (BDCs) are still present.

In Windows NT Server, domain controllers function in a single master model with the primary domain controller (PDC) as the single master. In other words, changes can be made only to the PDC and must then be replicated to all the backup domain controllers (BDCs). A BDC's database is not writeable, except for replication. When Windows Server 2003 is in the Windows 2000 mixed functional level and Windows NT BDCs are still in the domain, the BDCs will look for a PDC to replicate changes to them. Because there is no real PDC, the PDC emulator plays the role of (emulates) the PDC and replicates changes to the BDCs.

The PDC emulator still performs many functions when all Windows NT domain controllers have been upgraded and the Windows Server 2003 domain is in Windows Server 2003 functional level. These functions include being the final authority on password changes, which means that the PDC emulator must be contacted whenever a user's password is changed. The PDC emulator is also, by default, the domain master browser for the NetBIOS system that is essential for legacy clients and applications. In addition, the PDC emulator coordinates the time with other domain controllers. Because some of the PDC emulator's roles are closely tied to frequent changes that affect users, the PDC emulator should be located as close to the users as possible.

RID Master

There is one relative id (RID) master per domain. The RID master assures that all domain security IDs (domain SIDs) remain unique for each domain. A domain SID is comprised of two parts. The first part is the same for every object in the domain—this is called the SID. The second part is unique to each object in the domain—this is called the relative ID or RID.

Domain controllers must have RIDs to create objects. When a domain controller is initially created, it is given 500 RIDs by the RID master. Each object created on the domain controller uses one RID. When there are 50 RIDs remaining, the RID master refreshes the RID pool by sending the domain controller another 500 RIDs.

In a dynamic environment, the RID master should be as close to the users as possible. However, if this isn't possible, the issue is not critical—the RID pool traffic isn't bandwidth intensive.

Infrastructure Master

There is one infrastructure master per domain. The *infrastructure master* is responsible for keeping track of group-to-name references. Active Directory uses many different types of names to identify an object. One of those names is the LDAP name. The LDAP name of an object changes when the object is moved from one OU to another. However, the DNS name does not change nor does the object's globally unique ID (GUID). The infrastructure master keeps track of the real name of the object by using its GUID and relates that information back to all its other names depending on where it is in the Active Directory. Because of the infrastructure master, we can easily move an object from one OU to another without losing track of the object. The infrastructure master needs to focus on its own domain, so it should never be a Global Catalog server in a multi-domain network.

 You should know that there is only one schema master and domain naming master per forest and only 1 PDC emulator, RID master, and infrastructure master per domain.

Specifying the Server Specification to Meet System Requirements

Certainly, the domain controllers themselves are key components in the physical design of an Active Directory. These servers must have the proper hardware and software to be effective in a Windows Server 2003 network. In this section, we examine the following:

➤ Software editions

➤ Hardware requirements and recommendations

Software Editions

Microsoft actually makes four Windows 2003 operating systems. These operating systems, referred to as editions, include the following:

➤ Web Edition ➤ Enterprise Edition

➤ Standard Edition ➤ Datacenter Edition

Each edition is designed for use in a specific role in the network environment. We now examine the four Windows Server 2003 editions and their major roles.

Web Edition

Web Edition servers are not made for use as domain controllers. As their name implies, they are to be used as a Web servers. They are tuned for serving and hosting Web pages while maintaining vital security. Web servers are becoming increasingly important in today's interconnected world.

You should know that the Web Edition is not designed to be a domain controller.

Standard Edition

The Standard Edition can be a domain controller for a small organization, but Microsoft recommends that Standard Edition servers be used primarily for file and print servers and desktop application servers. They are not designed to be domain controllers for a large enterprise.

Enterprise Edition

Enterprise Edition is the recommended software for domain controllers for small, medium, and large networks. It can provide the high reliability and performance required for a domain controller. Enterprise Edition is available in a 32-bit version and a 64-bit version.

Datacenter Edition

Datacenter Edition is for huge business-critical and mission-critical applications and databases. It provides the highest levels of scalability, reliability, and manageability available. Datacenter Edition is available in a 32-bit version and a 64-bit version.

 It should be noted that the Web and Datacenter Editions are available only through original equipment manufacturers (OEMs) and cannot be purchased off the shelf as the Standard and Enterprise Editions can.

Hardware Requirements and Recommendations

There is a huge difference between a requirement and a recommendation. A *requirement* is simply the minimum that will allow the system to function in any capacity. This would certainly not be a good idea in a dynamic and growing network. The *recommended* specification is the minimum that was found to give acceptable performance in a typical network environment.

Table 6.1 lists the required and recommended minimums for hardware used for domain controllers in the three different operating systems. Web Edition is not included because it is not designed for use as a domain controller.

Table 6.1 Requirements and Recommendations for Domain Controllers			
Hardware Component	Standard Edition	Enterprise Edition	Datacenter Edition
Required CPU Speed	133MHz	133MHz 733MHz for 64-bit version	400MHz 733MHz for 64-bit version
Recommended CPU Speed	550MHz	733MHz	733MHz
Required RAM	128MB	120MD	512MD
Recommended RAM	256MB	256MB	1GB
Multi-Processor Support	Up to 4	Up to 8	8 required Up to 32

Designing Internet Connectivity for a Company

In today's interconnected world, most businesses require a connection to the Internet. The greatest challenge for a network administrator is to provide a connection that is transparent to a user while at the same time secure for the organization. There are many components from which we can choose to provide this connection. The components we choose will largely depend on the needs of the users and the number of users who are served by that component. In this section, we examine the most common components used to provide secure Internet access. These are the following:

➤ Internet Connection Sharing (ICS)

➤ Network address translation (NAT)

➤ Proxy server

➤ Firewall

Let's now examine each of these components and their relationship to the physical design of our network infrastructure.

Internet Connection Sharing

Internet Connection Sharing (ICS) is built into all Windows 2000 and Windows Server 2003 operating systems, including Windows 2000 Professional and Windows XP Professional. It provides an Internet connection hosted by one machine that can be used by many machines. This connection provides automatic address assignment and name resolution options.

You can configure Internet Connection Sharing through Routing and Remote Access on a server or through Network Connections on a client. The only additional hardware required is another network interface card for the computer hosting the ICS. Clients of ICS can be configured to obtain their IP addresses automatically, just as if they were getting them from a DHCP server.

When you configure the ICS host, the system sets up a private network with its IP address as 192.168.0.1/16. All clients set to obtain an address automatically will then receive an address in the 192.168.0.0/16 network. One of the host network interfaces will have the private address, and the other will have the address obtained from the Internet service provider (ISP).

Although ICS can be used with your server, it was designed for use when you have a small group of clients and no server, such as in a small remote office. In this case, one client hosts the connection to the Internet that all clients use. In a larger environment with a server, you would probably use a different component.

Network Address Translation

Small- to medium-sized networks use network address translation (NAT) services to provide users with access to the Internet. These services are transparent to the user. Their main benefit is that they hide the addresses used in the private network by translating every address that goes through them to an address that will be used on the Internet. This protects a network from spoofing. Another benefit is that the organization can have fewer registered IP addresses. This saves the organization money and saves IP addresses. You can actually have hundreds of private IP addresses translated to one registered address and give those hundreds of users simultaneous and separate access to the Internet.

Network address translation can be performed by many different components. Windows Server 2003 has NAT services built into Routing and Remote Access. When you use a Windows Server 2003 computer as a router, you can easily add the NAT services. You can find this selection by right-clicking on the server and then selecting Configure and Enable Routing and Remote Access. Figure 6.4 illustrates this configuration setting. You can also set up network address translation on firewalls, routers, and even some hubs.

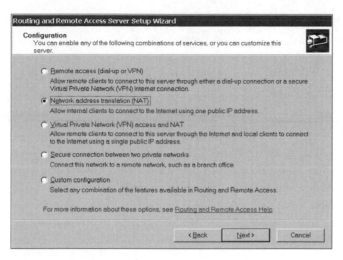

Figure 6.4   You can set a routing and remote access server for network address translation.

Proxy Server

Larger organizations generally use a proxy server to provide Internet access for their users. A *proxy server* performs network address translation by making the request for an address on behalf of the client, but can also provide more granular control of which users or user groups have access to the Internet and when they have access. In addition, a proxy server can be configured to filter and control access to certain Internet sites or groups of sites. Finally, proxy servers can cache the Internet requests from users. This cache can be used for greater security and control as well as to provide faster response to users seeking a frequently used site. Microsoft and many other software development companies offer proxy server products.

Firewall

As its name implies, a *firewall* provides a separation between two things or places. In this case, the firewall provides a separation of two networks. Typically, one of the networks is the Internet, but firewalls can be used between two private networks as well. There are basically two types of firewalls:

➤ Packet filtering

➤ Stateful inspection

We now discuss each of these and their effect on the physical design of our network.

Packet Filtering

Packet filtering is letting some packets go through the firewall while discarding (destroying) others. This can be performed in either direction (in or out) or in both directions at once. Some packet-filtering firewalls use software to make decisions, whereas others use hardware that is specifically designed for this purpose.

Firewalls typically filter by IP address, protocol, and port. For example, a firewall could be used to filter all ICMP (ping) traffic from entering your network and/or to filter all FTP (file transfer) traffic from leaving you network. The first example would protect the network from a denial of service attack using pings. The second example would protect you from a user sending valuable company information to some other company. In either case, the firewall examines each packet to make its decisions on whether to let the packet through or to discard it.

Stateful inspection is a firewall architecture that works at the network layer. Unlike static packet filtering, which examines a packet based on the information in its header, stateful inspection tracks each connection traversing all interfaces of the firewall and makes sure it is valid. This is also referred to as *dynamic packet filtering*.

Servers, as their name implies, are generally meant to serve! They are therefore vulnerable because they generally come out of the box with many services and ports open and ready for business. The Web Edition of Windows Server 2003 addresses this issue by closing many of these vulnerabilities during a default installation. A *firewall* is a server that is physically located between the Internet and the other servers in a network and provides the required security for the network. It makes sure that the packets that enter and leave the network are there for good reason, and it generally records everything that happens. A firewall can provide an additional authentication service for users attempting to send packets through it. The main benefit of a firewall is that it enables you to leave the services and ports on the servers on the inside of the network in their active and ready status.

Because a firewall is used to separate your network from other networks, it should be located on the perimeter of the network. In fact, all traffic in and out of the network should be routed through the firewall. Any traffic that can go around the firewall represents a security risk that should be avoided. That means the firewall must be able to perform at a pace that is fast and efficient, so as not to create a bottleneck. This should be taken into consideration when you choose between the many types of firewall hardware and software on the market.

Designing a Network and Routing Topology for a Company

Routing is the process of using protocols, sets of rules, to determine the destination of a packet and deliver the packet safely to its destination. The protocols used on a network are part of its logical and physical design. Certainly the most prominent protocol today, by far, is TCP/IP. We therefore need to understand TCP/IP addressing methods and standards and their effect on our network design. In addition, we need to choose an addressing scheme that can include registered and/or private addresses.

In this section, we examine the options available to us in regard to IP address assignment, which include

➤ Static assignment

➤ Automatic private IP address assignment (APIPA)

➤ Dynamic host configuration protocol (DHCP)

Static Assignment

You can assign a static IP address by typing it in the Internet Protocol (TCP/IP) Properties dialog for the connection, as illustrated in Figure 6.5.

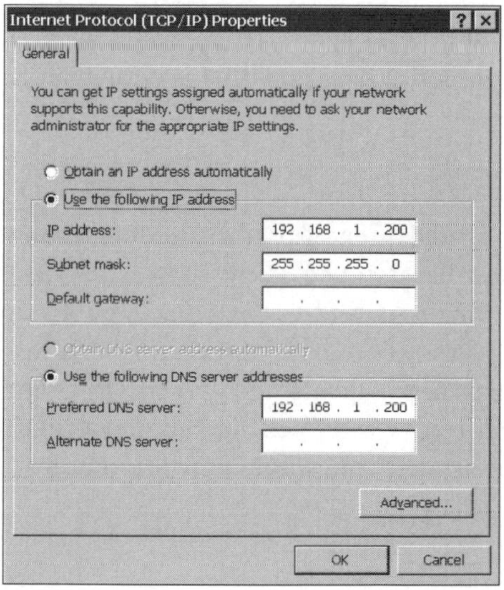

Figure 6.5 You can set a static address for a TCP/IP host.

You can assign a static address to any host on the network, but static address-es are typically used for the following:

➤ Servers

➤ Network printers

➤ Router interfaces

Let's now discuss each of these components and the reasons that a static IP address is the preferred option for each.

Servers

Modern networks use many different types of servers. Many of these servers, such as DNS, DHCP, and WINS servers, require a static address configuration. Not all servers require a static address, but it is generally accepted as good practice to give all servers a static address whether or not they require it.

Network Printers

Network printers are print devices that do not require a print server to func-tion on the network. They have their own network interface card (NIC) and can be assigned an IP address. Because these devices are static and clients need to find them quickly and easily, it makes sense to assign them static addresses, rather than have the addresses change and possibly cause connec-tion problems for the clients.

As a side note, these devices can easily be assigned IP addresses from a DHCP server by using an address from a reserved pool that is permanently assigned to the devices' MAC address.

Router Interfaces

Because router interfaces represent a fundamental part of the logical and physical network, they should always be assigned static addresses. Most routers don't have the capability to obtain an address automatically. Even if they do, you should take great care when considering this practice because router interfaces are configured on clients and servers. In other words, clients and servers rely on that router interface (default gateway) to be where they think it is! If it moves around, the whole network topology is disrupted.

Automatic Private IP Address Assignment

All Microsoft clients newer than Windows 95 OSR2 are set by default to obtain an IP address automatically as soon as they are installed and configured to use the network. There are many different ways in which they might obtain an address automatically. We discuss some of those methods later in this chapter. Microsoft clients, including Windows 98 and all newer clients, can also provide themselves with an automatic private IP address assignment (APIPA) if they find there are no network components available to provide them with a valid network address.

Automatic private IP addresses are set by the client and are chosen from the address range of 169.254.0.1/16 to 169.254.255.254/16. The address will be chosen at random and then pinged to ensure that no other client on the local subnet is using it. This is a convenient service to connect clients when a DHCP server is not available or when a small workgroup does not require automatic address assignment by other means. However, this method has serious limitations.

You should be aware that this service can allow clients to see each other, but it does not really connect any of the clients to the resources on the actual network. In other words, all clients that have addresses in this range can see each other, but none can see the network resources, which are on another subnet. Misery loves company! This could potentially create a troubleshooting nightmare for you if you don't immediately recognize the 169.254.0.0/16 network address. For this reason, some administrators choose to disable APIPA.

Dynamic Host Configuration Protocol

The easiest and most accurate way to assign addresses to clients in any network is dynamic host configuration protocol (DHCP). All clients set to obtain an IP address automatically will broadcast on the network to attempt to discover a DHCP server. When a DHCP server is available and properly configured, it responds to the client's request and assigns the client an IP address and potentially much more.

DHCP servers use scopes to determine the range of IP addresses to assign. Scope options can include the address of other servers and connections in the network. For example, a DHCP server can assign the client an IP address as well as the IP addresses of a DNS server, WINS server, and default gateway, just to name a few. You can configure a DHCP server to automatically assign client addresses based on many factors regarding the client. Those factors could include the physical subnet in which the client resides, the type of operating system on the client, and even the media access control (MAC) address of the client. Figure 6.6 illustrates some of the options available on a DHCP server.

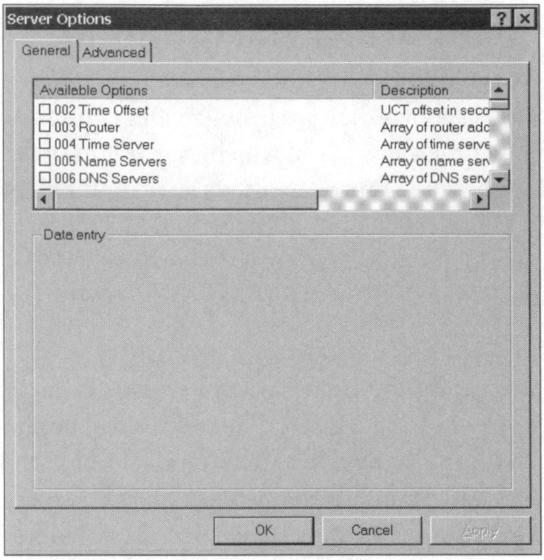

Figure 6.6   You can configure many options on a DHCP server.

Types of IP Addresses

There are two main types of IP addresses in any network:

➤ Public addresses

➤ Private addresses

In this section, we examine each of these types of addresses and the relation of each to the physical design of our network.

Public Addresses

Public IP addresses are real addresses that take up a part of the finite address space on the Internet. Therefore, they have to be assigned from the organizations that manage the Internet. One of these is the Internet Corporation for Assigned Names and Numbers (ICANN). It is a nonprofit corporation that was formed to assume responsibility for IP address space allocation and domain name management. Public IP addresses are registered through ICANN or other organizations that work through ICANN throughout the world. Other organizations include the InterNIC and the Internet Assigned Numbers Authority (IANA), which has its own department for each part of the world. In North America, we use the American Registry for Internet Numbers (ARIN). If all of this sounds confusing, that's because it is. But each entity has a Web site that can direct you to the correct site and assist you in registering IP addresses and domain names. All public addresses must be registered.

Using our current version of IP addressing (Version 4), which uses a 32-bit address, we have only a little more than 4 billion public IP addresses for the entire world! In the early 1990s, this seemed like a gigantic number of addresses and there were no concerns of running out. Today, only 10 years later, we have about 1 billion public addresses remaining. Changes in the way network addresses are issued have slowed the rate at which we're consuming the public IP addresses, but we will still run out at some point in the future. A new version of IP addressing (Version 6) is on the horizon. This will use a 128-bit address and provide an enormous number of IP addresses. In fact, the number is so large that it is difficult to comprehend. The number of IP addresses that will be provided by IP Version 6 is

340,282,366,920,938,463,463,374,607,431,768,211,456

This will provide at least 1,564 addresses for each square meter of the surface of the planet Earth!

Private IP Addresses

There is one more way that we can preserve our current IP address space. Using the technology that we have discussed—in particular, NAT, firewalls, and proxy servers—we can use significantly fewer public addresses. In a practical sense, we can use any address that we choose on the inside of our firewall, as long as that address is never seen on the outside. However, what if you and I both decide to use the same random address behind our firewalls, both of our firewalls fail, and our networks see each other? Then we would have an address conflict.

To prevent this from happening, some address ranges are filtered by Internet routers, marking them as nonroutable, and are therefore recommended for use as private internal IP address ranges only. These address ranges include the following:

➤ 10.0.0.0/8–10.255.255.255/8

➤ 172.16.0.0/16–172.32.255.255/16

➤ 192.168.0.0/16–192.168.255.255/16

All the network addresses, broadcast addresses, and host addresses in these address ranges are filtered from entering the backbone routers of the Internet. You should use these address ranges for internal use on your network.

You should know the private IP address ranges and the reason for their use.

Designing a Remote Access Infrastructure

As we stated in Chapter 5, "Creating the Logical Design for a Network Services Infrastructure," it's very important to continue to provide users with access to their files and folders on our network even when the users aren't in the office. The productivity of most companies depends on the ability to provide this access. In Chapter 5, we discussed the logical components of providing remote access while maintaining security. In this section, we discuss the physical components used for the same goals.

The physical components used to provide secure remote access include the following:

➤ Remote access servers

➤ Internet authentication servers

➤ Screened subnets

We now discuss each of these components and the relation of each to the physical design of our network.

Remote Access Servers

Remote access servers are specifically designed to provide a link between the services and protocols used by wide area networks (WANs) and those used by our local area network (LAN). These servers enable users to connect to the network from wherever they happen to be—provided that they have the proper credentials to authenticate the connection.

You can use the Routing and Remote Access tool on Windows Server 2003 to configure two main types of remote access. These include

➤ Dial-up access

➤ Virtual private network (VPN)

We now examine each of these types of remote access and the relationship of each to the physical design of our network infrastructure.

Dial-up Access

Remote access servers can use regular telephone lines, which are often referred to as the *public switched telephone network* (*PSTN*) or the *plain old telephone service* (*POTS*). In this case, a modem at the receiving end answers the modem at the sending end. In other words, the user's computer calls in and the other computers answer the call. This original method of remote access service is still used by many companies today; however, this method has some significant drawbacks.

First, dial-up access requires one modem for each simultaneous conversation. In a large network, with many remote access users, this can present a physical problem. Some companies have used integrated circuits that emulate many modems to overcome this physical limitation, but there is still a limit to what any device can provide. In addition, although some encryption can be used, the information transfer cannot be considered secure. Finally, dial-up through the PSTN is limited to a bandwidth of 53Kbps. Even though this might be fast enough to check email, we'll experience its limitations if we attempt to transfer large files!

Virtual Private Network

As its name implies, a virtual private network (VPN) is a secure communication channel through an inherently nonsecure medium, the Internet. To use a VPN, a user first makes a connection to an Internet service provider and then uses that connection to connect to the remote access server. Our remote access server is configured with *virtual ports* that receive the communication and forward it to the appropriate resources in our network. Figure 6.7 illustrates the use of virtual ports.

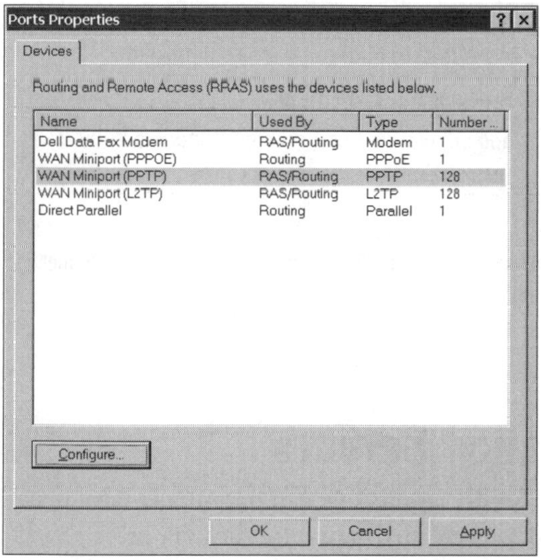

Figure 6.7 You can use virtual ports for remote access connections.

To provide a secure communication channel through a nonsecure medium, we overlay one protocol on top of another. This is called *encapsulation* or *tunneling*. There are two main tunneling protocols that can be used to provide this security:

➤ Point-to-point tunneling protocol (PPTP)

➤ Layer two tunneling protocol (L2TP)

These two tunneling protocols have some similarities, but many differences. PPTP is the oldest tunneling protocol and will probably be replaced by L2TP at some point in the future. L2TP offers many advantages over PPTP, including more flexibility, more efficient data transfer, and tunnel authentication (checking the other side) before each transmission. The only disadvantage of LT2P is that by default it cannot be used by clients earlier than Windows 2000 Professional. Because this will affect your decision as to whether to replace older clients, it should be considered part of the physical design of your network. Table 6.2 illustrates the similarities and differences of these two tunneling protocols.

Table 6.2 Comparison Chart of PPTP and L2TP Tunneling Protocols	
PPTP	**L2TP**
Internetwork must be IP based	Internetwork can be IP, Frame Relay, X.25, or ATM based
No header compression	Header compression for more efficient data transfer
No tunnel authentication	Tunnel authentication on each transmission
Built-in PPP encryption	Uses newer IPSec encryption
Can be used by all Microsoft clients	By default, can be used only by Windows 2000 Professional and newer clients

 You should know the main advantages and disadvantages of the two main tunneling protocols (PPTP and L2TP) for the test.

Internet Authentication Servers

In a network with many remote access servers, we can potentially have many remote access policies. As we discussed in Chapter 5, these policies can be centralized to one server. This Internet authentication server (IAS) should be physically located between the remote access servers (its clients) and a domain controller. This allows the IAS to contact the domain controller for authorization without disrupting other network components. Keeping the IAS physically close to a domain controller also ensures that it can communicate with the domain controller over a fast reliable link.

Screened Subnets

Many organizations use a combination of firewalls to create an area of the network that is neither completely on the inside nor completely on the outside. This area is referred to as a *screened subnet*, as illustrated in Figure 6.8. Servers that provide resources for clients on the inside as well as the outside are often placed into the screened subnet. Doing so means they are physically and logically closer to remote access users than they would be if they were all the way behind the firewalls. Servers that are sometimes placed into screened subnets include DNS, Web, FTP, email, and many others.

Screened Subnet

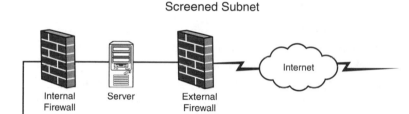

Internal Firewall   Server   External Firewall   Internet

Figure 6.8   Multiple firewalls create a screened subnet.

Servers that have vital information about the internal network, such as domain controllers, are not typically placed into a screened subnet. DNS servers in a screened subnet may contain an incomplete database as well. In other words, they might not have all the Active Directory records that the DNS servers on the inside of all of the firewalls have.

The multiple firewalls used with screened subnets enable you to control the traffic flow to and from all levels of the network. For example, FTP traffic can be allowed into and out of the first firewall, where the FTP server is located, but completely blocked on the second firewall. This type of control gives you many options as a remote access administrator.

Many companies use a firewall with multiple network interfaces to provide the same screened subnet. For example, a firewall with three NICs would be connected to the Internet with one interface and connected to the internal LAN with another, leaving the third interface connected to its own subnet. Servers placed on this subnet are accessible from the Internet (controlled by the firewall), but at the same time are protected without being on the internal network. Fewer and fewer sites are utilizing multiple firewalls for this purpose.

Exam Prep Questions

Question 1

> You're the domain administrator of a Windows Server 2003 network. You've decided to implement a DNS structure for your network, including a small remote office. The office does not have its own domain controller. Your main goal is to minimize all replication and zone transfer traffic on the slow link between your home office and the remote office. Which type of DNS server should you use in the remote office?
>
> ○ A. Active Directory–integrated
>
> ○ B. Secondary
>
> ○ C. Primary
>
> ○ D. Caching-only

Answer D is correct. Caching-only DNS servers do not host a zone and therefore do not have any zone transfer traffic. Active Directory–integrated zones can be hosted only on domain controllers. Even if you installed a domain controller at the remote office, you would create replication traffic for the Domain Controller; therefore, answer A is incorrect. Primary and secondary servers host a zone and create transfer traffic; therefore, answers B and C are incorrect.

Question 2

> Abbott Company is installing the first domain controller in the first Domain of its Active Directory. The company will be installing many more domain controllers and domains in the future. All domains will be in the same forest. Which Flexible Single Master Operation roles will be installed, by default, with the first domain controller and only with the first domain controller?
>
> ❑ A. PDC emulator
>
> ❑ B. Schema master
>
> ❑ C. Domain naming master
>
> ❑ D. RID master
>
> ❑ E. Infrastructure master

Answers B and C are correct. A PDC emulator and RID master will be installed with each new domain; therefore, answers A and C are incorrect.

Question 3

You're the domain administrator for a Windows Server 2003 network. You have a forest with many domains and have users who need access to resources in all the domains. You've installed many servers. Which servers will host a database of all the objects in all the domains that users can query to find resource information?

○ A. DNS servers

○ B. Global Catalog servers

○ C. All domain controllers

○ D. DHCP servers

Answer B is correct. DNS servers do not have a database that includes all the objects in all the domains; therefore, answer A is incorrect. Only domain controllers that are designated as Global Catalog servers have the required information; therefore, answers C and D are incorrect.

Question 4

You're the enterprise administrator for a large company. You have many types of DNS servers, including Windows NT, Windows 2000, and Windows Server 2003. Which statements are true regarding these servers?

❑ A. All servers can host an Active Directory–integrated zone.

❑ B. All servers can host a secondary zone to any other server.

❑ C. All servers can perform incremental zone transfer.

❑ D. Only Windows Server 2003 servers can use conditional forwarding.

Answers B and D are correct. Windows NT servers cannot host Active Directory–integrated zones; therefore, answer A is incorrect. Windows NT servers cannot perform incremental zone transfers; therefore, answer C is incorrect.

Question 5

> You're the network administrator for BFE Company. You're in charge of connecting 12 Windows XP Professional clients to the Internet. All clients are located in the same remote office. There are no other computers in the office. There is one DSL line connected to the office. You want to connect all clients to the DSL line with the least expense to BFE Company and the least administrative effort. Which service should you use?
>
> ○ A. Internet Connection Sharing
>
> ○ B. Network address translation
>
> ○ C. Proxy server
>
> ○ D. Internet authentication server

Answer A is correct. Internet Connection Sharing (ICS) is built-in to Windows XP Professional. It can be selected when establishing a new connection in network connections. Other clients can use ICS to connect through a client to the Internet. NAT services would require an additional component or a server; therefore, answer B is incorrect. Proxy server and Internet authentication server would require a server; therefore, answers C and D are incorrect.

Question 6

> You're the enterprise administrator for a new Active Directory forest. You're installing the second domain in the forest. Which two roles now need to be on separate servers? (Choose two.)
>
> ❑ A. PDC emulator
>
> ❑ B. Infrastructure master
>
> ❑ C. Domain naming master
>
> ❑ D. Global Catalog server

Answers B and D are correct. The Infrastructure Master should not be a Global Catalog server. The Infrastructure master servers keep track of the group-to-name reference for each individual domain and should only be focused on their own domain. A Global Catalog server contains all the objects in all the domains and a subset of the attributes for the objects. This combination does not work well together. Any other combination could function well on the same server; therefore, answers A and C are incorrect.

Question 7

You're the domain administrator for your company and are setting up a new domain controller. You have licenses only for Windows Server 2003 Web Edition software. How can you use Web Edition as a domain controller?

○ A. Install as Web Edition and then run DCPROMO.exe to upgrade.

○ B. You cannot use Web Edition for a domain controller.

○ C. Install the conversion package from the I386 folder.

○ D. Select Install as DC during the installation process.

Answer B is correct. Windows Server 2003 Web Edition can never be used as a domain controller; therefore, answers A, C, and D are incorrect.

Question 8

You're a member of a network design team. You're recommending an IP addressing strategy for a private network. Which of the addresses should not be used? (Choose two.)

❑ A. 192.169.0.1/16

❑ B. 10.1.1.1/8

❑ C. 172.34.1.5/16

❑ D. 192.168.255.254/16

Answers A and C are correct. Private addresses should be in one of three ranges. These include

➤ 10.0.0.0/8–10.255.255.255/8

➤ 172.16.0.0/16–172.32.255.255/16

➤ 192.168.0.0/16–192.168.255.255/16

Therefore, answers B and D are incorrect.

Question 9

You're the network administrator responsible for secure remote access services. You're considering two tunneling protocols: PPTP and L2TP. Which advantage will PPTP provide over L2TP?

- ○ A. More efficient data transfer
- ○ B. More flexibility with regard to clients
- ○ C. Tunnel authentication on each transmission
- ○ D. More flexibility with regard to protocols

Answer B is correct. The only benefit that PPTP provides is flexibility with regard to clients. L2TP is more efficient, more flexible with regard to protocols, and provides tunnel authentication with every transmission; therefore, answers A, C, and D are incorrect.

Question 10

You're the domain admin for a large sales organization. All the salespeople use laptops in and out of the office. You're responsible for setting up automatic IP addressing systems for the network. To which two components should you assign addresses automatically? (Choose two.)

- ❑ A. Laptops
- ❑ B. Remote access servers
- ❑ C. Network printers
- ❑ D. Sales support desktops

Answers A and D are correct. You should always use a static address assignment on servers; therefore, answer B is incorrect. You should always use a static address assignment on network printers; therefore answer C is incorrect.

Need to Know More?

 TechNet Windows 2003 Resources: `http://www.microsoft.com/technet/treeview/default.asp?url=/technet/prodtechnol/windows2000serv/default.asp`

 Microsoft Training and Certifications: Exams: `http://www.microsoft.com/traincert/mcpexams/default.asp`

 Microsoft Training and Certifications: View new and upcoming exams at `http://www.microsoft.com/traincert/mcpexams/status/new.asp`

 Internet Corporation for Assigned Names and Numbers: `http://www.icann.org`

Practice Exam 1

Now it's time to put to the test the knowledge you've gained from reading this book! Write down your answers to the following questions on a separate sheet of paper. You'll be able to take this sample test multiple times that way. After you answer all the questions, compare your answers with the correct answers in Chapter 8, "Answers to Practice Exam 1." The answer keys for both exams immediately follow each practice exam chapter. When you can correctly answer at least 54 of the 60 practice questions (90%) in each practice exam, you're ready to start using the PrepLogic Practice Exams CD-ROM at the back of this book. Using the practice exams for this book, along with the PrepLogic Practice Exams software, you can prepare yourself quite well for the actual 70-297 Microsoft certification exam. Good luck!

Please answer the questions following each case study based on the information provided in the case study.

Case 1: BFE, Inc.

BFE, Inc. Overview

BFE, Inc. is a medium-sized communications company that operates primarily in the Southeast. BFE's offices include a headquarters in Birmingham and small regional offices in Atlanta, Jacksonville, and Orlando.

Current LAN/Network

BFE currently has one Windows NT domain with some Windows Server 2003 member servers. Clients include Windows XP Professional, Windows 2000 Professional, Windows NT Workstation, and Windows 95. There are currently no servers in any of the regional offices. The company has 10Mbps connectivity in all LANs. There are several subnets in the headquarters office connected by routers that are not RFC 1542–compliant. Some subnets have only network printers and no clients.

Proposed LAN/Network

BFE has decided to upgrade the existing infrastructure to Windows Server 2003. Its main goals are the following:

➤ A DNS infrastructure with no zone transfer traffic.

➤ All clients must obtain IP addresses from DHCP servers.

➤ All client addresses should be registered dynamically in DHCP.

➤ Maintain name resolution support for legacy clients and applications.

➤ Reduce time for authentication of clients in regional offices.

➤ Incorporate as much of the existing infrastructure as possible into the new infrastructure.

Current WAN Connectivity

BFE has ISDN BRI connections from the headquarters location to each regional office. In addition, Birmingham and Atlanta are also linked with a full T-1.

Proposed WAN Connectivity

BFE is considering connecting all regional offices with T-1 links.

Directory Design Commentary

CIO: We have a special need for higher security in one department. We need to have a longer minimum password length for that department.

CEO: I want to be able to search quickly for any user or computer in my company from any office in my company.

Questions for Case 1

Question 1

One of the departments has a higher security risk and must therefore have a longer minimum password length requirement than any of the other departments. What should you do?

- ○ A. Set the minimum password length at each OU
- ○ B. Set up a group policy for the domain and block inheritance at the high security OU
- ○ C. Set up a separate domain for the high security department
- ○ D. Set up a group policy at domain level and use the No Override option

Question 2

Which components should you use for your new DNS structure? (Choose two.)

- ❏ A. Caching-only DNS server
- ❏ B. Standard primary zones
- ❏ C. Active Directory–integrated zones
- ❏ D. Standard secondary zones

Question 3

Where should you have DHCP relay agents?

- ○ A. All subnets.
- ○ B. All subnets except the one with that contains the DHCP server.
- ○ C. All subnets with clients set to obtain an IP address automatically, except the one that contains the DHCP server.
- ○ D. You do not need any DHCP relay agents with Windows Server 2003.

Question 4

Which services or files should be retained to provide NetBIOS name resolution for legacy clients? (Choose all that apply.)

- ❑ A. Windows NT DNS servers
- ❑ B. WINS
- ❑ C. LMHOSTS files
- ❑ D. User profiles

Question 5

Which clients can register their own A (host) records in DNS?

- ❑ A. Windows 95
- ❑ B. Windows XP Professional
- ❑ C. Windows NT Workstation
- ❑ D. Windows 2000 Professional

Question 6

Which clients can register their own PTR records in DNS?

- ○ A. Windows XP Professional and Windows 2000 Professional
- ○ B. All clients
- ○ C. Windows XP Professional
- ○ D. None of the clients

Question 7

Which statements are true with regard to your DHCP server? (Choose two.)

- ❑ A. The DHCP server can register all A records and PTR records for all clients.
- ❑ B. The DHCP server can register only PTR records for Windows XP Professional and Windows 2000 Professional clients.
- ❑ C. You can configure the DHCP server to register A records and PTR records for some clients and only PTR records for others.
- ❑ D. The DHCP server cannot register PTR records for Windows 95 clients.

Question 8

What should BFE do to increase the speed of logon authentication at the regional offices? (Choose two.)

❑ A. Install a domain controller in each regional office.

❑ B. Install T-1 links between the headquarters and all the regional offices in Jacksonville and Orlando.

❑ C. Install caching-only DNS servers at each regional office.

❑ D. Configure all clients in regional offices for NetBIOS name resolution.

Question 9

How should you enable quick searches of the Active Directory from all locations for the CEO? (Choose all that apply.)

❑ A. Install T-1 links to headquarters in Jacksonville and Orlando regional offices.

❑ B. Install a PDC emulator at each regional office.

❑ C. Use only standard primary DNS zones.

❑ D. Install domain controllers configured as global catalog servers at each regional office.

Question 10

Assuming that BFE has two domains, how many separate flexible single master operations (FSMO) roles will it have?

○ A. 2

○ B. 5

○ C. 8

○ D. 10

Question 11

Assuming that BFE installs domain controllers in each of the regional offices, how many sites should the company have?

- ○ A. 1
- ○ B. 4
- ○ C. 3
- ○ D. 2

Question 12

If the cost of the site link from Birmingham to Atlanta is set to the default, which of these costs would be appropriate for the links to the Jacksonville and Orlando offices? (Choose two.)

- ❏ A. 1000
- ❏ B. 50
- ❏ C. 25
- ❏ D. 250

Question 13

You install a new domain controller in Atlanta and configure the site links. You configure a cost of 100 for the T-1 and 1000 for the ISDN link. By default, which Birmingham to Atlanta link(s) will be used for Active Directory replication?

- ○ A. The T-1 link will be used exclusively as long as it is available.
- ○ B. Both the T-1 and the ISDN BRI link will be used at the same time.
- ○ C. The T-1 link and the ISDN BRI link will be load balanced proportionate to the bandwidth
- ○ D. Neither of the links will be used.

Question 14

Which replication protocol will be used within the headquarters site?

- ○ A. There is not enough information to know this
- ○ B. Remote Procedure Call over Internet Protocol
- ○ C. Simple Network Management Protocol
- ○ D. Transmission Control Protocol

Question 15

You want to use the existing Windows 2003 Standard Edition member server as a domain controller. Which should you do? (Choose all that apply.)

- ❑ A. Remove and reinstall the operating system, and select the Domain Controller option
- ❑ B. Back up any critical data on the server
- ❑ C. Upgrade the member server by running **adprep.exe** and **dcpromo.exe**
- ❑ D. Format the hard drive on the member server

Case 2: DataLink Corporation

Overview

DataLink Corporation is a large multinational company specializing in payroll administration, payroll tax filing, and human resources administration. DataLink has offices in the United States, Canada, Asia, and Europe. DataLink is in a growth mode and is currently researching office locations in Russia.

Current LAN/Network

DataLink has 100Mbps connectivity within all LAN locations. Headquarters is in New York City. There are regional offices in Miami, Atlanta, San Diego, Cleveland, Quebec, Hong Kong, and Lisbon. The company is currently using NT 4.0 domain controllers.

Client computers include NT workstations, Windows 95, Windows 98, Windows 2000 Professional, and Windows XP Professional. Some clients obtain an IP address automatically, whereas others have static addresses. Many salespeople use laptops to access resources from the field.

Current Domain and Management Infrastructure

DataLink currently has a separate domain for each location. All locations in the United States are managed by the same IT team. Locations outside the U.S. have their own IT management team at each location.

Current WAN Connectivity

Headquarters has a full T-1 link to all offices with the exception of the Hong Kong office, which has only an ISDN BRI link. Due to the nature of its business, DataLink transfers large files on a frequent basis and therefore requires the most available bandwidth possible. Primary and secondary DNS zones are used for fault tolerance. Zone transfer is not currently encrypted or secured.

Proposed LAN/Network

DataLink would like to upgrade all domain controllers to Windows Server 2003. The company's main goals are the following:

➤ Reduce administrative overhead where possible

➤ Eliminate nonsecure DNS zone transfer

➤ Establish and enforce group policies for all clients

➤ Provide secure remote access for sales team

➤ All clients should obtain addresses automatically

➤ All clients should register their own A (host) records

➤ All Active Directory replication should be scheduled

Directory Design Commentary

CIO: I'm not sure we need to have as many domains as we do now. I would like to examine consolidating some domains into others where possible.

CEO: We need to maintain complete autonomy in the Hong Kong office. It should be totally separate from the other offices.

CFO: Long-distance charges are through the roof because the sales team uses dial-up connections to headquarters every day. I would like to reduce these charges.

Questions for Case 2

Question 1

How many Windows Server 2003 forests should DataLink have in its new Active Directory infrastructure?

○ A. 1

○ B. 2

○ C. 3

○ D. 8

Question 2

How many Windows Server 2003 domains should DataLink have in its new Active Directory infrastructure?

- ○ A. There isn't enough information to know
- ○ B. 8
- ○ C. 2
- ○ D. 4

Question 3

Which type of namespace will be represented by the Hong Kong domain?

- ○ A. Child
- ○ B. Forest
- ○ C. Disjoint
- ○ D. Contiguous

Question 4

Which type of DNS zones should DataLink consider for its DNS infrastructure?

- ○ A. Active Directory–integrated
- ○ B. Standard primary and standard secondary
- ○ C. Stub
- ○ D. Caching-only

Question 5

You decide to create a new domain tree within the forest that contains the head-quarters domain. Which new features in Windows Server 2003 will make DNS name resolution more efficient to the disjointed namespace? (Choose two.)

- ❑ A. Incremental zone transfer
- ❑ B. Dynamic updates
- ❑ C. Stub zones
- ❑ D. Conditional forwarding

Question 6

Which clients will you be able to enforce Group Polices onto in the new infra-structure? (Choose all that apply.)

- ❑ A. Windows 98
- ❑ B. Windows 2000 Professional
- ❑ C. Windows XP Professional
- ❑ D. Windows NT Workstation

Question 7

Which Active Directory replication protocol(s) should be used between head-quarters and Hong Kong?

- ○ A. There isn't enough information to know
- ○ B. RPC over IP only
- ○ C. RPC and/or SMTP if needed
- ○ D. DLC

Question 8

Assuming that you use only the clients on which Group Policy can be enforced, which clients will be able to register their own A (host) records?

- ○ A. All clients
- ○ B. Only Windows XP Professional
- ○ C. Only Windows 2000 Professional
- ○ D. None of the clients

Question 9

Which type of remote access connectivity should the new infrastructure use?

- ○ A. SLIP
- ○ B. PPP
- ○ C. VPN
- ○ D. UDP

Question 10

Assuming a default installation, how many sites will be set up for the entire DataLink Corporation enterprise?

- ○ A. 1
- ○ B. 2
- ○ C. 8
- ○ D. There isn't enough information to know

Question 11

How many additional sites should DataLink administrators create?

- ○ A. 6
- ○ B. 8
- ○ C. 2
- ○ D. 4

Question 12

DataLink creates sites and site links for all regional offices, which connect them back to the headquarters. They accept all the defaults while creating the links. Which factor should be changed on the link connecting headquarters to Hong Kong?

- ○ A. Cost
- ○ B. Replication protocol
- ○ C. Bandwidth
- ○ D. Name

Question 13

Users in Hong Kong need to use resources in headquarters. How can this be done? (Choose all that apply.)

❑ A. Users can use the automatic two-way transitive trusts provided by Active Directory.

❑ B. Users will have to log on to the headquarters domain first.

❑ C. DataLink can set up a one-way external trust so that headquarters trusts Hong Kong.

❑ D. DataLink can upgrade the forest functional level to Windows 2003 and set up a two way transitive trust between the headquarters and Hong Kong forests.

Question 14

DataLink decides to raise the functional level of the United States domain to Windows Server 2003. Which tool(s) could the company use to raise the functional level? (Choose two.)

❑ A. Active Directory Sites and Services

❑ B. Active Directory Domains and Trusts

❑ C. Active Directory Users and Computers

❑ D. Domain Security Policy

Question 15

Which will have to be done before the forest with the headquarters location can be raised to Windows Server 2003 functional level?

○ A. All domains in the forest will have to be at Windows Server 2003 functional level.

○ B. All domain controllers in the DataLink Corporation enterprise will have to be a Windows Server 2003 functional level.

○ C. All clients will have to be upgraded to Windows XP Professional.

○ D. All member servers will have to be upgraded to Windows Server 2003.

Case 3: Layton Manufacturing Co.

Overview

Layton Manufacturing Company is a medium-size organization that operates in the northeastern United States. The company produces specialized plastics used in the automotive industry. Layton has its headquarters in Detroit and four regional plants in Milwaukee, Cleveland, Chicago, and Boston. Each plant produces the same specialized plastics using the same methods. Layton is considering further expansion to the southeast and possibly the northwest United States.

Current LAN/Network

Layton currently has a separate NT 4.0 domain for each of its offices. All IT administration is centralized to a team located in Detroit. The company has a single presence on the Internet as Layton.com.

Layton uses a single-master model and all regional office domains trust the headquarters domain. Each regional office contains the PDC for its own domain and BDCs for all five domains, including its own.

Clients include Windows 95, Windows 98, Windows NT Workstation, Windows 2000 Professional, and Windows XP Professional. All regional offices have 10Mbps connectivity. Layton headquarters has 100Mbps connectivity within it. Some clients obtain an IP address from a DHCP server, whereas others are statically configured.

Current WAN Network

Layton headquarters has full T-1 connections to all offices except Cleveland, which has an ISDN BRI connection. BDCs are configured to replicate with their PDC every night.

Proposed LAN/Network

Layton is considering upgrading the network to Windows Server 2003. The company's main goals are the following:

➤ Reduce the number of domain controllers to the minimum recommended with fault tolerance for authentication at each office.

➤ Reduce the number of domains to the minimum for their current needs.

➤ Reduce the number of trusts to a minimum.

➤ Increase security using group policies and IPSec for all possible clients.

➤ All clients should obtain IP addresses automatically.

➤ All client A (host) records should be dynamically registered in the DNS zones.

➤ All DNS zone traffic should be secure.

➤ Reduce DNS zone transfer traffic to a minimum.

➤ Maintain NetBIOS name resolution for legacy clients.

Directory Design Commentary

CIO: We need all the available bandwidth during the day. All Active Directory and WINS replication must be scheduled to take place at night.

CFO: We cannot afford, at this time, to replace any of the current client computers.

CEO: I need to be able to quickly search for any computer, printer, or user from any location in my company.

Questions for Case 3

Question 1

How many domains should Layton Manufacturing have in its new Active Directory infrastructure?

- ○ A. There isn't enough information to know
- ○ B. 1
- ○ C. 4
- ○ D. 5

Question 2

How should Layton set up its OU structure?

- ○ A. There isn't enough information to know
- ○ B. Functionally
- ○ C. Organizationally
- ○ D. Geographically

Question 3

How many domain controllers should Layton have, at a minimum, in its new Active Directory?

- ○ A. 4
- ○ B. 8
- ○ C. 10
- ○ D. 5

Question 4

How many sites should Layton's new Active Directory contain?

- ○ A. 4
- ○ B. There isn't enough information to know
- ○ C. 2
- ○ D. 5

Question 5

On which clients will Layton be able to use IPSec security policies? (Choose all that apply.)

- ❑ A. Windows NT Workstation
- ❑ B. Windows XP Professional
- ❑ C. Windows 95
- ❑ D. Windows 2000 Professional

Question 6

For which clients can Windows Server 2003 DHCP servers be configured to assign IP addresses and register A (host) records in DNS? (Choose all that apply.)

- ❑ A. Windows NT Workstation
- ❑ B. Windows 95
- ❑ C. Windows XP Professional
- ❑ D. None of the clients

Question 7

Which type(s) of zones should be used in Layton's new DNS infrastructure?

- ○ A. Standard primary and standard secondary
- ○ B. Stub
- ○ C. Active Directory–integrated
- ○ D. Caching-only

Question 8

Which replication protocol should Layton use between sites?

- ○ A. RPC over IP
- ○ B. SMTP
- ○ C. TCP
- ○ D. UDP

Question 9

You decide to add a full T-1 connection to Cleveland. You leave the ISDN BRI connection in place to be used as a backup. You configure the site link for the T-1 with a cost of 50. Which is an appropriate cost for the ISDN link to make sure it will be used only as a backup? (Choose all that apply.)

- ❏ A. The cost doesn't matter; the system will sense the bandwidth available.
- ❏ B. 51
- ❏ C. 25
- ❏ D. 10000

Question 10

How many flexible single master operations roles will the entire Layton enterprise have?

- ○ A. 25
- ○ B. 10
- ○ C. 1
- ○ D. 5

Question 11

You want to monitor Active Directory replication using a command-line tool. Which tool should you use?

- ○ A. Active Directory Users and Computers
- ○ B. Active Directory Sites and Services
- ○ C. **repadmin.exe**
- ○ D. ntdsutils

Question 12

What is the minimum number of global catalog servers required?

○ A. 5

○ B. 4

○ C. 1

○ D. 10

Question 13

Which type of replication should Layton use for WINS servers?

○ A. Push

○ B. Pull

○ C. Push/Pull

○ D. RPC

Question 14

How many trusts should be implemented in Layton's new Active Directory?

○ A. 5

○ B. 4

○ C. 1

○ D. 0

Question 15

Layton is considering purchasing a company in France. The new division of Layton Manufacturing will have IT management in France and a separate Internet presence as LaytonFrance.com. How should the new location in France be configured into Layton's Active Directory? (Choose all that apply.)

❑ A. As a new domain

❑ B. As a new forest

❑ C. As a new tree

❑ D. As a new OU

Case 4: Three Rivers Software Development Company

Overview

Three Rivers Software Development Company is a large organization with many offices in the U.S. as well as Canada, Japan, Australia, and Germany. Three Rivers produces software used specifically by pharmaceutical companies. Its products are cutting edge, so it has extensive security policies and procedures. Three Rivers is soon going to expand with new offices in London and France. Long-range plans include many more offices.

Current WAN/Network

Three Rivers currently has offices in the following locations:

➤ Pittsburgh (Headquarters)

➤ Birmingham

➤ San Diego

➤ Milwaukee

➤ Chicago

➤ Maui

➤ Tokyo

➤ Ontario

➤ Berlin

➤ Sydney

All LAN communications use at least a 10Mbps link. Some offices have 100Mbps connectivity throughout. Servers include Windows NT 4.0 domain controllers and Windows 2000 member servers. Clients include Windows 95, Windows 98, Windows 2000 Professional, Windows NT Workstation, and Windows XP Professional.

Current Domain and Management Infrastructure

Three Rivers currently has six domains. All offices in the U.S. are consolidated to one domain with one IT management team. Offices in each of the other countries have their own domain and their own IT management teams. Each office also has its own Internet presence. Each of the domains outside the U.S. trusts the U.S. domain, which contains the headquarters office. Headquarters does not currently trust any of the other domains nor do any of the other domains trust each other. The Sydney office is actually a partially owned subsidiary and must have complete autonomy from the headquarters office for legal reasons.

Current WAN/Network

Three Rivers headquarters office has full T-1 bandwidth to each of the other offices in the Unite States. In addition, it has full E-1 bandwidth to the office in Berlin. Each of the other offices outside the U.S. has ISDN BRI connectivity to the Pittsburgh (headquarters) office, with the exception of Sydney, which has only a 56K demand-dial connection. This link can be very unreliable at times.

Proposed WAN/Network

Three Rivers is considering upgrading its network to Windows Server 2003. The main goals are the following:

➤ Reduce the number of domains, if possible.

➤ Establish and maintain trust relationships between all domains.

➤ Eliminate WINS servers from the network, if possible.

➤ All DNS zone transfers should be secured and encrypted.

➤ Group policies should be enforced on all computers in the San Diego office and all possible computers in the other offices.

➤ All Active Directory replication within the United States should be scheduled.

➤ All clients should obtain addresses from DHCP servers.

➤ All client A (host) records should be dynamically registered.

Directory Design Commentary

CIO: We need to have the most secure remote access possible, regardless of the cost. Also, our headquarters office will use a minimum password length of eight characters, regardless of what the other U.S. offices use.

CFO: We cannot afford to upgrade all client computers at this time.

Security Officer: The San Diego office is a very high security installation. We must have a minimum password length of 12 characters instead of the 8-character minimum that headquarters uses. The clients must use IPSec for all communications.

Questions for Case 4

Question 1

How many domains should Three Rivers' new Active Directory infrastructure contain?

○ A. 5

○ B. 6

○ C. 2

○ D. There isn't enough information to determine

Question 2

How should the top-level organizational units in the domain that contains the headquarters be structured?

- ○ A. By function
- ○ B. By the organizational chart
- ○ C. By geographical location
- ○ D. By available bandwidth

Question 3

How should the Sydney office be represented in the new Active Directory infrastructure? (Choose all that apply.)

- ❑ A. As a separate domain
- ❑ B. As a separate tree
- ❑ C. As a separate forest
- ❑ D. As a separate OU

Question 4

How many new trusts will you need to create after upgrading all domain controllers in all domains to Windows Server 2003?

- ○ A. 5
- ○ B. 6
- ○ C. 12
- ○ D. 1

Question 5

If all offices currently have a mixture of legacy clients and newer clients, which office should be first to have all Windows 2000 Professional and/or Windows XP Professional clients?

- ○ A. Headquarters
- ○ B. Sydney
- ○ C. San Diego
- ○ D. There isn't enough information to determine

Question 6

Which type of DNS zones should be used in Three Rivers' new DNS infrastructure?

- ○ A. Active Directory–integrated
- ○ B. Standard primary and standard secondary
- ○ C. Stub
- ○ D. Caching-only

Question 7

Which Active Directory protocol should Three Rivers use for all offices in the United States?

- ○ A. RPC over IP
- ○ B. SMTP
- ○ C. TCP
- ○ D. UDP

Question 8

How should Active Directory replication be configured from Sydney to the other domains in the Three Rivers organization?

- ○ A. SMTP
- ○ B. RPC over IP
- ○ C. FTP
- ○ D. No replication is needed

Question 9

Which of Three Rivers' clients can dynamically register its own A (host) records in DNS? (Choose all that apply.)

- ❑ A. Windows 95
- ❑ B. Windows 2000 Professional
- ❑ C. Windows NT
- ❑ D. Windows XP Professional

Question 10

You decide to install a full T-1 from headquarters to the offices in Ontario to allow for more bandwidth for Active Directory replication. If the site link cost for the 56K link is still set to the default, which setting(s) would be acceptable for the T-1 line?

- ❑ A. 1
- ❑ B. 1000
- ❑ C. 10
- ❑ D. 100

Question 11

Three Rivers is considering purchasing new laptops. Which operating system should the new laptops use?

- ○ A. Windows XP Home Edition
- ○ B. Windows 98
- ○ C. Windows NT Workstation
- ○ D. Windows XP Professional

Question 12

You've decided to use an application that requires an efficient DNS reverse lookup zone. Which client can dynamically update its own PTR records in the DNS zone?

- ❑ A. None of the clients
- ❑ B. Windows XP Professional
- ❑ C. Windows 2000 Professional
- ❑ D. Windows NT Workstation

Question 13

Which clients will need to be upgraded to move toward eliminating WINS servers? (Choose two.)

❑ A. Windows 2000 Professional

❑ B. Windows 98

❑ C. Windows NT Workstation with Service Pack 6

❑ D. Windows XP Professional

Question 14

How many flexible single master operations (FSMO) roles will Three Rivers' entire organization contain?

○ A. 20

○ B. 17

○ C. 10

○ D. 22

Question 15

Three Rivers has implemented universal groups and applications that make frequent use of the global catalog. How many new global catalog servers should Three Rivers add, assuming that all domain controllers in the organization are still set to their default settings?

○ A. 1

○ B. 8

○ C. 5

○ D. 6

Answers to Practice Exam 1

Case 1: BFE, Inc.

1. C
2. A, C
3. C
4. B, C
5. B, D
6. D
7. A, C
8. A, B
9. A, D
10. C
11. B
12. A, D
13. A
14. B
15. B, C

Case 2: DataLink Corp.

1. B
2. D
3. B
4. A
5. C, D
6. B, C
7. B
8. A
9. C
10. B
11. A
12. A
13. C, D
14. B, C
15. A

Case 3: Layton Manufacturing Company

1. B
2. D
3. C
4. D
5. B, D
6. A, B, C
7. C
8. A
9. B, D
10. D
11. C
12. A
13. B
14. D
15. A, C

Case 4: Three Rivers Software Development Company

1. B	**6.** A	**11.** D
2. C	**7.** A	**12.** A
3. A, C	**8.** D	**13.** B, C
4. D	**9.** B, D	**14.** D
5. C	**10.** A, C	**15.** B

All answers for this chapter refer to the case studies in Chapter 7.

Case 1: BFE, Inc.

Question 1

The correct answer is C. Because account policies such as minimum password length are set at the domain level only, different policies require separate domains. Account policies set at the OU level are ignored when the user is logged on to the domain; therefore, answers A and B are incorrect. There can be only one account policy at the domain level; therefore, answer D is incorrect.

Question 2

The correct answers are A and C. Windows NT servers could be used for caching-only servers. Active Directory–integrated zones do not create zone transfer traffic because updates are sent with normal Active Directory replication. Standard primary zones and standard secondary zones create zone transfer traffic; therefore, answers B and D are incorrect.

Question 3

The correct answer is C. You need to have a DHCP relay agent in every subnet that has clients that are set to obtain an IP address automatically and that do not have a DHCP server in them. You do not need to have a DHCP relay agent in all subnets; therefore, answer A is incorrect. You do not need to have a DHCP relay agent in the subnets that have only network printers and no clients; therefore, answer B is incorrect. However, you must have some relay agents; therefore, answer D is incorrect.

Question 4

The correct answers are B and C. You must maintain the services of WINS and the LMHOSTS files as long as there are still legacy clients and/or applications that use NetBIOS name resolution. Windows NT DNS servers do not resolve NetBIOS names; therefore, answer A is incorrect. User profiles do not resolve NetBIOS names; therefore, answer D is incorrect.

Question 5

The correct answers are B and D. Only Windows 2000 and later clients can register their A records in DNS. Windows NT Workstation and Windows 95 clients cannot register their A records; therefore, answers A and C are incorrect.

Question 6

The correct answer is D. None of the clients can dynamically register its own PTR record in DNS. Only the DHCP server can register the PTR records dynamically; therefore, answers A, B, and C are incorrect.

Question 7

Answers A and C are correct. The DHCP server can be configured to dynamically register A records and PTR records for all clients or to register only records that clients request. In that case, Windows XP Professional and Windows 2000 Professional clients would request that their PTR records be registered but could register their own A records. The DHCP server can register PTR records for all clients; therefore, answers B and C are incorrect.

Question 8

Answers A and B are correct. Connectivity to the domain controllers is the key issue to speed up logon authentication. Installing domain controllers locally at each regional office or improving the connectivity between the offices would accomplish this goal. Caching-only DNS servers would not improve logon speed; therefore, answer C is incorrect. NetBIOS name resolution would not improve logon authentication in a Windows Server 2003 domain; therefore, answer D is incorrect.

Question 9

Answers A and D are correct. Because BFE, Inc. will have two domains, the key issue is a fast link to a global catalog server that contains all the objects in both domains. This can be accomplished by installing the T-1 links or by installing global catalog servers at each regional office. The PDC Emulator does not provide search capability; therefore, answer B is incorrect. Using only standard primary zones would not affect searches; therefore, answer C is incorrect.

Question 10

The correct answer is C. The flexible single master operations (FSMO) roles of Schema Master and Domain Naming Master are only one per forest. The PDC Emulator, RID Master, and Infrastructure Master roles are one per domain. As a result, there would be $(1×2) + (2×3) = 8$ FSMO roles. Therefore, answers A, B, and D are incorrect.

Question 11

The correct answer is B. They should have a separate site for headquarters and each regional office. Even the T-1 link from Birmingham to Atlanta is slow compared to the 10Mbps connectivity within each office. Each office connected to the other offices by a comparatively slow link (compared to LAN speed) should be a site; therefore, answers A, C, and D are incorrect.

Question 12

The correct answers are A and D. The cost for the link is inversely proportional to the bandwidth. The default cost of any link, including the link from Birmingham to Atlanta, is 100. In this case, 100 represents T-1 bandwidth of 1.544 Mbps. The ISDN BRI links are only 128Kbps (.128Mbps), so they should have a cost higher than 100; therefore, answers B and C are incorrect.

Question 13

The correct answer is A. The T-1 link has the lowest cost. Active Directory will use the link with the lowest cost for replication as long as it is available. In this case, the ISDN would be used only if the T-1 has failed. The links would not be shared; therefore, answer B is incorrect. The links would not be load balanced; therefore, answer C is incorrect. The lowest cost link will be used; therefore, answer D is incorrect.

Question 14

The correct answer is B. Remote Procedure Call over Internet Protocol (RPC over IP) will be used. Active Directory replication within sites (intra-site replication) always uses RPC over IP; therefore, answer A is incorrect because there is enough information to know this. Simple Mail Transport protocol is sometimes (although rarely) used between sites, but never within sites; therefore, answer C is incorrect. Transmission Control Protocol (TCP) is not a replication protocol; therefore, answer D is incorrect.

Question 15

The correct answers are B and C. A Windows Server 2003 Standard Edition member server can be converted to a domain controller, but you should always back up critical information before making any change to a server's configuration. You should run adprep.exe to prepare the domain for a Windows Server 2003 domain controller and then run dcpromo.exe on the member server to promote it to a Windows Server 2003 domain controller. There is no need to reinstall the operating system; therefore, answer A is incorrect. There is no need to format the hard drive on the member server; therefore, answer D is incorrect.

Case 2: DataLink Corp.

Question 1

The correct answer is B. They should have two forests. The Hong Kong location requires complete autonomy, so it must be a separate forest; therefore, answer A is incorrect. There is no need for three forests; therefore, answer C is incorrect. Each location (of 8 locations) does not need to be a forest; therefore, answer D is incorrect.

Question 2

The correct answer is D. All the offices in the U.S. should be combined into one domain. The other domains will be Quebec, Hong Kong, and Lisbon. Hong Kong will be a separate forest as well as a separate domain. There is enough information to know; therefore, answer A is incorrect. They do not need a separate domain for each location; therefore, answer B is incorrect. They should have one domain for each separate foreign location because they are managed by different IT teams and in different countries; therefore, answer C is incorrect.

Question 3

The correct answer is B. The Hong Kong database will represent a separate forest. A separate forest is not a child of an existing forest; therefore, answer A is incorrect. A disjointed namespace is part of the same forest, but in a different tree; therefore, answer C is incorrect. A contiguous namespace is part of the same tree in a forest; therefore, answer D is incorrect.

Question 4

The correct answer is A. Only Active Directory–integrated zones should be used. Standard primary and standard secondary zones create zone transfer and are not secure; therefore, answer B is incorrect. Stub zones have some zone transfer when their primary is changed; therefore, answer C is incorrect. Caching-only is not a type of zone, it is a type of server that does not host a zone; therefore, answer D is incorrect.

Question 5

The correct answers are C and D. These features, which are new to Windows Server 2003, will make name resolution more efficient with disjointed namespaces. Incremental zone transfers were introduced with Windows 2000 Server; therefore, answer A is incorrect. Dynamic updates were introduced with Windows 2000 Server; therefore, answer B is incorrect.

Question 6

The correct answers are B and C. These are the only clients on which you can enforce group policies. Windows 98 and Windows NT Workstation clients can exist in a Windows Server 2003 domain, but cannot use group policies; therefore, answers A and D are incorrect.

Question 7

The correct answer is B. RPC is the only protocol that should be used. There is enough information to know; therefore, answer A is incorrect. RPC over IP is the only Active Directory replication protocol that follows a schedule—SMTP ignores schedules; therefore, answer C is incorrect. DLC is not an Active Directory replication protocol; therefore, answer D is incorrect.

Question 8

The correct answer is A. All clients used will be able to register their own A (host) records. Windows 2000 Professional and Windows XP Professional clients can, by default, register their own A (host) records; therefore, answers B, C, and D are incorrect.

Question 9

The correct answer is C. This will help reduce long distance charges. SLIP (Serial Line Interface Protocol) is a legacy dial-up protocol that has been replaced by PPP. It is not supported on Windows Server 2003; therefore, answer A is incorrect. PPP (Point-to-Point Protocol) is a dial-up protocol and would still cause the sales team to incur long-distance expenses; therefore, answer B is incorrect. UDP (User Datagram Protocol) is not a remote access protocol; therefore, answer D is incorrect.

Question 10

The correct answer is B. One Default-First-Site-Name site will be set up, by default, for each Active Directory forest. There will be a Default-First-Site-Name for each of the two forests; therefore, answer A is incorrect. By default, there will not be a site for each location; therefore, answer C is incorrect. There is enough information to know; therefore, answer D is incorrect.

Question 11

The correct answer is A. Administrators should rename the Default-First-Site-Name sites and then create six more sites. The two sites that are created by default should not be deleted and should be renamed and used; therefore, answer B is incorrect. A site is required for each separate geographical area connected with the T-1 link; therefore, answers C and D are incorrect.

Question 12

The correct answer is A. The default cost of 100 should be increased. There are only two replication protocols from which to choose. Of these two, RPC over IP is the only protocol that follows a schedule; therefore, answer B is incorrect. You can set bandwidth on a site link; therefore, answer C is incorrect. The default name of the link will be DefaultIPSiteLink. This can be changed, but there is no need to do so because it is the only link for Hong Kong; therefore, answer D is incorrect.

Question 13

The correct answers are C and D. There are no automatic two-way transitive trusts between forests; therefore, answer A is incorrect. Users will not have to log on to the headquarters domain after the correct trusts are in place; therefore, answer B is incorrect.

Question 14

The correct answers are B and C. Active Directory Sites and Services cannot be used to raise the functional level of the domain; therefore, answer A is incorrect. The Domain Security tool cannot be used to raise the functional level of the domain; therefore, answer D is incorrect.

Question 15

The correct answer is A. Domain controllers in the Hong Kong forest have no effect on the ability to raise the functional level in the other forest with headquarters; therefore, answer B is incorrect. Clients and member servers have no effect on raising the functional level; therefore, answers C and D are incorrect.

Case 3: Layton Manufacturing Company

Question 1

The correct answer is B. Layton should have one domain. Because Layton is a medium-size business with all IT centralized to one location, has only one Internet presence, and because there are no other political reasons to have more than one domain, we know that Layton should have only one domain; therefore, answer A is incorrect. Layton only needs one domain; therefore, answers C and D are incorrect.

Question 2

The correct answer is D. The OUs should be set up by location. Because each of the plants performs the same functions, and because Layton is considering further expansion to other locations (not products), the organizational units should be set up by location; therefore, answer A is incorrect. Layton has simple functionality and we have no specific information about any other functions within headquarters or the plants; therefore, answer B is incorrect. We have no specific information about the organization and there is no mention of the company organization growing or expanding; therefore, answer C is incorrect.

Question 3

The correct answer is C. Layton should have at least two domain controllers in each site to provide the required fault tolerance at each office. Fault tolerance at each site requires that at least 10 domain controllers are used; therefore, answers A, B, and D are incorrect.

Question 4

The correct answer is D. Layton should have five sites: one for headquarters and one for each of the plants. Because all the offices are geographically separate and will be using comparatively slow links (compared to LAN speed), they should all be separate sites; therefore, answers A, B, and C are incorrect.

Question 5

The correct answers are B and D. Windows NT Workstation and older OS cannot use IPSec; therefore, answer A is incorrect. Windows 2000 Professional and newer clients can use IPSec; therefore, answer C is incorrect.

Question 6

The correct answers are A, B, and C. Windows Server 2003 DHCP servers can be configured to assign IP addresses to and register A (host) records for all of Layton's clients; therefore, answer D is incorrect.

Question 7

The correct answer is C. Only Active Directory–integrated zones should be used. One of Layton's requirements is that all DNS zone traffic must be secure. Standard primary and standard secondary zone transfer is not secure; therefore, answer A is incorrect. Stub zone transfer is not secure; therefore, answer B is incorrect. Caching-only is a type of server, not a type of zone; therefore, answer D is incorrect.

Question 8

The correct answer is A. Layton has only one domain and requires that all Active Directory replication be scheduled to run only at night. The SMTP replication protocol ignores schedules and can be used only between domain controllers in different domains; therefore, answer B is incorrect. TCP (Transmission Control Protocol) is not a replication protocol; therefore, answer C is incorrect. UDP (User Datagram Protocol) is not a replication protocol; therefore, answer D is incorrect.

Question 9

The correct answers are B and D. Any cost over 50 is appropriate. The system cannot sense the bandwidth available; therefore, answer A is incorrect. A cost of 25 on the ISDN link would make the system prefer the ISDN link and use the T-1 as a backup; therefore, answer C is incorrect.

Question 10

The correct answer is D. The number of flexible single master operations (FSMO) roles is based solely on the number of domains. In this case, one domain equals five FSMO roles; therefore, answers A, B, and C are incorrect.

Question 11

The correct answer is C. Active Directory Users and Computers is a GUI-based tool that is used to create and manage objects in the Active Directory; therefore, answer A is incorrect. Active Directory Sites and Services is a GUI-based tool that is used to manage Active Directory replication; therefore, answer B is incorrect. Ntdsutils is a command-line tool that is used to manage Active Directory; therefore, answer D is incorrect.

Question 12

The correct answer is A. To facilitate quick searches of the Active Directory from any office, you need to have a global catalog server at headquarters and at each of the four plants; therefore, answers B, C, and D are incorrect.

Question 13

The correct answer is B. Because all replication must be at night, WINS servers must be set to pull at night. Push replication happens after a defined number of changes to a database, which could happen during the day; therefore, answer A is incorrect. Push/pull would ensure that some replication happens on an interval, but would also allow replication after a defined number of changes; therefore, answer C is incorrect. RPC (Remote Procedure Call) is not a type of WINS replication; therefore, answer D is incorrect.

Question 14

The correct answer is D. Trusts are established between domains, not sites. Because Layton's new Active Directory should contain only one domain, there will be no need for trusts; therefore, answers A, B, and C are incorrect.

Question 15

The correct answers are A and C. LaytonFrance.com should be a new domain and a new tree in the existing forest. Because LaytonFrance.com will be owned by Layton Manufacturing, it should be in the same forest unless there is some political or legal consideration that requires complete autonomy; therefore, answer B is incorrect. Because LaytonFrance.com will have a separate Internet presence, it must be a new domain and not just a new OU; therefore, answer D is incorrect.

Case 4: Three Rivers Software Development Company

Question 1

The correct answer is B. Three Rivers will need to have two US domains because the San Diego office must have a 12-character minimum password requirement. In addition, because all the offices are in different countries with different languages and laws, and are managed by separate IT teams, they should be separate domains as well; therefore, answers A, C, and D are incorrect.

Question 2

The correct answer is C. Because all the logical information given is in relation to geographical locations, the parent organizational units should be arranged by location. This will also allow for the additional projected growth. There is no information available in regard to functions of Three Rivers; therefore, answer A is incorrect. The organizational chart should never be used as a guide to setting up an Active Directory; therefore, answer B is incorrect. Available bandwidth is a physical concern and would not be a consideration in regard to organizational units; therefore, answer D is incorrect.

Question 3

The correct answers are A and C. The Sydney office must have complete autonomy from the rest of the Three Rivers domains. The only way this is possible is for Sydney to be a separate domain in a separate forest. A separate tree in the same forest would have the same enterprise admins and schema admins, so it would not have complete autonomy; therefore, answer B is incorrect. A separate OU would be in the same domain structure and would not provide autonomy; therefore, answer D is incorrect.

Question 4

The correct answer is D. All the domains in the headquarters forest will, by default, have two-way transitive trust relationships with all the other domains. Because all the domain controllers will be Windows Server 2003, you can raise the functional level to Windows Server 2003 and create one forest trust that allows the Sydney forest to trust the headquarters forest and the headquarters forest to trust the Sydney forest. This single additional trust will meet the requirement that all domains have trust relationships; therefore, answers A, B, and C are incorrect.

Question 5

The correct answer is C. San Diego should be the first office to have all Windows 2000 Professional and/or Windows XP Professional clients. The San Diego office should be first because it is required to use group policies and IPSec. Clients prior to Windows 2000 Professional cannot support these features. Headquarters and Sydney are not required to use group policies or IPSec; therefore, answers A and B are incorrect. We have the information to know that San Diego needs the upgraded clients now; therefore, answer D is incorrect.

Question 6

The correct answer is A. Only Active Directory–integrated zones should be used. One of Three Rivers' requirements is that all DNS zone transfers must be encrypted and secured. Standard primary and standard secondary zone transfer can be encrypted but cannot be secured; therefore, answer B is incorrect. Stub zones require zone transfer for the few records they contain. This zone transfer cannot be secured; therefore, answer C is incorrect. Caching-only is a type of server that does not host any zones, not a type of zone; therefore, answer D is incorrect.

Question 7

The correct answer is A. Only RPC over IP should be used. One of Three Rivers' requirements is that all replication must be scheduled. SMTP replication ignores schedules; therefore, answer B is incorrect. TCP (Transmission Control Protocol) and UDP (User Datagram Protocol) are transport protocols and not replication protocols; therefore, answers C and D are incorrect.

Question 8

The correct answer is D. No replication is needed because Sydney will be a totally separate forest. SMTP (Simple Mail Transport Protocol) is used between domain controllers that are in different domains and sites but in the same forest; therefore, answer A is incorrect. RPC over IP is used within domains or between domains that are in the same forest; therefore, answer B is incorrect. FTP (File Transfer Protocol) is not an Active Directory replication protocol; therefore, answer C is incorrect.

Question 9

The correct answers are B and D. Windows 95 clients cannot register their own A (host) records in DNS; therefore, answer A is incorrect. Windows NT Workstation clients cannot register their own A (host) records in DNS; therefore, answer C is incorrect.

Question 10

The correct answers are A and C. The default cost of all links is 100, so the default for the 56K line will have been 100. The T-1 must be set for a cost less than 100 so it will be the preferred link; therefore, answers B and D are incorrect.

Question 11

The correct answer is D. Because the CIO requires the most secure remote access available, the new laptops should either use the Windows XP Professional operating system or the Windows 2000 Professional operating system so that they can use the new security features of L2TP with IPSec and be controlled by group policies; therefore, answers A, B, and C are incorrect.

Question 12

The correct answer is A. No client can update its own PTR record in the DNS zone. However, the DHCP server can update PTR records for all clients; therefore, answers B, C, and D are incorrect.

Question 13

The correct answers are B and C. Clients prior to Windows 2000 Professional (legacy clients) have to be upgraded. In addition, all legacy applications that use NetBIOS name resolution also have to be upgraded or replaced. Clients prior to Windows 2000 Professional use NetBIOS name resolution and therefore need WINS. Windows 2000 Professional and Windows XP Professional clients can instead use SRV records in DNS servers; therefore, answers A and D are incorrect.

Question 14

The correct answer is D. Each forest contains two flexible single operations (FSMO) roles: Schema Master and Domain Naming Master. Each domain contains three FSMO roles: PDC Emulator, RID Master, and Infrastructure Master. Three Rivers' organization has two forests and six domains total. The formula would then be (2×2)+(6×3)= 4 + 18 = 22; therefore, answers A, B, and C are incorrect.

Question 15

The correct answer is B. The first domain controller in each new forest is the only domain controller that becomes a global catalog (GC) server by default. All other domain controllers can be configured by the administrator to be a GC. In an Active Directory that uses universal groups and other applications that make frequent use of GCs, each site should contain its own GC. Three Rivers has 10 sites, but only the two sites with the forest root domains contain GCs by default. They will need to add a GC to each site that does not contain a GC, for a total of 8 new GCs; therefore, answers A, C, and D are incorrect.

Practice Exam 2

Please answer the questions following each case study based on the information provided.

Case 1: HW, Inc.

HW, Inc. Overview

HW, Inc. is a small company that designs women's apparel. The head office is located in Boston. In the past few years, the company's clothing line has taken off and warehouses/stores have been opened in Phoenix, Manhattan, Tampa, and San Francisco.

Current LAN/WAN Network

All locations have a T3 connection to the head office in Boston. Each location, including Boston, is currently using Windows NT 4.0 domain controllers. HW, Inc. consists of a single Windows NT 4.0 domain. Locations are connected to the head office using routers that are not 1542-compliant.

Most workstations are running Windows 2000 Professional. Some workstations in the head office are still running Windows 95. IP addresses are statically assigned by each local administrator.

There is a central IT group within the head office that oversees most administration. Each location has a network administrator responsible for performing day-to-day tasks.

Proposed LAN/WAN Network

HW, Inc. would like to upgrade all its domain controllers to Windows Server 2003. The company would also like to achieve the following:

➤ Reduce the administration associated with IP addressing

➤ Reduce the administration associated with running DNS on the network

➤ Allow for name resolution for all hosts

➤ Enforce company-wide security settings

➤ Implement secure remote access for members of the Sales group

Active Directory Design Commentary

CEO: We need to maintain complete autonomy over the different locations.

IT Manager: Local administrators are responsible for performing day-to-day administrative tasks. However, I would like to further limit their scope of authority so that they are capable of administering only their own location.

Owner: Due to the increased demand for Internet sales, we'd like to consider establishing an Internet presence in the future. We've registered the HWInc.com domain name and would like to use it internally.

Questions for Case 1

Question 1

How many domains should be created for HW, Inc?

○ A. 1

○ B. 2

○ C. 4

○ D. 5

Question 2

How many top-level OUs should be created?

○ A. 2

○ B. 3

○ C. 4

○ D. 5

Question 3

Based on the WAN connectivity currently in place, how many Global Catalog servers are required?

○ A. 1

○ B. 2

○ C. 3

○ D. 4

Question 4

When designing the DNS infrastructure, what type of zones should be configured?

○ A. Primary

○ B. Secondary

○ C. Active Directory–integrated

○ D. Stub

Question 5

You're planning the Active Directory sites for the new infrastructure. If multiple sites are configured, which replication protocol should be used when configuring the site links?

- ○ A. SMTP
- ○ B. FTP
- ○ C. RPC over IP
- ○ D. Kerberos

Question 6

The IT manager wants to use dynamic update to reduce administration of zone files. What must be done to update A records for Windows 95 clients?

- ○ A. Install the Active Directory client
- ○ B. Enable the DHCP server to perform updates on their behalf
- ○ C. Configure the Windows 95 clients to update their own A records
- ○ D. Enable secure updates on the DNS server

Question 7

What type of OU infrastructure should be created?

- ○ A. Functional
- ○ B. Geographical
- ○ C. Organizational
- ○ D. Role-based

Question 8

Which of the following offers an IP address solution for HW, Inc.?

- ❑ A. Install DHCP servers within each office location
- ❑ B. Install a single DHCP server and configure a relay agent within each location.
- ❑ C. Install a single DHCP server within the head office
- ❑ D. Configure each workstation to automatically obtain an IP address and use APIPA

Question 9

A DNS server is installed on the network. Some users report that they cannot access network resources. During your investigation, you discover that the problem is affecting only Windows 95 clients. What should you do?

- ○ A. Configure the Windows 95 clients with the IP address of the DNS server
- ○ B. Configure a HOSTS file on each Windows 95 workstation
- ○ C. Install a WINS server on the network
- ○ D. Enable dynamic updates on the DNS server

Question 10

HW, Inc. has recently purchased another clothing company. The company already has its own Internet presence that needs to be maintained. The company currently uses the same internal and external namespace and would like to continue to do so. What should you do?

- ○ A. Create a new forest for the company
- ○ B. Create a child domain under the HWInc.com root domain
- ○ C. Create a new tree within the existing forest
- ○ D. Configure an OU for the new company within the HWInc.com domain

Question 11

A domain-wide group policy is being configured. The IT manager is concerned that local administrators might be able to configure policies at the OU level that could affect the settings of the domain-wide policy. What should you do?

- ○ A. Enable the Block Inheritance option on each OU.
- ○ B. Remove the Apply Group Policy permission for the local administrators.
- ○ C. Enable the No Override option for the domain-wide policy.
- ○ D. Nothing. Policies are not inherited from parent to child container.

Question 12

What feature can the IT manager use to ensure that the local administrator within each site is limited to administering local users and resources?

○ A. Inheritance

○ B. Group Policy

○ C. Delegation of authority

○ D. Organizational units

Question 13

HW, Inc. has recently partnered with a men's clothing line. Each company will maintain its own Active Directory forest. What must be done for users within the HWInc.com domain to access resources within the other forest?

○ A. Configure shortcut trusts between the forest root domains.

○ B. Nothing. Two-way transitive trusts are automatically established between forest root domains.

○ C. Configure a two-way external trust.

○ D. Configure a one-way external trust.

Question 14

Which of the following DNS names should you choose for the forest root?

○ A. boston.hwinc.com

○ B. hwinc.net

○ C. hwinc.com

○ D. boston.hwinc.net

Question 15

During the migration process, users will still need access to resources in the Windows NT 4.0 domain. How can this be supported?

○ A. Configure a two-way transitive trust.

○ B. Configure a shortcut trust.

○ C. Nothing. Two-way transitive trusts are automatically created.

○ D. Configure a one-way nontransitive NTLM trust.

Case 2: FKB Consulting

FKB Consulting Overview

FKB Consulting is a large firm that provides consulting services in several different areas. The company consists of the following divisions: Consulting, Sales, Finance, Accounting, and Managers.

FKB Consulting has a corporate head office located in New York. Several branch offices are located throughout the United States. The company also has a small presence in Canada.

FKB Consulting has recently partnered with another firm, DKB consulting. Each company has its own presence that needs to be maintained.

LAN/WAN Structure

The existing infrastructure is to be upgraded from Windows NT to Windows Server 2003. Two domain controllers are running Windows NT Server 4.0. Workstations are running various operating systems, from Windows 95 to Windows XP. There are no plans yet to upgrade the workstations. There are already two DNS servers on the network running BIND 8.2.2. There are no plans to upgrade them.

The locations within the United States are connected using DSL connections. The small office located in Canada is connected to the head office using a 56kbps frame relay connection that is already heavily utilized. The company is currently looking into upgrading this connection. However, there are no immediate plans to move ahead with this.

Current Domain/Management Structure

The existing infrastructure consists of five separate domains—one for each department. Each domain has its own IT group.

Proposed LAN Structure

The company plans to upgrade all domain controllers to Windows Server 2003. The BIND DNS servers will remain on the network with no plans to upgrade them.

The company would like to reduce the number of domains in the current infrastructure. Resources must be shared between the two companies.

DNS zone transfers should be secure.

The administrators should be able to configure which users can dynamically update the zone file.

Legacy clients must be able to resolve hostnames.

Directory Design Commentary

CEO: The link between the Canada office and the head office is heavily saturated. Users in this location need all the available bandwidth.

CFO: Server hardware will be upgraded to meet the hardware requirements for Windows Server 2003. This year's budget does not allow for workstations running legacy operating systems to be upgraded.

IT Manager: Each domain currently has its own administrator. I'd like to enable them to continue to administer their own department, and at the same time have the ability to limit the scope of their administration. A standard password policy and audit policy should be configured for the entire organization.

Questions for Case 2

Question 1

How many forests will be created for the company?

◯ A. 1

◯ B. 2

◯ C. 3

◯ D. 4

Question 2

How many domains will be created in the new infrastructure?

◯ A. 1

◯ B. 2

◯ C. 4

◯ D. 5

Question 3

How many sites will be created in the new infrastructure?

◯ A. 1

◯ B. 2

◯ C. 4

◯ D. 5

Question 4

FKB currently has BIND 8.2.2 DNS servers. Can these DNS servers support the new Active Directory infrastructure?

○ A. No. Windows Server 2003 DNS must be used.

○ B. No. BIND 8.2.2 only supports SRV records.

○ C. Yes. All versions of BIND support SRV records and dynamic updates.

○ D. Yes. BIND 8.2.2 supports SRV records and dynamic updates.

Question 5

DKB Consulting has its own DNS infrastructure. The company plans to upgrade its DNS servers to Windows Server 2003. What type of zone should be configured to allow administrators to control which users can update the zone file?

○ A. Primary

○ B. Secondary

○ C. Stub

○ D. Active Directory–integrated

Question 6

Traffic needs to be controlled over the frame relay connection. Which of the following options would work best?

○ A. Use RPC over IP as the replication protocol and configure a link cost

○ B. Use SMTP as the replication protocol and configure a replication schedule

○ C. Use RPC over IP as the replication protocol and configure a replication schedule

○ D. Use SMTP as the replication protocol

Question 7

How many top-level organizational units should be configured?

○ A. 2

○ B. 4

○ C. 5

○ D. 6

Question 8

What must be done before the domain controllers can be upgraded to Windows Server 2003?

○ A. Upgrade the Windows NT Server 4.0 directly to Windows Server 2003

○ B. Install the latest service pack on the domain controllers

○ C. Upgrade the domain controllers to Windows 2000

○ D. Perform a clean installation of Windows Server 2003 because there is no upgrade path

Question 9

How many Global Catalog servers should be implemented?

○ A. 1

○ B. 2

○ C. 4

○ D. 5

Question 10

A research and development department is being added. Users in this department are responsible for creating, testing, and modifying company software. The applications installed will make several modifications to the schema. The IT manager does not want all users to be affected by the modifications. What should you do?

○ A. Create a child domain for the new department

○ B. Create a new organizational unit for the department

○ C. Create a new forest for the department

○ D. Create a new root domain within the existing forest for the new department

Question 11

Which of the following platforms can update their own host records with the DNS servers?

❑ A.   Windows 95

❑ B.   Windows NT Workstation 4.0

❑ C.   Windows 2000

❑ D.   Windows XP

Question 12

The company needs to support clients that use NetBIOS names for locating network services. Which of the following solutions can be used?

❑ A.   DNS

❑ B.   WINS

❑ C.   HOSTS

❑ D.   LMHOSTS

Question 13

The IT manager wants to implement group policies throughout the company. Place the following in the order that group policies are applied

        Local

        Computer

        Domain

        Site

        User

        Organizational Unit

1. _____

2. _____

3. _____

4. _____

5. _____

Question 14

The administrator for the Sales OU is configuring a GPO for software distribution. However, the IT group should not be affected by the policy settings. What technique can be used to solve this problem?

○ A. Use filtering with security groups

○ B. Use the No Override option

○ C. Use the Block Inheritance option

○ D. Rearrange the OU structure so that it is based on groups rather than departments

Question 15

Don is a member of the Research and Development department. He's trying to update the Active Directory schema but is receiving an error message. What could be causing the problem?

○ A. Don is not logged on locally to the schema master.

○ B. Don is not a member of the Schema Admins group.

○ C. Don is not a member of the Enterprise Admins group.

○ D. The default schema cannot be changed.

Case 3: Good Nature, Inc.

Good Nature, Inc. Overview

Good Nature, Inc. is a large manufacturer of bath and body products. The head office is located in Minneapolis, Minnesota. Regional offices are located in Los Angeles, Phoenix, Tampa, and Chicago.

The head office currently has the following departments:

➤ Accounting

➤ Human Resources

➤ IT

➤ Manufacturing

➤ Advertising

➤ Sales

➤ Marketing

Each regional office has the following departments:

➤ IT

➤ Manufacturing

➤ Sales

➤ Marketing

Good Nature has recently acquired a chain of day spas. The two companies must maintain a separate Internet presence but still be able to share resources.

Current LAN/WAN Structure

Workstations are running a variety of platforms, including Windows 95, Windows 98, Windows NT Workstation 4.0, and Windows 2000 Professional. Most servers are running Windows NT Server 4.0, but a few are still running Windows NT Server 3.51.

Regional offices are connected to the head office using 1.5mbps T1 connections. The T1 connections are not heavily utilized at this point.

The different office locations are connected using routers. Routing tables are currently maintained by the administrators, but the routers support dynamic routing.

Proposed WAN Structure

The company is looking into using DSL and VPN connections to the head office to reduce costs. However, a remote access solution must be in place before this will happen.

Directory Services Commentary

CIO: We would like to maintain a centralized approach to creating user accounts. Accounts should be created in the head office. However, due to the number of calls received from regional offices, we would like to delegate some authority to the local IT groups so that they can reset passwords and perform other various day-to-day tasks.

IT Director: All offices are connected using routers. Static routes are currently implemented, but with expansion of the company being planned in the future, static routes will be a serious overhead. Also, to reduce the administrative overhead associated with maintaining our DNS servers, host records should be dynamically updated. IP addresses should also be assigned automatically. Currently none of the routers forward broadcasts.

CEO. We would like to implement tighter security in regard to client computing environments and implement domain-wide policies with local administrators being able to apply further restrictions. GNDaySpas requires an application that will alter the schema. We do not want to be affected by this.

Question 1

How should Active Directory be structured for Good Nature?

- ○ A. Two forests
- ○ B. One forest, one domain
- ○ C. One forest, two domain trees
- ○ D. One forest, one domain tree

Question 2

One of the departments in Good Nature requires more complex passwords than all other departments. What should you do?

- ○ A. Place the department within its own forest
- ○ B. Place the department within its own domain
- ○ C. Place the department within its own OU and configure an account policy at the OU level
- ○ D. Place the department within its own domain tree

Question 3

Place the appropriate operation masters on each domain. Some may be used more than once.

Domains:

Goodnature.com

Accounting.goodnature.com

GNDaySpas.com

Operation Masters:

Schema master

RID master

Domain naming master

PDC emulator

Infrastructure master

Goodnature.com

_____

Accounting.goodnature.com

_____

GNDaySpas.com

_____

Question 4

Which of the following are benefits of using L2TP as opposed to PPTP for VPN connections?

- ❑ A. More efficient data transfer
- ❑ B. Provides support for a variety of platforms
- ❑ C. Tunnel authentication for each transmission
- ❑ D. Provides support for a variety of protocols

Question 5

A user in the GNDaySpas domain attempts to install an application that will integrate within Active Directory. The installation will add new classes to the schema. However, the installation fails. What is most likely causing the problem?

- ○ A. There is no schema master within the domain.
- ○ B. The user is not a member of the Schema Admins group.
- ○ C. The Active Directory schema cannot be updated.
- ○ D. The application is not supported.

Question 6

The IT administrators want users to be able to perform searches for resources throughout the network as quickly as possible. What should you do?

- ○ A. Place a domain naming master in each region
- ○ B. Move the role of Global Catalog to another server
- ○ C. Install a DNS server within each region
- ○ D. Enable a Global Catalog within each region

Question 7

One of the domains within the forest has two member servers. These member servers host resources that all users in the forest need access to. What should you do?

- ○ A. Create local groups on each member server. Place users in global groups. Add the global groups to the local groups.
- ○ B. Create global groups on each member server. Place users in domain local groups. Add the domain local groups to the global groups.
- ○ C. Create domain local groups on each member server. Place users in global groups. Add the universal groups to the domain local groups.
- ○ D. Create global groups on each member server. Place users in local groups. Add the local groups to the global groups.

Question 8

How should group policies be implemented for the company?

- ○ A. Configure policies at the OU level.
- ○ B. Configure a single domain-wide policy and enable the Block Inheritance option.
- ○ C. Configure a domain-wide policy and enable the No Override option.
- ○ D. Configure multiple policies at the domain level.

Question 9

How should you implement the administration of group policies?

- ○ A. Enable local regional administrators to edit GPOs at the domain level.
- ○ B. Enable domain administrators to edit GPOs at the OU level.
- ○ C. Enable local regional administrators to create and edit GPOs at the OU level.
- ○ D. Enable local regional administrators to edit GPOs at the OU level.

Question 10

What is one of the most important aspects to consider when determining the number of domains to create?

- ○ A. Account policies
- ○ B. The location of domain resources
- ○ C. The amount of bandwidth available
- ○ D. The number of users within a company

Question 11

Which of the following factors require that multiple domains be created?

- ❑ A. Separate internal namespaces
- ❑ B. Account policies
- ❑ C. Delegation of authority
- ❑ D. Multiple Global Catalog servers

Question 12

DKP International is expanding and a new office is being opened in Europe. The IT director for the company wants to know if a new domain is required for the new location. Which of the following should be considered?

- ❑ A. Security requirements
- ❑ B. Number of users
- ❑ C. Number of local resource
- ❑ D. WAN connectivity
- ❑ E. Operating systems in use

Question 13

Which of the following would offer an IP addressing solution for the company?

- ❑ A. Install a single DHCP server to be used by all workstations.
- ❑ B. Install a single DHCP server. Place a DHCP relay agent on each subnet without a DHCP server.
- ❑ C. Place a DHCP server on each subnet.
- ❑ D. Install the DHCP relay agent.

Question 14

Static routes are no longer suitable for the company. Which of the following can be implemented?

- ❑ A. OSPF
- ❑ B. ICMP
- ❑ C. PPTP
- ❑ D. RIP

Question 15

Good Nature has no immediate plans to upgrade client workstations. What should you do to enable name resolution with the least amount of administrative overhead?

- ○ A. Configure LMHOSTS files on each workstation
- ○ B. Implement a WINS solution
- ○ C. Configure each workstation with a HOSTS file
- ○ D. Purchase routers that can forward NetBIOS name broadcasts

Case 4: DKP Int'l

DKP Int'l. Overview

DKP Int'l is a medium-size provider of school supplies. The company manufactures pencils, pens, erasers, and other miscellaneous items. DKP Int'l has decided to upgrade to Windows Server 2003.

DKP is merging with a company called Paper Trailz. Paper Trailz is a manufacturer of paper products such as notebooks, calendars, and day planners. Paper Trailz is also upgrading to Windows Server 2003 as part of the merger.

Current LAN/WAN Structure

The head office is located in Chicago. This is where all administrative staff is currently located. The head office contains approximately 800 workstations. Regional offices are located in Denver, San Francisco, and Orlando. These three offices are all connected to the head office. Production facilities are located throughout the United States. These offices are connected to regional offices using 56kbps connections.

All workstations run Windows 95. Some users have portable computers that are running Windows 2000 Professional.

The network currently uses Windows NT Server 4.0. There are four domains configured: one for the head office and three for the regional offices. A complete trust model has been implemented.

Paper Trailz currently uses a single Windows NT 4.0 domain.

DKP Int'l has registered the domain name of DKP.com. The company would like to use this for the forest root domain name.

Each regional office has a local administrator. However, all the high-end technical administrators are based in the head office.

Proposed LAN/WAN Environment

The company has no plans to upgrade any of the existing WAN connections.

Local administrators should have limited authority with the ability to reset passwords, unlock accounts, and manage some local resources.

Because Paper Trailz (papertrailz.com) already has an Internet presence, this should be maintained.

DKP plans to implement remote access in the future so that users can access the regional domains from their home offices. This brings up security concerns. Centralized administration of remote access is preferred. Only members of the Managers group and the Sales group should have remote access permissions. Managers should have access at any time, whereas members of the Sales group should have access only during weekday business hours.

Directory Service Commentary

CEO: There are too many people with administrative privileges, which dates back to when the company was first established.

IT Manager: The local IT support in each of the regional offices should have limited administrative privileges.

CIO: The new company should be able to maintain its current Internet presence However, the two companies need to be able to easily share resources.

Question 1

You're designing the DNS naming strategy for DKP Int'l. Which of the following points should you consider?

- ❏ A. The company plans to have an Internet presence.
- ❏ B. The number of users within the company.
- ❏ C. Paper Trailz' existing Internet presence.
- ❏ D. IT administrators in regional offices will have limited privileges.

Question 2

How many Active Directory forests will be required?

- ○ A. 1
- ○ B. 2
- ○ C. 3
- ○ D. 5

Question 3

Paper Trailz needs to maintain its current domain name. Users in this company should also still be able to manage their own resources. Users in both companies need to share resources. How should you proceed?

- ○ A. Create a child domain called papertrailz.dkp.com under the forest root dkp.com for the new company.
- ○ B. Create an OU for Paper Trailz within the dkp.com domain.
- ○ C. Create a new forest root called papertrailz.com.
- ○ D. Create a new tree within the dkp.com forest for Paper Trailz.

Question 4

How many domains would you create for DKP Int'l?

- ○ A. One domain
- ○ B. Two domains: one for DKP Int'l and one for Paper Trailz.
- ○ C. Four domains: One for each regional office and one for the head office.
- ○ D. Five domains: One for the head office, one for each regional domain, and one for Paper Trailz.

Question 5

Which of the following servers must exist within the Paper Trailz domain?

- ❑ A. Schema master
- ❑ B. Global Catalog
- ❑ C. RID master
- ❑ D. PDC emulator
- ❑ E. DNS server

Question 6

What kind of organizational unit model is appropriate for DKP Int'l?

- ○ A. Functional
- ○ B. Organizational
- ○ C. Geographical
- ○ D. Hybrid

Question 7

Two domains are created for DKP Int'l: dkp.com and papertrailz.com. dkp.com is the forest root domain. Which of the following information will be replicated between the two domains?

- ❏ A. Schema naming context
- ❏ B. Domain naming context
- ❏ C. Sysvol
- ❏ D. Global Catalog
- ❏ E. Configuration naming context

Question 8

One of the administrators in Chicago makes a change to the properties of a user's account. How long until the change appears on other domain controllers within Chicago?

- ○ A. 5 seconds
- ○ B. 5 minutes
- ○ C. 10 minutes
- ○ D. 15 minutes
- ○ E. 60 minutes

Question 9

DKP Int'l hopes to implement remote access in each of the regional offices so that users can access the network from home offices. Administration of the remote access servers should be done by the IT group in the Chicago office. What should you do?

- ❑ A. Configure remote access servers in each of the regional offices
- ❑ B. Configure a single remote access server in the head office
- ❑ C. Configure an IAS server in the head office
- ❑ D. Configure multiple remote access servers in the head office
- ❑ E. Configure an IAS server in each of the regional offices

Question 10

During the migration to Windows Server 2003, users in a Windows NT 4.0 regional domain need access to resources in a Windows Server 2003 domain. What should you do?

- ○ A. Nothing. Two-way transitive trusts are automatically configured.
- ○ B. Manually configure two-way transitive trusts between domains.
- ○ C. Manually configure a shortcut trust between domains.
- ○ D. Configure a one-way NTLM trust between domains.

Question 11

Remote access policies consist of various elements. In what order are policy elements evaluated against a connection attempt?

- ○ A. Conditions, profile, permissions
- ○ B. Conditions, permissions, profile
- ○ C. Profile, conditions, permissions
- ○ D. Permissions, conditions, profile

Question 12

DKP is implementing remote access policies for its company so that users can remotely access the regional domains. Two policies are created: one for the Sales group that limits access during the weekdays from 8 a.m. to 5 p.m. and one for the Managers group. Jim is a member of both the Sales group and the Managers group. When he connects to the remote access server at 5 p.m., access is denied. What should you do?

- ○ A. Remove Jim from the Sales group
- ○ B. Edit the properties of Jim's user account to grant remote access
- ○ C. Edit the permissions of the remote access policy to grant access
- ○ D. Change the order of the remote access policies so that the policy created for the Managers group is listed first

Question 13

You're the network administrator for DKP Int'l. A new sales office is being opened in a remote location. The office will maintain only 10 workstations. You're in charge of connecting 10 Windows XP Professional clients to the Internet. There are no other computers in the office. One DSL line is connected to the office. You want to connect all clients to the DSL line with the least expense to the company and the least administrative effort. Which service should you use?

- ○ A. Internet Connection Sharing
- ○ B. Network address translation
- ○ C. Proxy server
- ○ D. Internet authentication server

Question 14

DKP Int'l is installing the first domain controller for the Paper Trailz domain. The domain will host several domain controllers. Which Flexible Single Master Operation roles will be installed, by default, on the first domain controller (and only on the first domain controller) within the Paper Trailz domain?

- ❑ A. PDC emulator
- ❑ B. Schema master
- ❑ C. Domain naming master
- ❑ D. RID master

Question 15

One of the domains is running in mixed mode. Mary's Dial-In permissions are set to the default setting. When she attempts to access the network through the remote access server, all attempts are denied. Which could you do to allow Mary access to the network through the RAS?

- ○ A. Change her permissions to Allow
- ○ B. Change her profile to Allow
- ○ C. Change her permissions to Control Access Through Remote Access Policy
- ○ D. Change the domain to native mode

Answers to Practice Exam 2

All answers for this chapter refer to the case studies in Chapter 9.

Case 1: HW, Inc.

1. A	**6.** B	**11.** C
2. D	**7.** B	**12.** C
3. A	**8.** A, B	**13.** D
4. C	**9.** C	**14.** C
5. C	**10.** C	**15.** D

Case 2: FKB Consulting

1. A	**6.** D	**11.** C, D
2. A	**7.** C	**12.** B, D
3. B	**8.** B	**13.**
4. D	**9.** B	**14.** A
5. D	**10.** C	**15.** B

Case 3: Good Nature, Inc.

1. A	**6.** D	**11.** A, B
2. B	**7.** C	**12.** A, D
3.	**8.** C	**13.** B, c
4. A, C, D	**9.** C	**14.** A, D
5. B	**10.** A	**15.** B

Case 4: DKP Int'l

1. A, C	**6.** C	**11.** B
2. A	**7.** A, E	**12.** D
3. D	**8.** A	**13.** A
4. B	**9.** A, C	**14.** A, D
5. C, D, E	**10.** D	**15.** A

Case 1: HW, Inc.

Question 1

The correct answer is A. Because the company currently uses a single domain and wants to maintain this, only a single domain needs to be created. When designing Active Directory, a single domain is recommended (but not always feasible). Also, company-wide security settings are required, one domain should be created. Therefore, answers B, C, and D are incorrect.

Question 2

The correct answer is D. Five separate OUs should be created. One OU will be created for each of the five different geographical locations. The company wants to enable each administrator in the various locations to perform administrative tasks. This can be achieved by creating an OU for each location and granting each administrator permission over the appropriate OU. Therefore answers A, B, and C are incorrect.

Question 3

The correct answer is A. Because all locations are connected by T1 links, only a single Global Catalog server is required. Multiple Global catalogs can be created. However, multiple GCs are usually implemented when locations are connected by slow links. Therefore answers B, C, and D are incorrect.

Question 4

The correct answer is C. By storing zone data within Active Directory, administration of DNS can be reduced through secure dynamic updates. Also, it will not be necessary to maintain two separate replication topologies. Zone information can be replicated using the active directory replication topology.

Primary and stub zones can both be converted to Active Directory–integrated. However, if the zone information is stored locally, administration of DNS is not reduced. Therefore, answers A and D are incorrect. Answer B is incorrect because secondary zones can not be converted to Active Directory–integrated.

Question 5

The correct answer is C. Because the different locations are connected via high speed connections, RPC over IP should be used for the replication protocol if multiple sites are created. Answer A is incorrect because SMTP is normally used for slow, unreliable connections. Answer B and D are incorrect because they are not replication protocols.

Question 6

The correct answer is B. Windows 95 clients do not support dynamic updates, so a DHCP server must be configured to perform updates on behalf of clients. Answer A is incorrect because the Active Directory client does not provide this functionality. Answer C is incorrect because Windows 95 clients cannot be configured to update resource records. Answer D is incorrect because secure updates are enabled to limit those users and groups that can update the DNS zone file.

Question 7

Answer B is correct. Because the administrative model is based on the different business locations, the OU structure should model this and be based on geographical locations. Answer A and C are incorrect because these models would not allow the company to maintain its current administrative model. Answer D is incorrect; role-based is the same as functional.

Question 8

Answers A and B are correct. Because the routers do not forward broadcasts, a DHCP server can be placed within each location or a single DHCP server can be implemented and the DHCP relay agent enabled in each location. Answer C is incorrect because requests for IP addresses will not be forwarded by the routers. Answer D is incorrect because APIPA does not include the IP address of the default gateway, so communication is limited to the local subnet.

Question 9

Answer C is correct. Windows 95 clients use NetBIOS for locating network services. A WINS server is required to resolve NetBIOS names to IP addresses. Answers A and B are incorrect because DNS and HOSTS files are used to resolve domain names to IP addresses. Answer D is incorrect because dynamic updates are enabled so clients can dynamically update their own resource records.

Question 10

The correct answer is C. By establishing a new tree within the forest, the new company can maintain a separate namespace. Answer A is incorrect because a new forest is unnecessary. Answers B and D are incorrect because these two solutions would not allow the new company to maintain a separate namespace.

Question 11

The correct answer is C. By enabling the No Override option for a Group Policy Object, any settings configured at a lower level in the hierarchy will not be able to override the settings. Answer A is incorrect because the Block Inheritance option is set on an OU to change the default behavior of how policy settings are inherited. When this option is configured, policy settings configured for a parent container are not inherited by a child OU. Answer B is incorrect because this solution would exempt the Administrators group only from being affected by policy settings. Answer D is incorrect because policies are inherited from parent container to child container by default.

Question 12

The correct answer is C. Delegation of authority is used to grant individuals or groups certain administrative rights over a container or object. Answer A is incorrect because inheritance defines how settings such as permissions are inherited from parent to child. Answer B is incorrect because Group Policy is a tool used to control the user and computer environment. Answer D is incorrect because OUs are created to organize objects within a domain.

Question 13

The correct answer is D. By configuring a one-way external trust, users from a domain in one forest will be able to access resources from a domain in a remote forest. Answer B is incorrect because trusts are not automatically established between forests. Answer A is incorrect because shortcut trusts are established between domains in a single forest. Answer C is incorrect because the question does not state that users in the new forest need access to resources in the HW, Inc forest.

Question 14

The correct answer is C. The company has already registered this name on the Internet and wants to use the same name internally and externally. Answers A, B, and D are incorrect because they would not allow the company to use the same name internally and externally.

Question 15

The correct answer is D. One-way nontransitive NTLM trusts must be configured between Windows Server 2003 domains and Windows NT 4.0 domains. Answers A and C are incorrect because transitive trusts do not exist between Windows Server 2003 and Windows NT 4.0. Answer B is incorrect because shortcut trusts are created between Windows Server 2003 domains in the same forest.

Case 2: FKB Consulting

Question 1

The correct answer is A. Only a single forest structure is required. Answers B, C, and D are incorrect because multiple forests are not required for this scenario.

Question 2

The correct answer is A. Only a single domain is required. Answer B, C, and D are incorrect because multiple domains are not required.

Question 3

The correct answer is B. Two sites are required; the location in Canada should be placed within its own site because there is a slow connection to the head office. Answer A is incorrect because the location in Canada should be placed in its own location—the 56kbps link is too slow to support regular replication. Answers C and D are incorrect because this many domains are not required.

Question 4

The correct answer is D. DNS BIND 8.2.2 supports both SRV records and dynamic updates. The current version of BIND servers implemented by the company can support the Windows Server 2003 Active Directory infrastructure. Therefore answers A, B, and C are incorrect.

Question 5

The correct answer is D. Secure updates can only be configured for those zones that are Active Directory–integrated. Answers A and C are incorrect because the primary and stub zone must be Active Directory–integrated to support secure updates. Answer B is incorrect because secondary zones are not stored within Active Directory.

Question 6

The correct answer is D. Because the speed of the link is only 56kbps, SMTP must be used as the replication protocol. SMTP ignores all schedules. Answers A and C are incorrect because RPC over IP can not be used reliably with links as slow as 56kbps. Answer B is incorrect because SMTP ignores the schedules configured for a site link.

Question 7

The correct answer is C. An OU should be created for each of the different departments. Answers A and B are incorrect because an OU is required for each of the departments to allow the company to continue using its current administrative model. Answer D is incorrect because this many OUs are not required.

Question 8

The correct answer is B. Computers running Windows NT 4.0 must have the latest service pack installed (Service Pack 5 at a minimum). Answer A is incorrect because Service Pack 5 must be installed before the computers can be upgraded. Answers C and D are incorrect because computers running Windows NT 4.0 can be upgraded directly to Windows Server 2003.

Question 9

The correct answer is B. At least two Global Catalogs should be place in each of the domains. Answer A is incorrect because a Global Catalog should also be place in Canada because of the slow connection. Answers C and D are incorrect because this many Global Catalogs are not required.

Question 10

The correct answer is C. The schema policy is shared between all domains within a forest. Therefore, a second forest must be configured because a test environment should be kept completely separate from the live, business-critical infrastructure. Answers A, B, and D are incorrect because these solutions would not allow the department to maintain its own schema policy. A single schema policy is shared between all domains in a forest.

Question 11

The correct answers are C and D. Windows 2000 and Windows XP can update their own A records with a DNS server. Answers A and B are incorrect because these two platforms do not support dynamic updates.

Question 12

The correct answers are B and D. Both WINS and LMHOSTS provide solutions for users to resolve NetBIOS names to IP addresses. Answers A and C are incorrect because DNS and HOSTS files are used to resolve domain names to IP addresses.

Question 13

The correct order is Local, Site, Domain, OU. Group policies cannot be applied to the computer or users container.

Question 14

The correct answer is A. Filtering using security groups enables you to configure the permissions of a GPO to apply to only specific users and groups. Answers B and D are incorrect because these solutions do not allow the granularity required. These options do not enable you to specify which users and groups a GPO should apply to. Answer C is incorrect because the restructuring of the current OU structure is not required.

Question 15

The correct answer is B. To make any changes to the schema, you must be a member of the Schema Admins group. Answer A is incorrect because you do not need to be logged on locally to the schema master to make schema updates. Answer C is incorrect because you must be a member of the Schema Admins group. Answer D is incorrect because the default schema can be changed.

Case 3: Good Nature, Inc.

Question 1

Answer A is correct. Two forests are required, so Good Nature is not affected by the modifications made to the schema. Answers B, C, and D are incorrect because these solutions would not meet the business requirements.

Question 2

Answer B is correct. Password policies are configured at the domain level. Therefore, the department must be placed within its own domain to meet this business requirement. Answer A is incorrect because placing the department within its own domain is unnecessary. Answer C is incorrect because this solution would not permit the company to implement two password policies. Answer D is incorrect because there is no requirement for the department to have its own namespace.

Question 3

Goodnature.com:

Schema Master

RID Master

Domain Naming Master

PDC Emulator

Infrastructure Master

GNDaySpas.com:

Schema Master

RID Master

Domain Naming Master

PDC Emulator

Infrastructure Master

Accounting.goodnature.com:

RID Master

PDC Emulator

Infrastructure Master

Two of the FSMO roles are forest-wide: the schema master and the domain naming master. That means each forest will contain a single schema master and a single domain naming master. The remaining three FSMO roles are domain-wide.

Question 4

Answers A, C, and D are correct. L2TP provides more efficient data transfers, support for more protocols, and tunnel authentication for each transmission. Answer B is incorrect; PPTP provides support for more platforms than L2TP at present.

Question 5

Answer B is correct. To update the Active Directory Schema, you must be a member of the Schema Admins group. Answer A is incorrect because the first domain controller within a forest automatically assumes the role of schema master. Answer C is incorrect because the schema can be updated by a user with the correct permissions. Answer D is incorrect because this is not the likely cause of the application failing to install as it tries to update the schema.

Question 6

Answer D is correct. A Global Catalog is used to perform directory searches. Placing a Global Catalog within each region will enable users to perform faster searches. Answer A is incorrect because the domain naming master is not used for performing searches and there can be only one per forest. Answer B is incorrect because moving the role to another server would not speed up directory searches. Answer C is incorrect because DNS servers are used to resolve hostnames.

Question 7

Answer C is correct. Domain local groups should be created on each member server hosting network resources. Users should be placed into universal groups. The universal groups can be added to the domain local groups. Therefore answers A, B, and D are incorrect.

Question 8

Answer C is correct. A single domain-level policy should be created. With the No Override option set, any policies created by OU administrators will not be able to interfere with the domain-level policy. Answer A is incorrect because the company wants to implement domain level policies. Answer B is incorrect because the Block Inheritance option is used to ensure that policies configured on a parent container are not inherited by the child container. Answer D is incorrect because local administrators need the ability to configure group policies for their own region.

Question 9

Answer C is correct. The company wants to give local regional administrators the ability to create and edit GPOs at the OU level. Answer A is incorrect because this would give local regional administrators too much authority. Answer B is incorrect because the local administrators require the ability to create and edit GPOs at the OU level. Answer D is incorrect because local regional administrators also need to be able to create GPOs.

Question 10

Answer A is correct. One of the most important things to consider when determining the number of domains is the account policies because only one account policy can be configured per domain. Therefore answers B, C, and D are incorrect.

Question 11

Answers A and B are correct. If a company requires two separate namespaces or if it requires two different account policies, multiple domains will be required. Answer C is incorrect because delegation of authority can be done within a domain using organizational units. Answer D is incorrect because there can be multiple global catalogs per domain.

Question 12

Answers A and D are correct. When assessing the requirements for a new domain, you should consider the security requirements and WAN connectivity. Both of these might warrant the creation of additional domains. Therefore answers B, C, and E are incorrect.

Question 13

Answers B and C are correct. Because the network is routed, you have two options: A DHCP server can be placed on each subnet or you can place a DHCP server on one subnet and enable the DHCP relay agent on the remaining subnets. Therefore, answers A and D are incorrect.

Question 14

Answers A and D are correct. Dynamic routing can be implemented by configuring a routing protocol such as OSPF or RIP. Answers B and C are incorrect because neither of these is a routing protocol.

Question 15

Answer B is correct. Pre–Windows 2000 clients will use NetBIOS name to locate network resources. Therefore, a method of NetBIOS name resolution must be implemented. A WINS solution would require the least amount of administrative overhead. Answer A is incorrect because configuring LMHOSTS files would increase the administrative overhead. Answer C is incorrect because HOSTS files are used to resolve hostnames. Answer D is incorrect because this would increase the cost.

Case 4: DKP Int'l

Question 1

Answers A and C are correct. DKP Int'l is planning to have an Internet presence and Paper Trailz has an existing Internet presence. Both companies require different domain names. This needs to be considered when planning the DNS naming strategy. Answer B is incorrect because the number of users within the company has no effect on the DNS naming strategy. Answer D is incorrect. Although this might affect the number of domains created, it will not affect the DNS names that are used within the new infrastructure.

Question 2

Answer A is correct. Only a single forest is required. Answers B, C, and D are incorrect because no requirements are outlined in the case scenario that would warrant the creation of multiple forests.

Question 3

Answer D is correct. By creating a new tree within the dkp.com forest, Paper Trailz can maintain its existing domain name and continue to administer its own resources. Because the domain is still in the forest, a two-way transitive trust is configured, which allows users to share resources. Answers A and B are incorrect because neither solution allows the company to maintain its current domain name. Answer C is incorrect because multiple forests are not required.

Question 4

Answer B is correct. Two domains are required, one in each forest: one for DKP Int'l and one for Paper Trailz. Therefore, answers A, C, and D are incorrect.

Question 5

Answer C, D, and E are correct. The Paper Trailz domain requires a DNS server, RID master, and PDC emulator. Answers A and B are incorrect because these roles are assumed by the first domain controller in the forest root domain.

Question 6

Answer C is correct. An organizational unit based on geographical locations would be most appropriate. Answer A, B, and D are incorrect because these models would not allow the company to distribute administrative tasks as it currently does.

Question 7

Answers A and E are correct. The schema naming context, Global Catalog, and configuration naming context are replicated between domains. Answers B and C are incorrect because this information is not replicated between domains. Answer D is incorrect; because there is only a single Global Catalog, no Global Catalog data is being replicated.

Question 8

Answer A is correct. Intrasite replication occurs every 5 seconds. This is the default replication interval, but it can be changed by editing the Registry. Answers B, C, D, and E are incorrect because they do not represent the correct values.

Question 9

Answers A and C are correct. Remote access servers should be placed in each of the regional offices. By installing an IAS server in the head office and configuring the RAS servers as RADIUS clients, remote access authentication and accounting information can be centralized. Answers B, D, and E are incorrect because they do not meet the requirements of the company.

Question 10

Answer D is correct. To allow users in a Windows NT domain to access resources in a Windows Server 2003 domain, one-way NTLM trusts must be configured. Answer A is incorrect because two-way transitive trusts are not automatically configured. Answers B and C are incorrect because these types of trusts cannot be configured between Windows NT and Windows Server 2003 domains.

Question 11

Answer B is correct. Policy elements are evaluated in the following order: conditions, permission, profile. Answers A, C, and D are incorrect because they do not represent the correct order in which policy elements are evaluated.

Question 12

Answer D is correct. By changing the order in which the policies are evaluated, Jim will not be affected by the policy configured. Answer A is incorrect. Although this would solve the problem, Jim more than likely needs to be a member of the Sales group. Answers B and C are incorrect because Jim can already gain remote access during business hours.

Question 13

Answer A is correct. The simplest way to connect the workstations to the Internet using a single connection is to enable Internet Connection Sharing on a workstation. Answers B, C, and D are incorrect because Windows XP Professional does not include these technologies.

Question 14

Answers A and D are correct. The first domain controller in the domain assumes the roles of PDC emulator and RID master. Answers B and C are incorrect because these roles are assumed by the first domain controller within the forest root domain.

Question 15

Answer A is correct. For the user to be granted remote access permission, the permission must be changed from Deny to Allow. Answer B is incorrect because dial-in permissions cannot be configured through user profiles. Answer C is incorrect because this option is not available when running in mixed mode. Answer D is incorrect because raising the domain functionality would not grant the user remote access permission.

What's on the CD-ROM

This appendix provides a brief summary of what you'll find on the CD-ROM that accompanies this book. For a more detailed description of the PrepLogic Practice Exams, Preview Edition exam simulation software, see Appendix B, "Using the PrepLogic Practice Exams, Preview Edition Software." In addition to the PrepLogic Practice Exams, Preview Edition software, the CD-ROM includes an electronic version of the book in Portable Document Format (PDF) and the source code used in the book.

The PrepLogic Practice Exams, Preview Edition Software

PrepLogic is a leading provider of certification training tools. Trusted by certification students worldwide, PrepLogic is the best practice exam software available. In addition to providing a means of evaluating your knowledge of this book's material, PrepLogic Practice Exams, Preview Edition features several innovations that help you improve your mastery of the subject matter.

For example, the practice tests enable you to check your score by exam area or domain to determine which topics you need to study further. Another feature gives you immediate feedback on your responses in the form of explanations for correct and incorrect answers.

PrepLogic Practice Exams, Preview Edition exhibits all the full-test simulation functionality of the Premium Edition, but offers only a fraction of the total questions. To get the complete set of practice questions, visit www.preplogic.com and order the Premium Edition for this and other challenging exam training guides.

For a more detailed description of the features of the PrepLogic Practice Exams, Preview Edition software, see Appendix B.

An Exclusive Electronic Version of the Text

As mentioned previously, the CD-ROM that accompanies this book also contains an electronic PDF version of this book. This electronic version comes complete with all figures as they appear in the book. You can use Acrobat's handy search capability for study and review purposes.

Using the PrepLogic Practice Exams, Preview Edition Software

This book includes a special version of the PrepLogic Practice Exams software—a revolutionary test engine designed to give you the best in certification exam preparation. PrepLogic offers sample and practice exams for many of today's most in-demand and challenging technical certifications. A special Preview Edition of the PrepLogic Practice Exams software is included with this book as a tool for assessing your knowledge of the training guide material and to give you the experience of taking an electronic exam.

This appendix describes in detail what PrepLogic Practice Exams, Preview Edition is, how it works, and what it can do to help you prepare for the exam. Note that although the Preview Edition includes all the test simulation functions of the complete retail version, it contains only a single practice test. The Premium Edition, available at www.preplogic.com, contains a complete set of challenging practice exams designed to optimize your learning experience.

The Exam Simulation

One of the main functions of PrepLogic Practice Exams, Preview Edition is exam simulation. To prepare you to take the actual vendor certification exam, PrepLogic Practice Exams, Preview Edition is designed to offer the most effective exam simulation available.

Question Quality

The questions provided in PrepLogic Practice Exams, Preview Edition are written to the highest standards of technical accuracy. The questions tap the content of this book's chapters and help you review and assess your knowledge before you take the actual exam.

The Interface Design

The PrepLogic Practice Exams, Preview Edition exam simulation interface gives you the experience of taking an electronic exam. This interface enables you to effectively prepare to take the actual exam by making the test experience familiar. Using this test simulation can help eliminate the sense of surprise or anxiety you might experience in the testing center because you will already be acquainted with computerized testing.

The Effective Learning Environment

The PrepLogic Practice Exams, Preview Edition interface provides a learning environment that not only tests you through the computer, but also teaches the material you need to know to pass the certification exam. Each question includes a detailed explanation of the correct answer, and most of these explanations provide reasons for the other answers being incorrect. This information helps reinforce the knowledge you already have and provides practical information you can use on the job.

Software Requirements

PrepLogic Practice Exams requires a computer with the following:

➤ Microsoft Windows 98, Windows Me, Windows NT 4.0, Windows 2000, or Windows XP

➤ A 166MHz or faster processor

➤ A minimum of 32MB of RAM

➤ 10MB of hard drive space

As with any Windows application, the more memory your computer has, the better the software performs.

Installing PrepLogic Practice Exams, Preview Edition

You install PrepLogic Practice Exams, Preview Edition by following these steps:

1. Insert the CD that accompanies this book into your CD-ROM drive. The Autorun feature of Windows should launch the software. If you have Autorun disabled, select Start, Run. Go to the root directory of the CD and select setup.exe. Click Open, and then click OK.

2. The Installation Wizard copies the PrepLogic Practice Exams, Preview Edition files to your hard drive. It then adds PrepLogic Practice Exams, Preview Edition to your desktop and the Programs menu. Finally, it installs test engine components to the appropriate system folders.

Removing PrepLogic Practice Exams, Preview Edition from Your Computer

If you elect to remove PrepLogic Practice Exams, Preview Edition, you can use the included uninstallation process to ensure that it is removed from your system safely and completely. Follow these instructions to remove PrepLogic Practice Exams, Preview Edition from your computer:

1. Select Start, Settings, Control Panel.

2. Double-click the Add/Remove Programs icon to display a list of software installed on your computer.

3. Select the PrepLogic Practice Exams, Preview Edition title that you want to remove. Click the Add/Remove button to remove the software from your computer.

How to Use the Software

PrepLogic is designed to be user friendly and easy to learn. Because the software has a smooth learning curve, your time is maximized because you can start practicing with it almost immediately. PrepLogic Practice Exams, Preview Edition has two major modes of study: Practice Exam and Flash Review.

In Practice Exam mode, you can develop your test-taking abilities and knowledge by using the Show Answer option. While you're taking the test, you can display the answers along with detailed explanations of why they are right or wrong. This feature helps you better understand the material presented.

Flash Review mode is designed to reinforce exam topics rather than quiz you. In this mode, you're shown a series of questions but no answer choices. You can click a button that reveals the correct answer to each question and a full explanation for that answer.

Starting a Practice Exam Mode Session

Practice Exam mode enables you to control the exam experience in ways that actual certification exams do not. To begin studying in Practice Exam mode, click the Practice Exam radio button in the main exam customization window to enable the following options:

➤ *The Enable Show Answer button*—Clicking this button activates the Show Answer button, which enables you to view the correct answers and a full explanation for each question during the exam. When this option is not enabled, you must wait until after your exam has been graded to view the correct answers and explanation for each question.

➤ *The Enable Item Review button*—Clicking this button activates the Item Review button, which enables you to view your answer choices. This option also facilitates navigation between questions.

➤ *The Randomize Choices option*—You can randomize answer choices from one exam session to the next. This makes memorizing question choices more difficult, thereby keeping questions fresh and challenging longer.

On the left side of the main exam customization window is the option to select the preconfigured practice test or create your own custom test. The preconfigured test has a fixed time limit and number of questions. With a custom test, you can configure the time limit and number of questions in your exam.

The Preview Edition on this book's CD-ROM includes a single preconfigured practice test. You can get the compete set of challenging PrepLogic practice exams at `www.preplogic.com` to make certain you're ready for the big exam.

You click the Begin Exam button to begin your exam.

Starting a Flash Review Mode Session

Using Flash Review mode is an easy way to reinforce topics covered in the practice questions. To begin studying in Flash Review mode, click the Flash Review radio button in the main exam customization window. Then select the preconfigured practice test or create your own custom test.

You click the Begin Exam button to begin a Flash Review mode session.

Standard PrepLogic Practice Exams, Preview Edition Options

The following list describes the function of each button you see across the bottom of the window:

NOTE

Depending on the options, some buttons are grayed out and inaccessible—or they might be missing completely. Buttons that are relevant to the mode you're in are active.

➤ *Exhibit*—This button is visible if an exhibit is available to support the question. An *exhibit* is an image that provides supplemental information that is necessary to answer a question.

➤ *Item Review*—This button leaves the question window and opens the Item Review window, from which you can see all questions, your answers, and your marked items. You can also see correct answers listed here, when appropriate.

➤ *Show Answer*—This option displays the correct answer, with an explanation of why it is correct. If you select this option, the current question is not scored.

➤ *Mark Item*—You can select this check box to flag a question that you need to review further. You can view and navigate your marked items by clicking the Item Review button (if it is enabled). When your exam is being graded, you are notified if you have any marked items remaining.

➤ *Previous Item*—You can use this option to view the previous question.

➤ *Next Item*—You can use this option to view the next question.

➤ *Grade Exam*—When you have completed your exam, you can click Grade Exam to end your exam and view your detailed score report. If you have unanswered or marked items remaining, you are asked whether you would like to continue taking your exam or view the exam report.

Seeing Time Remaining

If your practice test is timed, the time remaining is displayed in the upper-right corner of the application window. It counts down the minutes and seconds remaining to complete the test. If you run out of time, you are asked whether you want to continue taking the test or end your exam.

Getting Your Examination Score Report

The Examination Score Report window appears when the Practice Exam mode ends—as a result of time expiration, completion of all questions, or your decision to end the exam early.

This window provides a graphical display of your test score, with a breakdown of scores by topic domain. The graphical display at the top compares your overall score with the PrepLogic Exam Competency Score. The PrepLogic Exam Competency Score reflects the level of subject competency required to pass the particular vendor's exam. Although this score does not directly translate to a passing score, consistently matching or exceeding this score does suggest that you have the knowledge needed to pass the actual vendor exam.

Reviewing Your Exam

From the Your Score Report window, you can review the exam you just completed by clicking the View Items button. You can navigate through the items and view the questions, your answers, the correct answers, and the explanations for those questions. You can return to your score report by clicking the View Items button.

Contacting PrepLogic

If you would like to contact PrepLogic for any reason, including getting information about its extensive line of certification practice tests, you can do so online at www.preplogic.com.

Customer Service

If you have a damaged product and need to contact customer service, please call 800-858-7674.

Product Suggestions and Comments

PrepLogic values your input! Please email your suggestions and comments to feedback@preplogic.com.

License Agreement

YOU MUST AGREE TO THE TERMS AND CONDITIONS OUT-LINED IN THE END USER LICENSE AGREEMENT ("EULA") PRESENTED DURING THE INSTALLATION PROCESS. IF YOU DO NOT AGREE TO THESE TERMS, DO NOT INSTALL THE SOFTWARE.

Glossary

. . . .

Active Directory

Active Directory is implemented as a service that enables network administrators to centrally organize and manage objects such as users, computers, printers, applications, and profiles.

Active Directory–Integrated Zones

Active Directory–integrated zones are DNS zones that are located on a DNS server that is also a domain controller. Since domain controllers replicate information to each other on an ongoing basis, the DNS server can piggyback its information onto the Active Directory replication. This eliminates the need for zone transfer and conserves available bandwidth.

Administrative Model

The administrative model implemented by a business essentially determines who holds the decision-making authority and who is responsible for implementing decisions. The most common administrative models are centralized and decentralized.

Automatic Private IP Addressing

Automatic Private IP Addressing (APIPA) is a service that provides an IP address to a client when the client is set to obtain an address automatically and a DHCP server is unavailable. The addresses range from 169.254.0.1 to 169.254.255.254.

BIND

BIND (Berkeley Internet Name Domain) is a Unix-based DNS service. Windows Server 2003 DNS is capable of interoperating with various versions of BIND.

Caching-Only DNS Servers

Caching-only DNS servers are servers with DNS installed and set with forwarders but no zone information. These servers are generally used with a small remote office that has a relatively slow link to the main office. They resolve queries and cache the responses without the need for zone transfer. This conserves bandwidth on the slower link.

Conditional Forwarding

Conditional forwarding is a new feature in Windows Server 2003 that forwards DNS name resolution requests to specified servers based on the hostname requested. It is used to make the process of name resolution more efficient.

Delegation

The act of assigning administrative duties and responsibilities to other individuals and groups within a business. Delegation eliminates the need to have one user or group responsible for all network administration.

DHCP

Dynamic Host Configuration Protocol (DHCP) is a service that dynamically assigns IP addresses and other IP configuration settings to clients that connect to a network.

DNS Servers

DNS servers are name servers responsible for a portion of the domain namespace. Client resolvers contact the DNS servers to map domain names to IP addresses (known as *name resolution*).

Domain

A domain is the main administrative unit within Active Directory. It's a collection of computer, user, and group accounts that are maintained by the domain administrator and share a common directory database.

Domain Local Group

A domain local group is used to assign users permissions to resources within the domain in which the group is created. This type of group can contain user accounts, universal groups, and global groups from any domain in the forest.

Dynamic DNS

Dynamic DNS (DDNS) is a service that dynamically registers hostnames when a computer connects to a network.

Dynamic Updates

Dynamic updates enable computers running Windows 2000, Windows XP, and Windows Server 2003 to automatically update their own A records with the DNS server.

Filtering

Filtering is a feature that enables an administrator to exclude certain security groups from being affected by a group policy by limiting the scope of the policy.

Firewall

A firewall is hardware, software, or a combination of the two, that dynamically filters packets into and out of a network. Firewalls are an essential component for a secure network design.

Flexible Single Master Operations

Flexible Single Master Operations (FSMO) are roles that must be performed as single master. These roles include schema master, domain naming master, PDC emulator, RID master, and infrastructure master.

Forest

A forest is one or more Windows Server 2003 domains that share a common schema, configuration container, and Global Catalog. Two-way transitive trusts are automatically established between domains in the same forest.

Global Catalog

The Global Catalog is a list of all the objects in the Active Directory and a subset of all the attributes of all the objects. It is used by users, administrators, and applications to search the Active Directory.

Global Catalog Server

Global Catalog servers are domain controllers that also replicate the Global Catalog. This can be set in the NTDS settings for the server. You should have at least one Global Catalog server per site.

Global Group

A global group is used to assign users permission to resources throughout the forest. This type of group can contain user accounts from the domain in which the group is created.

Group Policy Object

A Group Policy Object (GPO) is simply a collection of Group Policy settings. It's basically a container for the policy settings specified in the Group Policy snap-in.

ICANN

The Internet Corporation of Assigned Names and Numbers (ICANN) is the official registry for IP addresses and domain names. ICANN and its associated registries are responsible for ensuring that IP addresses and domain names remain unique throughout the world.

Incremental Zone Transfer

Incremental zone transfer (IXFR) is the capability to transfer only what has changed on a DNS database on each transfer, rather than the entire database. This capability allows for more frequent zone transfer and therefore keeps the zone information more current and accurate.

Internet Connection Sharing

Internet Connection Sharing (ICS) allows an Internet connection hosted by one machine to be shared by many machines.

Kerberos

Kerberos version 5 is an industry-standard authentication protocol supported by Windows Server 2003. The Kerberos protocol is the default authentication protocol used by clients within a Windows Server 2003 forest.

NetBIOS Name Resolution

NetBIOS name resolution is the process of resolving a user-friendly NetBIOS name to an IP address and vice versa.

Network Address Translation

Network Address Translation (NAT) is a service that translates an IP address that is valid for one network to an IP address that is valid for another connected network.

Organizational Unit

An organizational unit (OU) is a logical container object used to organize objects within a domain. OUs can contain users, groups, computers, printers, data, and other OUs.

Proxy Server

A proxy server is used in larger networks for network address translation. Proxy servers also provide more control over which users have access to the Internet and what sites they can access. In addition, proxy servers cache Internet requests from users. These caches can be used to provide greater security and to provide faster response to users seeking a frequently used site.

RAS

Remote Access Services (RAS) enable a user to access resources from the network by connecting through telephone lines, cable modems, or any other connection medium.

Remote Access Policies

Remote access policies control authentication and authorization to a remote access server. They contain three elements: conditions, permissions, and profile.

Scope

In terms of Active Directory, the scope determines the areas within a company that will be included in the design plan. Scope can also be used in the context of permissions and privileges. The scope of one's privileges determines what objects you have the right to administer.

Screened Subnet

A screened subnet is a special private network between two firewalls. It is used to provide a balance of security and accessibility of servers that are used on the Intranet and from the Internet. Also known as a *DMZ*.

Site

A site is a group of IP subnets connected by high-speed reliable links. Sites are created to control the replication process across slow links. Creating sites enables an administrator to take advantage of the physical network and optimize replication and Active Directory access.

SRV Records

In Windows Server 2003 (as well as Windows 2000), the DNS service locator records (SRV records) are used to locate servers that are running specific services. SRV record support is mandatory to support Active Directory with Windows Server 2003 domain controllers.

Stub Zone

A stub zone is a small, read-only copy of a zone. It contains only the SRV record, name server record, and glue A host record for the zones. Stub zones are used in non-contiguous namespaces to make name resolution more efficient.

Tree

Within a forest, domains that share a contiguous namespace form a tree. After a tree has been established within a forest, any new domains added to an existing tree will inherit a portion of its namespace from its parent domain.

Trust

A trust is the logical link between two domains that allows for passthrough authentication. A user from a trusted domain is granted access to resources in the trusting domain.

Universal Group

A universal group is a type of security group that is used to grant users access to resources throughout the forest. Universal groups can contain user accounts, global groups, and universal groups from any domain within the forest.

Virtual Private Network

A virtual private network (VPN) is a secure communication channel through a nonsecure medium—the Internet. This is accomplished through protocol encapsulation.

WINS

Window Internet Name Systems (WINS) is a service that dynamically registers NetBIOS names and resolves NetBIOS names to IP addresses.

Zone

A zone is a discrete, contiguous portion of a DNS namespace. An administrator or a group of administrators typically has responsibility for maintaining a zone.

Index

B-C

J-K-L

M

Q-R